I0821336

The Theology of the Heidelberg Catechism

COLUMBIA SERIES IN REFORMED THEOLOGY

The Columbia Series in Reformed Theology represents a joint commitment of Columbia Theological Seminary and Westminster John Knox Press to provide theological resources for the church today.

The Reformed tradition has always sought to discern what the living God revealed in Scripture is saying and doing in every new time and situation. Volumes in this series examine significant individuals, events, and issues in the development of this tradition and explore their implications for contemporary Christian faith and life.

This series is addressed to scholars, pastors, and laypersons. The Editorial Board hopes that these volumes will contribute to the continuing reformation of the church.

Columbia Theological Seminary wishes to express its appreciation to the following churches for supporting this joint publishing venture:

Central Presbyterian Church, Atlanta, Georgia
First Presbyterian Church, Franklin, Tennessee
First Presbyterian Church, Nashville, Tennessee
First Presbyterian Church, Quincy, Florida
First Presbyterian Church, Spartanburg, South Carolina
First Presbyterian Church, Tupelo, Mississippi
North Avenue Presbyterian Church, Atlanta, Georgia
Riverside Presbyterian Church, Jacksonville, Florida
Roswell Presbyterian Church, Roswell, Georgia
South Highland Presbyterian Church, Birmingham, Alabama
Spring Hill Presbyterian Church, Mobile, Alabama
St. Simons Island Presbyterian Church, St. Simons Island, Georgia
St. Stephen Presbyterian Church, Fort Worth, Texas
Trinity Presbyterian Church, Atlanta, Georgia
University Presbyterian Church, Chapel Hill, North Carolina

COLUMBIA SERIES IN REFORMED THEOLOGY

The Theology of the Heidelberg Catechism

A Reformation Synthesis

LYLE D. BIERMA

First edition
Published by Westminster John Knox Press
Louisville, Kentucky

13 14 15 16 17 18 19 20 21 22—10 9 8 7 6 5 4 3 2 1

Book and cover design by Drew Stevens

Library of Congress Cataloging-in-Publication Data

Bierma, Lyle D.
The theology of the Heidelberg Catechism : a reformation synthesis / Lyle D. Bierma.—First edition
p. cm. — (Columbia series in Reformed theology)
Includes bibliographical references and index.
ISBN 978-0-664-23854-4 (alk. paper)
1. Heidelberger Katechismus. I. Title.
BX9428.B55 2013
238'.42—dc23

2012047963

PRINTED IN THE UNITED STATES OF AMERICA

♾ The paper used in this publication meets the minimum requirements of the American National Standard for Information Sciences—Permanence of Paper for Printed Library Materials, ANSI Z39.48-1992.

Westminster John Knox Press advocates the responsible use of our natural resources. The text paper of this book is made from 30% post-consumer waste.

CONTENTS

ACKNOWLEDGMENTS

For their roles in this project, I would like to express my profound gratitude to the following: the administration and Board of Trustees of Calvin Theological Seminary, Grand Rapids, Michigan, for a sabbatical in the spring and summer of 2009 to begin work on this book; the Editorial Board of the Colombia Series in Reformed Theology, whose feedback in the early stages of the writing process proved invaluable; Donald McKim and Julie Tonini, editors at Westminster John Knox Press who were most gracious in their encouragement and support along the way; Erika Lundbom, the copy editor, who provided a sharp eye and many helpful suggestions; Todd Rester, PhD student at Calvin Seminary, who prepared the index; and especially the hundreds of college and seminary students whom I have had the privilege of teaching courses in creeds and confessions over the past thirty-three years and from whom I have learned so much. It is to these students that this volume is dedicated.

Lyle D. Bierma

Calvin Theological Seminary
Grand Rapids, Michigan

ABBREVIATIONS

AC	Augsburg Confession
BSLK	*Die Bekenntnisschriften der evangelisch-lutherischen Kirche*, 4th ed.
CO	*Calvini Opera*
CR	*Corpus Reformatorum* (Bretschneider/Bindseil)
EO (1552)	*Examen ordinandorum* (German edition)
EO (1554)	*Examen ordinandorum* (Latin edition)
GC	Genevan Catechism (Calvin)
HC	Heidelberg Catechism
Institutes (1536)	*Institutes of the Christian Religion: 1536 Edition* (Battles)
Institutes (1559)	*Calvin: Institutes of the Christian Religion* (McNeil/Battles)
LC	Larger Catechism (Ursinus)
LW	*Luther's Works*
OS	*Opera Selecta* (Calvin)
SBC	Second Brief Confession of Faith (Beza)
SC	Smaller Catechism (Ursinus)
WA	*Weimar Ausgabe*

1
INTRODUCTION

During the 400th anniversary year of the Heidelberg Catechism in 1963, *The Christian Century* ran an editorial overflowing with praise for this age-old manual of Christian doctrine. The catechism was "the most attractive, 'the most sweet-spirited' of the confessions of faith that came out of the Protestant Reformation." More than that, it survived "as the most ecumenical of the Protestant confessions," since, according to the editorialist, it was written to mediate the views of Lutherans and Reformed at a time when Germany was being torn apart by theological controversy. As such, the HC might still be "the confession of faith which can serve as the doctrinal basis for denominational reunion," but at the very least it deserved "the careful study of all ecumenical-minded Protestants."[1]

The Christian Century was not the only voice in the early 1960s to portray the HC as a kind of ecumenical statement of faith. James I. McCord, then president of Princeton Theological Seminary, also wrote on the occasion of the HC's quatercentenary that the catechism could be considered "the most ecumenical confession of the Reformation period," in part because "it is remarkably free from dogmatic definition and, except for the mooted question 80, is singularly nonsectarian in character."[2] Columbia Theological Seminary professor Shirley Guthrie saw the HC as "'ecumenical' in the best sense of the word" because "it generally is not a polemic *against* anything or anyone but simply a positive statement of what *Christians* (not just 'Calvinists') believe."[3] For the Dutch scholar Arie Lekkerkerker, "a certain ecumenical intent" behind the production of the HC was due to Heidelberg's location on the theological fault line between Lutheran and Reformed Protestantism.[4] And according to New Brunswick Seminary president Howard Hageman some years later, Zacharias Ursinus, the main author of the HC, demonstrated an ability to capture "the central thrusts of Reformation theology" that united several Protestant traditions and to avoid many of the "theological eccentricities" that divided them.[5] All of these statements echoed Karl Barth's claim already in the late 1940s that "the Heidelberg Catechism is a document which expresses a *general evangelical comprehension*." Apart from the HC's stance on the omnipresence of the ascended Christ, the relationship between physical and spiritual washing in baptism, and the nature of Christ's presence in the Lord's

Supper, there are no exclusively Reformed doctrines in the catechism, and "a reasonable Lutheran should also be able to stand on this ground."[6]

As the 400th anniversary of the HC came and went, however, so did most of the discussion about its ecumenical nature and potential. Now that we have reached the 450th anniversary, it is worth asking why so few ecumenically minded people during the last fifty years have given the catechism the careful study that *The Christian Century* had called for and whether such study would still be of any ecumenical value today. A major barrier to viewing the HC as a kind of ecumenical document is that for most of its history it has been identified almost exclusively with the Reformed branch of Protestantism. Within sixty years of its publication, the German text had been translated, often multiple times, into Latin, Dutch, English, Hungarian, French, Greek, Romansch, Czech, and Spanish for use by Reformed congregations in the regions of Europe where those languages were read or spoken.[7] At the Reformed Synod of Dort in the Netherlands in 1618–19, not only the Dutch delegates but also the foreign representatives from England, Scotland, Switzerland, and various parts of Germany declared their approval of the HC as a Reformed confession.[8] In the centuries that followed, the catechism traveled with Reformed emigrants and missionaries to every corner of the globe, and today it is one of the most widely used and deeply loved statements of the Christian faith in global Reformed Protestantism. In North America alone, there are at least twelve denominations with European Reformed or Presbyterian roots that still recognize the HC as one of their confessional documents: the Canadian and American Reformed Churches, Christian Reformed Church in North America, Free Reformed Churches of North America, Heritage Reformed Congregations, Hungarian Reformed Church in America, Netherlands Reformed Congregations, Presbyterian Church (U.S.A.), Protestant Reformed Churches in America, Reformed Church in America, Reformed Church in the United States, United Church of Christ (one of whose four feeder streams was the former German Reformed Church), and the United Reformed Churches in North America. In the words of John W. Nevin, the HC "became *the* Catechism emphatically of the Reformed Church, the counterpart in full of Luther's Catechism."[9]

This Reformed ecclesiastical identity of the HC has been buttressed over the past 150 years by a body of scholarship that finds in the catechism a distinctly Reformed theological character as well.[10] Leading the way was Karl Sudhoff who, in his magisterial biography of Caspar Olevianus and Zacharias Ursinus in the mid-nineteenth century, concluded that the HC was in full accord with other Reformed confessions not only in its view of the sacraments but also in all other points of doctrine, including perseverance of the saints and predestination.[11] During the 350th anniversary year of the HC (1913), A. E. Dahlmann described the HC as "a clear, definite and popular statement of Reformed doctrine over against Lutheranism,"[12] and a year later August Lang put it even more pointedly: "In its characteristic features, the Heidelberg Catechism is not Lutheran, nor Melanchthonian, nor Zwinglian, nor Bullingerian, nor Bucerian, but Calvinistic."[13] Friedrich Winter, in a comparative study of the Augsburg Confession and the HC in 1954, determined that "the HC was by and large a product of Calvinian theology,"[14] and Gustav Benrath concurred on the 400th anniversary of the HC that "the Heidelberg Catechism is and remains Calvinian."[15] A couple of years later, Fred Klooster asserted before the Evangelical Theological Society that, contrary to the 1963 editorial in *The Christian Century*, the doctrinal heritage of the HC is not multifaceted but "a distinctly *Reformed* Protestantism . . . rather than Lutheran, Melanchthonian or Zwinglian."[16] More recently, Klooster has maintained in a comprehensive commentary on the HC that in its general disposition and many of its features the catechism is "thoroughly Calvinistic."[17]

Others, too, have claimed that the HC is Reformed in its theology but that it had its roots in the Zurich rather than the Genevan reformation. The first to advance this thesis was the Dutch scholar Maurits Gooszen, who in two major works in the 1890s maintained that the HC reflected the "original Reformed Protestantism" of northern Switzerland, particularly the spirit of Heinrich Bullinger, whose "soteriological-biblical" approach to theology was markedly different from the more "intellectual-speculative" method of John Calvin.[18] Among the relatively few who have followed this line of argument is G. P. Hartvelt, who detected a major influence on the HC not only from Bullinger himself but from two of his kindred spirits in Heidelberg, university theologian Petrus Boqinus and court physician Thomas Erastus.[19] Joachim Staedtke and Walter Hollweg have also argued for the strong, though not exclusive, influence of Bullinger on the HC.[20]

Nevertheless, despite the long-standing use of the HC in Reformed and Presbyterian circles and the scholarly claims for its Reformed, even Calvinist, theology, there are at least three things that point us back in the direction of the "ecumenical" interpretation of the HC that people were suggesting fifty years ago: (1) another line of research that is often overshadowed by the scholarship that we have recounted above; (2) the historical context out of which the HC arose; and (3) the text of the catechism itself.

First of all, there is another body of scholarship from the past century and a half that considers the HC not distinctively Reformed at all but rather a combination of elements from the Reformed and Lutheran (often Melanchthonian) traditions. One of the first to suggest this was Johannes Ebrard, who in a history of the doctrine of the Lord's Supper in 1846 described the Palatinate reformation in general and the eucharistic teaching of the HC in particular as "Melanchthonian-Calvinian."[21] The very next year, the American Mercersburg theologian John W. Nevin characterized the HC as "German Calvinistic, or Semi-lutheran we may say, in its theological constitution and spirit."[22] The spirit he had in mind here was likely that of Melanchthon, as he indicated in a rhapsodic description of the HC four years later:

> The Catechism is no cold workmanship merely of the rationalizing intellect. It is full of feeling and faith. . . . A rich vein of mysticism runs everywhere through its doctrinal statements. A strain of heavenly music seems to flow around us at all times, while we listen to its voice. It is moderate, gentle, soft, in one word, *Melanchthonian*, in its whole cadence.[23]

Another Mercersburg theologian of the time, Philip Schaff, used similar language: "Here the mind of Melanchthon and the mind of Calvin joined hands and the Heidelberg Catechism bears the clear marks of both. It unites Melanchthonian mildness and fervor with Calvinian power and depth."[24] Nearly a century later, yet another theologian in the Mercersburg tradition, Bard Thompson, not only revived the Ebrardian term "Melanchthonian-Calvinian" (though now in reverse order as "Calvino-Melanchthonian") to describe the HC but claimed that "the Heidelberg Catechism marks the complete development of a synthesis of Melanchthonian and Calvinist doctrine."[25] J. F. G. Goeters, too, identified the catechism, broadly speaking, as the "amalgamation" (*Verschmelzung*) of Melanchthonianism and Calvinism into a third theological type that he termed "German Reformed."[26] And most recently, Eberhard Busch has put it this way:

> The Philippistic and the Calvinist directions coincided in the will to resist the splitting of the Protestant church into two confessions, despite existing differences in their understandings. The writers of the catechism were imbued with this desire of their teacher [Melanchthon]. One could easily call their text a union confession, formulated in view of the confessional age already approaching, as an attempt to work against Protestant division.[27]

Others broadened the synthesis beyond Melanchthonianism and Calvinism. Max Göbel's famous encomium to the HC in the nineteenth century suggested four sources: "The Heidelberg Catechism blended Lutheran intimacy, Melanchthonian clarity, Zwinglian simplicity, and Calvinian fieriness all into one."[28] In addressing the question whether the HC was primarily Melanchthonian (Heppe), Bullingerian (Gooszen) or Calvinian (Lang), Staedtke concluded that, to a certain degree, all three were true. The HC was an "eclectic composition," shaped by influences from several sides.[29] Neuser, like Göbel, detected the imprint of four "fathers" of the document—Luther, Melanchthon, Calvin, and Zwingli and his followers—with Calvin's influence by far the strongest.[30] For Jan Rohls, the text of the HC represented an "integration of very diverse doctrines"[31] from Melanchthon, Calvin, and the Zwinglian tradition; Ulrich Hutter likewise saw the author of the HC staking out middle ground between Wittenberg, Zurich, and Geneva.[32] More recently, Willem Verboom concluded in a comprehensive study of the theology of the HC that the catechism reflects a combination of some of the characteristic views of several major reformers, such as Melanchthon (on law), Bullinger (on covenant), and Calvin (on creation).[33]

Even some of those who have argued in the strongest terms for the Calvinist nature of the catechism have been willing to concede at least some Lutheran influence on the text. Lang, for example, found convergences with the Lutheran reformation primarily in the HC's structural contrast between law and gospel in parts 1 and 2 and in the christocentric orientation of the catechism, according to which the believer's only comfort lies not in the knowledge of God or the covenant of God but in the one sacrifice of Christ on the cross.[34] Winter could locate only a few places where the HC differed from Calvin, but he granted that the HC was not wholly untouched by Lutheran influences, including the way it treats the relationship between faith, the Holy Spirit, sacrament, and Word.[35] Benrath likewise saw the catechism moving at least a short distance away from Calvin and toward Lutheran theology.[36]

A second factor that points toward a more ecumenical reading of the HC is the historical background and context of the catechism, which in turn may help to shed light on the third factor, the text of the HC itself. The three narratives of the Palatinate reformation as a whole, the religious development of Elector Frederick III, and the theological pilgrimage of Zacharias Ursinus, the primary author of the HC, indicate a pattern that could serve as a guideline for determining the theological pedigree of the catechism itself.

The Palatinate was one of the more prominent states of the Holy Roman Empire in the sixteenth century.[37] It was actually divided into two sub-territories, the Lower Palatinate in the Rhineland, with Heidelberg as its capital, and the Upper Palatinate in northern Bavaria. Both were under the rule of the Count Palatine, who also served as one of the seven electors responsible for the selection of the Holy Roman Emperor. Like several other parts of the German empire, the Palatinate changed its state religion from Catholicism to Protestantism during the sixteenth century, but the reformation there "underwent the longest incubation phase of any major German territory."[38] Lutheran and South German Reformed influences had seeped into the region during the reign of Elector Louis V (reigned 1508–44), but it was not until 1546, nearly thirty years after Luther's Ninety-five Theses, that the Palatinate officially became Protestant under the leadership of Louis's brother, Elector Frederick II (reigned

1544–56). The reformation in the German empire suffered a major setback when a league of Protestant princes was defeated by the emperor in 1547 and many Catholic practices were reinstated in their territories under the Augsburg Interim (1548). With the Peace of Augsburg (1555), however, Protestantism was again fully legalized in the empire, at least in those states whose rulers were willing to enforce adherence to the Lutheranism of Melanchthon's AC. When Louis's and Frederick's nephew Otto Henry (reigned 1556–59) came to the throne, therefore, the Palatinate was poised to enter a significant new phase of reform.

Looming large over this next phase of reform was the figure of Philip Melanchthon, himself a native of the Lower Palatinate.[39] Born in the little town of Bretten in 1497, he pursued his education in Bretten, Pforzheim, and Heidelberg—all in the Lower Palatinate—and was awarded a bachelor's degree from Heidelberg University at the age of fourteen before transferring to the university in Tübingen. When the reformer returned to Heidelberg on a visit in 1524, he was honored by the university faculty with a silver goblet in recognition of his many achievements. The next year both Elector Louis V and the peasants of the Palatinate asked him to arbitrate in the peasant uprisings in the area, a service he willingly performed but with little success.

Following Luther's death in 1546, German Lutheranism experienced a bifurcation into two major theological parties: the Gnesio-Lutherans, who vigorously defended what they claimed to be the pure doctrine of Luther, and the Philippists or Melanchthonians, who with their leader had been willing to make concessions to Catholicism during the Interim and to modify some of Luther's teachings. Elector Otto Henry's sympathies clearly lay with the Philippist party, and his reforms in the Palatinate bore that stamp. In 1556 he introduced a new Lutheran church order that not only designated Melanchthon's AC as the doctrinal standard for the Palatinate but also included excerpts from Melanchthon's *Examen ordinandorum* (German, 1552; Latin, 1554), a catechism-like text for use in preparing ministerial candidates for ordination.[40] As far back as the rule of Louis V, the Palatine electors had been soliciting advice from Melanchthon, but Otto Henry went a step further and invited Melanchthon to join the faculty of Heidelberg University and assist with the reform of the Palatinate at close quarters. Melanchthon turned down the offer. He did, however, continue as a long-distance advisor, convincing Otto Henry in 1557, for example, to appoint his (Melanchthon's) former student Tilemann Heshusius as head of the theological faculty in Heidelberg, and assisting with the reorganization of the university a year later.[41]

Although Otto Henry's reform of the Palatinate was shaped to a large extent by the authority of Philip Melanchthon and his moderate form of Lutheranism, the elector did not hesitate to invite to his territory leaders from a variety of Protestant backgrounds, including Reformed.[42] It is not clear whether his motive was to build a nucleus of Protestant unity in the Palatinate or only to fill political, educational, and ecclesiastical vacancies with people of excellent reputation, regardless of their theological persuasion.[43] It is also possible that he was simply not "a fine connoisseur of theological subtlety."[44] In any case, among those he appointed to important posts during his short reign were not only fellow Philippists like Michael Diller, who became an influential member of the Palatinate consistory, but also the Strasbourg Lutheran pastor Johannes Marbach and the Gnesio-Lutheran professor Tilemann Heshusius, who ended up as head of the theological faculty and chief superintendant of the Palatine church. What is even more striking, however, is that he employed Stephan Zirler (or Cirler) and Thomas Erastus, both sympathetic to the Zurich reformation, as his private secretary and personal physician, respectively; Christoph Ehem and François Baudouin, both with Calvinist leanings, as professors of law at the university; and Petrus Boquinus, who has been variously described as a Calvinist and a Bullingerian,[45] as professor of New Testament.

When Otto Henry died after just three years on the throne, therefore, most of the major Protestant parties of the day already had a foothold in the Palatinate—Gnesio-Lutherans, Philippists, Zwinglians (perhaps better termed late Zwinglians or Bullingerians), and Calvinists. The task of bringing them together was left to Elector Frederick III (reigned 1559–76), who, like his predecessor, began his reign as a convinced Philippist. Frederick had been born and raised a Roman Catholic but was converted to the Lutheran faith by his first wife, Maria, during the early years of their marriage. Even before becoming elector of the Palatinate, however, he found himself moving away from the Gnesio-Lutheranism of his wife and son-in-law, Duke John Frederick of Saxony, and toward the more moderate expression of Lutheranism represented by Melanchthon. As governor of the Upper Palatinate (1556–59) and duke of Palatinate-Simmern (1557–59), Frederick introduced Otto Henry's church order and other Melanchthonian reforms into these ancillary territories. He also become a supporter of Melanchthon's so-called altered version of the AC (1540) and was one of the signatories to the Frankfurt Recess, a statement of Protestant confessional unity drawn up by Melanchthon in 1558.[46]

When Frederick III arrived in Heidelberg in 1559, he soon became embroiled in an acrimonious debate over the Lord's Supper. The principal antagonists were Gnesio-Lutheran Tilemann Heshusius, general superintendent of the Palatinate churches, and the Calvinist William Klebitz, a student at the university and deacon at the Holy Spirit Church in Heidelberg. Heshusius vociferously defended a doctrine of the oral manducation of the body of Christ in the sacrament and attacked anything less as Zwinglian. Frederick intervened to try to restore the peace and ultimately dismissed both men from Heidelberg, but his disillusionment with Heshusius's brand of Lutheranism had deepened. In the aftermath of the controversy, he sought Melanchthon's judgment on how he had handled the dispute, and Melanchthon replied in a "Responsio" with a strong endorsement of Frederick's actions. The Wittenberg reformer also suggested that Christians not try to penetrate the mystery of the union between sign and signified in the Lord's Supper but simply embrace the Pauline affirmation in 1 Corinthians 10:16 that the bread of the Supper is a *koinonia* (participation, fellowship, communion) with the body of Christ. Frederick considered Melanchthon's response important enough to have it published a year later in both its original Latin and a German translation.[47]

Upon Melanchthon's death in early 1560, Frederick III found himself looking more and more to the Zurich and Genevan reformations for inspiration, advice, and personnel. It may be going too far to say that he became a convert to Calvinism,[48] but he personally experienced and then engineered in the Palatinate what Gunnoe has called a "shift from a Philippist/Gnesio-Lutheran theological axis to a Philippist-Reformed theological axis."[49] During a formal disputation on the Lord's Supper between Gnesio-Lutheran and Reformed theologians in Heidelberg in June 1560, Frederick seems to have become increasingly attracted to the Reformed position. And in early 1561 he was instrumental in getting the German Protestant princes at the Naumburg Conference to agree to Melanchthon's "Variata" (altered) version of the AC as an acceptable interpretation of the "Invariata" (unaltered) version of 1530. This allowed for an understanding of the presence of Christ in the Lord's Supper that more closely approximated, or at least did not rule out of hand, the Reformed point of view.[50]

During the early 1560s, Gnesio-Lutheran advisors, pastors, and professors either began leaving the Palatinate voluntarily or were released by the elector from their positions. Frederick filled the vacancies with Philippist and especially Reformed personnel, among whom were the Calvinists Wenceslaus Zuleger, chairman of the Heidelberg consistory; Caspar Olevianus, rector of the Sapience College (a pastoral training school), professor of dogmatics at the university, and later pastor of two Heidelberg churches; Immanuel Tremellius, professor of Old Testament at the university; and Zacharias Ursinus, Olevianus's successor at both the Sapience College and the university.[51]

As part of this transformation of the Palatinate into a Melanchthonian-Reformed territory, Elector Frederick ordered the preparation of a new catechism for his realm in early 1562. The challenge he faced as a Lutheran territorial prince was to design a form of confessional unity for the Philippists, Calvinists, and Zwinglians in his realm that could fit within the bounds of Melanchthon's AC, to which all non-Catholic states in

Germany had to subscribe. Fortunately, Frederick now had a diverse group of Melanchthonian, Zwinglian, and Calvinist functionaries that he could draw on to forge such a consensus. In his preface to the catechism, he refers to "the advice and cooperation of our entire theological faculty in this place, and of all superintendents and distinguished servants [chief ministers] of the Church, [through whom] we have secured the preparation of a summary course of instruction or catechism of our Christian Religion."[52] The first group that he identifies as part of the production team, the "entire theological faculty," comprised the three professors at the university: Tremellius and Ursinus, both Calvinists, and Boquinus, whom, as we have already seen, some have characterized as a Calvinist and others as a Bullingerian.

The second part of the team, "all [the] superintendents," consisted of nine men who functioned much like bishops in the Roman Catholic Church. The superintendents from that time period whose names we know are Olevianus, a Calvinist; Johannes Velvanus, who had Melanchthonian, Zwinglian, and Calvinist sympathies; Johannes Willing and Johannes Sylvanus, both of whom leaned toward the Zurich reformation; and Johannes Eisenmenger, a close friend and collaborator of the South German Lutheran reformer Johannes Brenz.[53]

The third and final group, the "chief ministers of the Church," included, among others, Olevianus and Diller, a Melanchthonian who gradually moved in a Calvinist theological direction. Olevianus, Diller, and Boquinus were also part of the *Kirchenrat* (church council or consistory), which consisted of three ministers and three laymen and had responsibility for regulating Palatine ecclesiastical affairs. If, in fact, the entire consistory was involved in the preparation of the HC, the other three members would have been the laymen Zirler and Erastus, both influenced by the Zurich reformation, and Zuleger, a Calvinist.[54]

The member of this large drafting committee who likely functioned as the primary author of the HC was Zacharias Ursinus,[55] whose pilgrimage from Philippism to Calvinism mirrored that of Frederick III and the Palatinate reformation as a whole.[56] Ursinus was born in 1534 into a Lutheran family in the Silesian city of Breslau. He was probably catechized there as a child by the Melanchthonian preacher Ambrosius Moibanus, who had helped to introduce the Reformation to Breslau in the 1520s. In 1550, at the age of fifteen, Ursinus enrolled at Wittenberg University, where he became a student, friend, and theological ally of Philip Melanchthon, even accompanying his teacher to Torgau when the plague descended on Wittenberg in 1552. His deep devotion to his mentor becomes clear in a letter he wrote to a friend when the Gnesio-Lutherans accused Melanchthon of abandoning Luther's teaching and moving closer to Calvin:

> I am of the opinion that Dr. Philip teaches what is right, and has been fortunate enough to teach us in a holy and pure way, the real substance of the holy sacrament. Dr. Philip never swerves, but sticks to what is true, secure, important and necessary, never losing sight of what is sublime and divine. Personally, I do not hesitate to confess that I have benefited and learned more from his impressive method of teaching than from the vague commentaries of his opponents.[57]

After completing his studies in Wittenberg in 1557, Ursinus embarked on a study tour of the major centers of the Reformation to become acquainted with some of the leaders of the evangelical movement. His first stop was in Worms, where he joined Melanchthon at a religious colloquy between Roman Catholics and Protestants. He then began an extended journey to Strasbourg, Basel, Zurich, Bern, Lausanne, and finally Geneva, where he met John Calvin and received a set of the reformer's works as a personal gift. Stopping again in Zurich on the way home, he became better acquainted with Bullinger, Zwingli's successor and the most influential leader of the Zurich church, and with the Italian Calvinist Peter Martyr Vermigli, who seems to have made the greatest theological impact on Ursinus.

In 1558, Ursinus began his professional teaching career at the gymnasium in Breslau. However, his use of Melanchthon's *EO* as a classroom textbook and his budding relationships with several leading Reformed theologians led several Gnesio-Lutheran ministers in the city to suspect him of heterodoxy, especially because he supported Melanchthon's rejection of Christ's bodily presence in the eucharistic elements. To explain his position on the sacraments and defend himself against the accusations of the Gnesio-Lutherans, Ursinus prepared 123 "Theses on the Sacraments" (1559),[58] some of which he derived from his teacher Melanchthon. The theses so impressed Melanchthon that he is reported to have said that he had "never seen anything so brilliant as in this work."[59]

Tensions between the two Lutheran parties in Breslau precipitated Ursinus's departure in April 1560, just a week after the death of Philip Melanchthon. The coincidence of these two events—the death of his longtime mentor and his exodus from Breslau—seems to have represented for Ursinus a critical point in his movement away from Lutheranism and into the Reformed orbit. In the fall he made his way back to Zurich, where he took up studies with Vermigli for nearly a year before accepting an invitation from Elector Frederick III to join his team of reformers in the Palatinate. When Ursinus arrived in Heidelberg in the fall of 1561, therefore, he had made a long journey, theologically as well as geographically, from Wittenberg to Heidelberg by way of Geneva and Zurich. Nevertheless, most scholars agree that Melanchthon left a stamp on Ursinus's doctrine, pedagogy, and approach to reform that was never eradicated by later Reformed influences.[60]

What clues, then, might this overview of the historical *context* of the HC provide to the theological shape of the *text*? Running through the stories of the Palatinate reformation, the religious development of Frederick III, and the theological pilgrimage of Zacharias Ursinus is a common theme that was articulated already in the seventeenth century by Heidelberg professor Heinrich Alting. In a lecture to his students on the Protestant Reformation, Alting noted that the churches of Saxony and other nearby German territories—Denmark, Norway, Sweden, Poland, and Lithuania—all recognized Wittenberg as their mother. Zurich enjoyed that distinction among the churches in Switzerland, southern Germany, France, England, Scotland, the Netherlands, parts of Poland and Lithuania, Hungary, and Transylvania. But the Protestant church in the Palatinate was different, he said. It could actually claim both cities as mother—Wittenberg with respect to the origin and early growth of the Palatinate church, and Zurich with respect to its further refinement.[61] The church in the Palatinate consisted, so to speak, of a Lutheran (Melanchthonian) foundation onto which elements of a Reformed superstructure had been erected.

As we have seen, Alting's postulate about the Palatinate church was true also of Frederick III, Zacharias Ursinus, and indeed the entire territorial reform movement in which they played a part. All three had roots in the Melanchthonian Lutheran tradition, but over time they opened themselves up to and absorbed Reformed influences from both Zurich and Geneva. Should it not be the case, then, that what we have found in the context of the HC is likely to be reflected in the text? Should we not expect that in a document commissioned by Frederick and composed by Ursinus to function as the flagship of the reformation in the Palatinate, we would encounter traces of the same grafting of Reformed branches onto a Lutheran vine that we found in the Palatine reformation in general and in those individuals who helped to lead it?

It is the burden of this book to show that this is indeed the case. The text of the HC follows essentially the same pattern as its historical context, substantiating the body of scholarship that has portrayed the HC not as a distinctively Reformed confession but as a statement of theological synthesis around which the several Protestant parties in the Palatinate could unite. What we intend to add to this body of research, however, is a detailed demonstration of *how* the HC integrates textual and/or thematic elements from both the Lutheran and Reformed traditions in all of its major doctrines. Time and again, the text and theology of the HC draw from some of the foundational documents of the Lutheran tradition: Luther's Small Catechism of 1529, which was already in wide use in the Palatinate in the years leading up to the HC; Melanchthon's AC, to which the Palatinate was confessionally bound under the Peace of Augsburg; and Melanchthon's *Examen ordinandorum*, a catechetical work that Otto Henry incorporated into his Palatinate church order of 1556. But the HC also draws on and interweaves strands of text from the Reformed tradition, particularly from Calvin's Genevan Catechism (1545), the north-German Lasco catechisms of the 1540s and 1550s, and two confessions by Theodore Beza (1560). Furthermore, as we examine the doctrines of the HC, we will note the variety of ways that the author works toward integration and synthesis: establishing common ground, finding middle positions, toning down controversial points, stating viewpoints positively without explicit rejection of alternatives, and sometimes simply combining elements of both traditions into a single formulation. At the end, we will return to the questions highlighted during the 400th anniversary in 1963: how ecumenical this sixteenth-century confessional project really was and what implications the HC's attempt at theological synthesis might have for ecumenical activity today.

In developing this interpretation, the next seven chapters will analyze the major theological topics that arise in the HC in the sequence of its 129 questions and answers. Chapter 2 focuses on the HC's theme of comfort and threefold structure (HC 1–2), chapter 3 on law and gospel (HC 3–19), chapter 4 on providence and predestination (HC 20–28), chapter 5 on Christ and the Holy Spirit (HC 29–64), chapters 6 and 7 on the sacraments and covenant, respectively (HC 65–85), and chapter 8 on gratitude and good works (HC 86–129). The last chapter ("Ecumenical Reflections on the Heidelberg Catechsim") examines, as we have said, how ecumenical this 450-year-old document was for its time and what insights it might provide for those Reformed and Presbyterian churches that still subscribe to it and are at the same time involved in the contemporary ecumenical movement. An appendix at the back contains a translation of the HC recently prepared and adopted by three of the Reformed denominations that recognize the HC as one of their confessions: the Presbyterian Church (U.S.A.), the Reformed Church in America, and the Christian Reformed Church in North America. It is this "ecumenical" translation that is cited throughout the book.

2

THEME AND STRUCTURE OF THE HEIDELBERG CATECHISM

Q/A 1–2

1 Q. What is your only comfort in life and in death?

A. That I am not my own, but belong—body and soul, in life and in death—to my faithful Savior, Jesus Christ. He has fully paid for all my sins with his precious blood, and has set me free from the tyranny of the devil. He also watches over me in such a way that not a hair can fall from my head without the will of my Father in heaven; in fact, all things must work together for my salvation. Because I belong to him, Christ, by his Holy Spirit, assures me of eternal life and makes me wholeheartedly willing and ready from now on to live for him.

2 Q. What must you know to live and die in the joy of this comfort?

A. Three things: first, how great my sin and misery are; second, how I am set free from all my sins and misery; third, how I am to thank God for such deliverance.[1]

These first two questions and answers of the Heidelberg Catechism introduce, respectively, the theme and basic structure of the rest of the document, providing the reader with an overview of the catechism as a whole. As we shall see in this chapter, this theme and structure both have deep, though not exclusive, roots in the Lutheran tradition, especially the works of Philip Melanchthon.[2]

THEME OF COMFORT

Judging by the number of times the word *comfort* is used in the HC, one would hardly guess that it serves as the theme of the entire catechism. After occurring twice in noun form in the first two questions, it appears only four more times in the rest of the document and then only as a verb: "How does Christ's return 'to judge the living and the dead' *comfort* you?" (Q 52); "[The Holy Spirit] makes me share in Christ and all his benefits, *comforts* me, and will remain with me forever" (A 53); "How does 'the resurrection of the body' *comfort* you?" (Q 57); and "How does the article concerning 'life everlasting' *comfort* you?" (Q 58).[3]

It is in HC 1, of course, that the idea of our "only comfort in life and in death" is first introduced and explained. Christian comfort (German: *Trost*) is a trust, confidence, or what Klooster calls "a certainty-outside-of-ourselves"[4] that derives not simply from belonging to Christ but from belonging to a Christ who saves us from sin and the devil's power, who watches over us in such a way that everything works together for our salvation, and who by his Holy Spirit assures us of salvation and changes the direction of our hearts and lives. This christological and soteriological emphasis is repeated in the other four references to comfort later on. According to HC 52, our comfort derives from looking with confidence to Christ the returning judge, who has already elected us and saved us from the curse, and who will take us to himself in the joy and glory of heaven. HC 53 uses language reminiscent of HC 1 when it speaks of the comforting work of the Holy Spirit. The resurrection of the body (HC 57) comforts us by assuring us that we who belong to Christ will go immediately to him after death and will someday enjoy new bodies patterned after his. And even though HC 58's interpretation of "the life everlasting" does not explicitly mention the Christian's connection to Christ, it still has a soteriological focus: the salvation that we enjoy in part in this life will be brought to perfection in the life to come.

We encounter the notion of comfort even more frequently, however, in places where the term itself is not used. True faith is a "sure knowledge" and a "wholehearted trust" that we are saved through Christ (A 21). We can "trust" the Father in such a way that we "do not doubt" that he will turn adversity to our good (A 26), and we can have "good confidence" that nothing will separate us from his love (A 28). By being joined to Christ and his anointing, our struggle against sin and the devil is with a "free conscience" (A 32). When we are under fierce spiritual assault, we can be "assured" that Christ our Lord has already experienced and thus delivered us from the anguish (German: *Angst*) of hell (A 44). Christ's resurrection and ascension benefit us by providing us with a variety of spiritual "pledges" (A 45, A 49). The doctrine of justification provides a threefold antidote to the three accusations of a troubled conscience (A 60). Through our participation in the sacraments, the Holy Spirit "confirms" our faith (A 65) and "confirms" for us that our whole salvation rests on the sacrificial work of Christ (A 67). Baptism was given to remind and "assure" us that Christ's sacrifice was for us personally (HC 69) and that our spiritual washing is real (A 73). Likewise, the Lord's Supper reminds and "assure[s]" us that we share in Christ's sacrifice and gifts (HC 75) and in his true body and blood (A 79). By his Holy Spirit, Christ is renewing us so that we may be "assured" of our faith by its fruits (A 86). Our prayers should rest on the "unshakeable foundation" that God will listen to our prayers for the sake of Christ our Lord (A 117). We address God in prayer as Father to awaken in us a reverence and "trust" that God has become our Father through Christ (A 120). And the little word *Amen* means that what we have prayed shall "truly and surely" be, for "it is . . . sure" that God listens to our prayers (A 129).

In the end, however, it is not really the frequency of the term *comfort* and its synonyms that determines its role as the leitmotiv of the catechism. Rather, it is how it is linked in HC 2 to the three major divisions of the catechism: to live and die in the joy of this comfort, we must know our misery (part 1), our deliverance (part 2), and the proper path of gratitude (part 3). All of the remaining 127 questions and answers are divided into those three parts and thus relate ultimately, though often indirectly, to the theme of comfort.

What were the theological and textual sources for the HC's opening question on comfort? It has long been suggested that Ursinus and the drafting committee drew from a variety of earlier catechisms and other documents in their work, most notably Ursinus's own Smaller Catechism (1561 or 1562) and, to a lesser extent, his Larger Catechism (1562).[5] Parts or all of some ninety of the HC's 129 questions and answers are based on the text of the SC, and there are several parallels to the LC as well.[6] The dependence of the HC on these two source catechisms is apparent already in the opening words of HC 1, which shows clear linguistic similarities to the lead questions in the SC and LC:

SC 1 Q. What is the comfort by which your heart is sustained in death as well as in life?
A. That God has truly pardoned all my sins because of Christ and has given me eternal life, in which I may glorify him forever.[7]

LC 1 Q. What firm comfort do you have in life and in death?
A. That I was created by God in his image for eternal life, and after I willingly lost this in Adam, out of his infinite and gracious mercy God received me into his covenant of grace, so that because of the obedience and death of his Son sent in the flesh, he might give me as a believer righteousness and eternal life. It is also that he sealed his covenant in my heart by his Spirit, who renews me in the image of God and cries out in me, "Abba, Father," by his Word, and by the visible signs of this covenant.[8]

It is striking that even though the question in HC 1 clearly follows the language of these two source texts, the answer is quite different from those of the earlier catechisms. Furthermore, there is no mention of comfort in the SC's counterparts to HC 52 (Christ's return), 53 (the Holy Spirit), 57 (resurrection of the body), and 58 (life everlasting).[9] Indeed, the SC employs the word *comfort* only three times in its 118 questions and answers, once in the opening question and twice in answers dealing with the assurance of election (SC 51, 52). The situation is a little different with the LC, where *comfort* is found in only six of the 323 questions and answers. Four of these uses (LC 1, 103, 110, and 131) have parallels in HC 1, 52, 53, and 58, respectively; the other two occur in answers on the offices of Christ (LC 64) and justification (LC 141). Unlike the HC, however, the LC never connects the comfort idea to the basic structure of the document or suggests it as a main theme, and the SC does so only indirectly.

What other texts, then, might lie behind HC 1, and what might have inspired Ursinus and the drafting committee to adopt comfort as the central theme of the HC? For answers to those questions we need to look to both the Lutheran and Reformed traditions. A likely Lutheran source for at least part of HC 1 is Luther's own Small Catechism of 1529. As Goeters and Neuser have noted, the famous first lines of the answer in HC 1 show remarkable similarities to Luther's explanation of the second article of the Apostles' Creed:[10]

> That I am not my own, but belong—body and soul, in life and in death—to my faithful Savior, Jesus Christ. He has fully paid for all my sins with his precious blood, and has set me free from the tyranny of the devil. (HC 1)
>
> I believe that Jesus Christ . . . is my Lord. He has redeemed me . . . He has purchased and freed me from all sins, from death, and from the power of the devil . . . with his . . . precious blood . . . in order that I may belong to him. (Small Catechism[11])

The parallel language of key phrases in the two texts is all the more striking when one compares their original German texts:

> He has set me free [*mich . . . erlöset hat*] (HC 1)
> He has redeemed me [*mich . . . erlöset hat*] (Small Catechism)
>
> He has fully paid for all my sins [*für alle meine Sünden*] (HC 1)
> He has purchased and freed me from all sins [*von allen Sünden*] (Small Catechism)
>
> from the tyranny of the devil [*aus aller Gewalt des Teufels*] (HC 1)
> from the power of the devil [*von der Gewalt des Teufels*] (Small Catechism)
>
> with his precious blood [*mit seinem theuren Blute*] (HC 1)
> with his . . . precious blood [*mit seinem . . . theuren Blute*] (Small Catechism)
>
> That I belong [*eigen bin*] . . . to my faithful Savior, Jesus Christ (HC 1)
> that I may belong [*eigen sei*] to him (Small Catechism)

What is especially noteworthy here is Luther's use of the language of being possessed by Christ or "belonging to" Christ, an image that becomes a key component of the comfort theme in HC 1.

Scholars have also pointed to a parallel between the opening words of Ursinus's three catechisms and the first question of a 1547 Lutheran catechism by another one of Melanchthon's students, Joachim Mörlin:

> Q. **What is your comfort above everything on earth?**
>
> A. Even though I know that by nature I am as much a child of wrath as everyone else (Eph. 2), nevertheless I have since become another person and a Christian by being baptized as a child into Jesus Christ, my precious Savior, according to his command (Mark 10).[12]

The way the question is phrased certainly suggests that it could have influenced the opening words of the SC, LC, and HC. The problem is that this question was actually not in the 1547 edition of Mörlin's catechism; it appeared only later in a revised edition in 1566, three years after the publication of the HC.[13] Nevertheless, the fact that within a space of three years, two of Melanchthon's students, Ursinus and Mörlin, would open their catechisms with an emphasis on comfort suggests that we should examine how important this motif was in the works of their teacher.

Comfort in the sense of assurance of salvation is indeed a major theological theme in Melanchthon's corpus,[14] especially in two of his works associated with the reformation in the Palatinate. First of all, as a Lutheran territory under the strictures of the Peace of Augsburg, the Palatinate recognized Melanchthon's AC as its official doctrinal statement. Any new territorial catechism would have to respect its boundaries. We should hardly be surprised, therefore, if the confessional standard that provided the theological framework for the HC likewise emphasized the doctrine of comfort.

What we find in the Latin text of the AC is at least fourteen (and in the German text eleven) explicit uses of the term *comfort* in a variety of contexts.[15] In article III on the Son of God, for example, it is stated that the ascended Christ rules over all creatures "so that through the Holy Spirit he may make holy, purify, strengthen, and *comfort* all who believe in him."[16] Article XII on repentance affirms that faith "*comforts* the heart [*conscientiam*] and puts it at peace."[17] The twentieth article on faith and good works refers to the doctrine of justification through faith in Christ as "very *comforting* to and beneficial for timid and terrified consciences."[18] Likewise, the Mass was instituted and should be used "as a *comfort* to terrified consciences" (article XXIV).[19] In the practice of confession, "how *comforting* the word of absolution is" and "necessary . . . for terrified consciences. . . . We should joyfully find *comfort* in the absolution, knowing that through such faith we obtain forgiveness of sins" (article XXV).[20] By contrast, many of the traditions of

Catholic piety taught "nothing about the *comfort* of God's grace" and only obscured "Christian teaching concerning more important matters, such as faith, *comfort* in spiritual trials, and the like" (article XXVI).[21] In short, as de Reuver has put it, "the phrase 'comfort of the conscience' occurs time and again [in the AC]—and at the most salient moments. That indicates how closely . . . this Lutheran confession . . . is connected to the Reformed 'comfort book' of Heidelberg by a similar underlying spiritual tone."[22]

The comfort theme is even more prominent in another of Melanchthon's works, the *EO*, a catechetical preparatory manual for ordinands that Otto Henry had incorporated into his Palatinate church order of 1556 and Ursinus had used in his teaching in Breslau in the late 1550s. As Hollweg has noted, there are a number of linguistic parallels between this document and the HC,[23] so it is quite possible, even likely, that the *EO* left a mark on Ursinus and on the HC that included Melanchthon's frequent references to comfort throughout.[24] As with the HC later on, the common thread running through these references in the *EO* (1552) is their soteriological focus. According to Melanchthon, people experience the divine judgment of the law "when the conscience falls into a terror and despair so great that it brings with it bodily and eternal death if no *comfort* is forthcoming through knowledge of Christ the Lord from the gospel."[25] Our "poor, miserable nature is sinful"; nevertheless, "in the knowledge of our sin and terror-stricken consciences, we have *comfort*" through the gospel of the Mediator, who came to destroy the devil's work and accomplish "the great work of our deliverance."[26] Or again:

> The gospel proclaims this eternal, gracious *comfort*: that God surely and for the sake of his Son Jesus Christ, by grace and without any merit of our own, wishes to grant us forgiveness of sins, impute to us righteousness and accept us, and through his Son Jesus Christ give us the Holy Spirit and make us heirs of eternal salvation.[27]

"In this deep *comfort* that fills your heart, the Son of God gives you his Holy Spirit and works in you life and joy in God."[28] This comes in part from the testimony of the Spirit in our hearts that we are children of God, by which we "experience genuine *comfort* in God."[29] And thus "*comforted* through faith and trust in Christ the Lord," we now also "desire to be obedient to him."[30]

This is but a small sampling of the more than fifty occurrences of the term *comfort* in the *EO*. The language of comfort, misery, deliverance, assurance, and obedience here sounds very similar to the introductory questions and answers of the SC, and especially the HC. Indeed, the blending in HC 1 of this Melanchthonian parlance with phrases from Luther's Small Catechism gives the opening lines of the HC an unmistakably Lutheran flavor.[31] Even more significant, however, is the *pervasive-*

ness of the comfort motif in the *EO*—quite possibly part of the inspiration for the thematic role it came to play in the HC.

As deep as the Lutheran roots of HC 1 might have been, however, we should not overlook the influence also of a collection of Reformed sources. This is the body of catechetical literature produced in the mid-sixteenth century by the reformer Johannes à Lasco and his co-workers, Marten Micronius and Jan Utenhove, for the Reformed churches in Emden, Germany, and several Dutch refugee congregations in London.[32] Lasco's (Large) Emden Catechism of 1546 (Dutch translation, 1551), for example, contains the following questions and answers in its exposition of the first article of the Apostles' Creed, "I believe in God the Father almighty":

> **Q. Why does Scripture call God a "Father" and "almighty"?**
> A. For the awakening and firm establishment of our faith and for the special *comfort* of all believers.
>
> **Q. What *comfort* does that little word "Father" bring with it?**
> A. A very special *comfort*, to be heard in life and death: namely, that the most high God, the Father of our Lord Jesus Christ, wants to be our Father as well.
>
> **Q. What *comfort* does it bring us to confess that our God is almighty?**
> A. If we hold on to that in faith, we become certain and *comforted* that we may rely completely on him, whom no one can withstand.[33]

What is most striking here, of course, is not just the fivefold use of the word *comfort* but the reference in the second of these answers to a comfort "in life and death," a phrase later found in SC 1, LC 1, and HC 1.

A few years later, Micronius began his *Een corte undersouckinghe des gheloofs* (*A Brief Examination of the Faith*, 1553), a Dutch translation of part of Lasco's liturgical treatise *Forma ac Ratio* (1553), with the following question and answer:

> **Q. How are you assured in your heart that you are a member of the church of Christ?**
> A. From the fact that the Holy Spirit testifies to my spirit that I am a child of God. . . . Furthermore, I also feel moved by the Spirit of God to obedience to the divine commandments.[34]

There is no mention of comfort here, but the reference in the answer to a twofold operation of the Holy Spirit has a familiar ring to it. It bears a clear similarity to the last lines of HC 1, which affirm that by the Holy Spirit Christ does two things for the believer: he "assures me of eternal life" and "makes me wholeheartedly willing and ready from now on to live for him."

Micronius actually does employ the term *comfort* in two later questions in *A Brief Examination of the Faith*:

> Q. **What comfort do you have in [the communion of saints, forgiveness of sins, resurrection of the body, and life everlasting]?**
>
> A. First, that all Christ's benefits belong in equal measure to all saints and believers. Second, that they receive forgiveness of their sins from God the Father as often as they desire it in the name of Christ through a firm faith with a humble heart. Finally, that however much they are despised here, on the last day they will rise in their own bodies to eternal life.
>
> Q. **What comfort do you have in [the Lord's Supper]?**
>
> A. That through the sacrifice of the body and blood of Christ I have forgiveness of my sins and am nourished unto eternal life as certainly as I eat the bread from the minister at the table of the Lord and drink the cup that is given me; and just as my body is naturally sustained through daily food and drink.[35]

The first of these bears no resemblance to HC 1, but it does adumbrate the connection between comfort and the resurrection of the body in HC 57 and between comfort and the life everlasting in both LC 131 and HC 58. The second question and answer not only contains similar language to parts of HC 75, 76, and 79 on the Lord's Supper, but it also explicitly links comfort and the certainty of salvation, which in the HC are connected this clearly only in HC 1.

Finally, Lasco's Small Emden Catechism of 1554 also contains a couple questions that are of interest here:

> [3] Q. **How are you certain that you are a true Christian and share in such benefits of Christ [as are listed in the previous answer]?**
>
> A. First, from the testimony of the Holy Spirit, who testifies to my spirit . . . that I am a child of God. Second, from the will and desire to serve God the Lord, which, by the Holy Spirit, I experience in my inmost self.[36]
>
> [24] Q. **Where, then, shall this poor, condemned person, frightened by that law, seek comfort?**
>
> A. Not in himself or in any other creature in heaven or on earth, but only through faith in the one Mediator and Savior Jesus Christ, who is revealed to us through the holy Gospel.[37]

The first of these answers, of course, parallels the references in *A Brief Examination of the Faith*, and later in HC 1, to the double work of the Holy

Spirit. The second question and answer is especially remarkable because, like HC 1, it not only asks where our comfort is to be found but also identifies the source of that comfort not in ourselves but in the Mediator and Savior Jesus Christ.

It is, of course, true that like the SC, LC, and HC, the word *comfort* is found relatively infrequently in these north-German sources—five times in the (Large) Emden Catechism, twice in *A Brief Examination of the Faith*, and just a single time in the Small Emden Catechism. Unlike the three works by Ursinus, however, the Emden catechisms do not give the idea of comfort a very prominent place. They neither locate it in the first question and answer nor assign it a thematic role by attaching it to the structure of the document as a whole. Indeed, the one text with material that sounds the most like HC 1, the Small Emden Catechism, leads off with a teleological, not a soteriological, question ("Why were you created as a human being?"),[38] and its lone reference to comfort does not occur until Q 24. Comfort is at most a minor theological concept buried deep in the text, and it does not seem to play a role beyond the limited contexts in which it appears. Nevertheless, these Reformed catechisms from northwest Germany provide us with several possible sources for some of the language of the question in SC 1, LC 1, and HC 1; for parts of the opening and closing lines of the answer in HC 1; and for the linkage between comfort and three of the doctrines of the Apostles' Creed in LC 103, 110, 131, and HC 57.

When it comes to the choice of comfort as the overall theme of the HC, therefore, it is the Lutheran tradition that probably had the greater impact on Ursinus. However, when it comes to the actual language of the HC's opening question and answer on comfort, we find woven through the text strands of material from both Lutheran and Reformed sources. In this respect, HC 1 serves as a paradigm of much of the rest of the catechism.

THREEFOLD STRUCTURE

We move now from the central theme of the HC, introduced in the first question and answer, to the threefold structure of the catechism outlined in HC 2:

> **Q. What must you know to live and die in the joy of this comfort?**
>
> A. Three things: first, how great my sin and misery are; second, how I am set free from all my sins and misery; third, how I am to thank God for such deliverance.

The obvious textual source of HC 2 is the third question and answer of Ursinus's *Catechesis minor*, or SC (1561 or 1562), which seems to have served as a base text for the HC:

> **Q. What does God's Word teach?**
> A. First, it shows us our misery; second, how we are delivered from it; and third, what gratitude ought to be shown to God for this deliverance.

As in HC 2, this answer introduces the major divisions of the catechism to follow.

What, then, were the roots of this tripartite structure in the SC? Four sources in particular have competed for this distinction—three Lutheran and one Reformed, and two of which were connected in some way to the Palatinate in the years immediately preceding the HC. The oldest of these texts was proposed by August Lang over a century ago, namely, an early catechetical work by Martin Luther titled "Eine kurze Form der zehn Gebote . . ." ("A Short Form of the Ten Commandments . . .," 1520).[39] There Luther introduces a threefold structure to the document with the use of a medical metaphor:

> Three things a person must know in order to be saved. First, he must know what to do and what to leave undone. Second, when he realizes that he cannot measure up to what he should do or leave undone, he needs to know where to go to find the strength he requires. Third, he must know how to seek and obtain that strength. It is just like a sick person who first has to determine the nature of his sickness, then find out what to do or to leave undone. After that, he has to know where to get the medicine which will help him do or leave undone what is right for a healthy person. Third, he has to desire to search for this medicine and to obtain it or have it brought to him.
>
> Thus the commandments teach man to recognize his sickness . . . and so he will recognize himself to be a sinful and wicked person. The Creed holds before him and teaches him where to find the medicine, the grace, that will help him to keep the commandments; and the Creed points him to God and his mercy, given and made plain to him in Christ. Third, the Lord's Prayer teaches him how to desire, obtain, and have this medicine brought to him, namely, with proper, humble, comforting prayer . . . In these three are the essentials of the entire Bible.[40]

The parallels here to the first two parts of the HC are striking, especially when one considers that the HC, too, links the law to part 1 and the creed to part 2. According to Lang, Ursinus simply replaced Luther's concepts of "sickness" and "medicine" with the terms *misery* and *deliverance* and then filled out the triad with the Reformed notion of gratitude.[41]

A second possible source text was suggested in the late nineteenth century by Maurits Gooszen, namely, Philip Melanchthon's first edition of the *Loci communes theologici* ("Theological Commonplaces," 1521).[42] Gooszen alleged that the *Loci* derives its shape from three major movements: from sin and the law; to grace and the gospel; to repentance, love, and the sacraments,[43] an arrangement that was itself impressed upon Melanchthon by the general outline of Paul's Epistle to the Romans.[44]

In the early twentieth century, Johann Reu called attention to yet a third possible source titled "A Brief Orderly Summary of the Right True Doctrine of Our Holy Christian Faith," a Lutheran digest of Christian doctrine first published in Regensburg in 1547 and reprinted in Heidelberg in 1558.[45] Although the "Summary" was anonymous, it did contain a foreword by the Gnesio-Lutheran Nicholas Gallus, a former student of Melanchthon's who later became a strong critic of his teacher's theology. This treatise was reprinted in Heidelberg in 1558 and undoubtedly became a part of the catechetical literature in use in the Palatinate in the five years leading up to the HC.[46]

What is striking about this document is that its subsections are organized under the three main doctrinal headings of law and sin, gospel and faith, and good works[47] and that in the explanations of each section we encounter the actual terms *misery*, *deliverance*, and *thankfulness*, respectively.[48] The "Summary" then concludes with a "Brief Christian Confession for Young Children and Simple People," which is also divided into three parts:

> First, I confess that I am a poor, sinful creature.
> Second, I confess and I believe that . . . our Lord Jesus Christ . . . has . . . obtained and merited forgiveness of my sins and eternal life.
> Third, I confess that for such great grace and goodness I should be truly thankful to God.[49]

The tripartite structure of the "Summary" as a whole, the language of misery, deliverance, and gratitude, and the threefold division of the brief confession at the end all led Reu to conclude that one of the HC's most celebrated features, its three part systematic arrangement, had its origins in this Lutheran catechism.[50]

In the 1960s Walter Hollweg offered a fourth hypothesis, contending that two Reformed confessions by Theodore Beza, the "Confession of the Christian Faith" (*Confessio fidei christianae,* 1560) and "A Second Brief Confession of Faith" (*Altera brevis fidei confessio*, 1560), significantly influenced the structure, content, and even some of the phraseology of the HC.[51] Hollweg laid the groundwork for his argument by highlighting Beza's close ties to the Heidelberg community. Already in the years before the publication of the HC, Beza had developed friendly relations with the Palatinate electors Otto Henry and Frederick III, consistory member Michael Diller, university professor Peter Boquinus, and future contributors to the HC Ursinus and Olevianus. Between 1557 and 1559 Beza personally visited Heidelberg four times and during these visits became increasingly involved in the Protestant eucharistic debates in the region.[52]

Beza's trip to Heidelberg in November 1559 led to yet another significant, if unexpected, development. At the apparent suggestion of Elector Frederick III, an intermediary informed Beza of the need in the Palatinate for a brief summary of the Genevan understanding of the Protestant faith that was not as difficult or diffuse as some of the other Swiss theological works. Less than half a year later, in March 1560, Beza's *Confessio chrisitanae fidei*, a Latin revision of his *Confession de la foi chrestienne* (1559), was published in Geneva. In the preface, he indicated that he had sought to steer a middle course between the breadth of Calvin's *Institutes*, on the one hand, and the brevity of the GC, on the other—precisely what his Palatinate contacts had asked of him. Beza's shorter version of the *Confessio*, the *Altera brevis fidei confessio*, was also well known in Heidelberg. Like the longer confession, it was first composed in French in 1559 (*Autre briefve confession de foy*) and was appended to the French and Latin editions of the longer *Confessio*. In 1561 it was translated from French into Dutch and accompanied Peter Dathenus's Dutch refugee congregation in its move from Frankfurt to Heidelberg that same year. A German translation of the French text, probably prepared by Caspar Olevianus, was published in Heidelberg in 1562, and the very next year this translation was reprinted in Heidelberg as an appendix to a German translation of the Gallican Confession.[53]

All of this data, says Hollweg, suggests that the authors of the HC *could* have used Beza's two confessions as resources in carrying out their assignment. That they did in fact do so, he argues, can be seen from the several organizational and linguistic similarities between these confessions and the HC. Most relevant to the structure of the HC is a parallel Hollweg noted between the threefold division of the catechism and the threefold work of the Holy Spirit in articles 17–21 of the "Second Brief Confession": the first work of the Spirit relates to awareness of sin through the law, the second to salvation through the gospel, and the third to sanctification.[54] Hollweg acknowledged the difference between the third element here (sanctification) and the third heading of the HC ("Gratitude"), but he maintained that the substructure of the HC required that sanctification be treated in part 2 under the exposition of the Apostles' Creed (see HC 24: "God the Holy Spirit and our Sanctification"). Nevertheless, the themes of gratitude, good works, and prayer in part 3 still had their roots in the two Bezan confessions.[55]

Should the threefold structure of the HC, then, be traced to Luther, Melanchthon, an anonymous Lutheran catechism from Regensburg, or Beza? Each of these options is certainly a possibility but none is entirely satisfactory. The least likely source text is probably Melanchthon's 1521 *Loci,* in which the threefold division that Gooszen detected there is not at all transparent to the reader and in which Melanchthon himself never attempts to make it transparent. Moreover, there is no integration of the latter portion of this work with the theme of gratitude.

If a source with so little explicit evidence for a triadic arrangement could have inspired such a structure in the HC, then so also could any number of other documents, such as, for example, Luther's Small Catechism of 1529. In an expanded paraphrase of this catechism in 1566, Melanchthon's former student Joachim Mörlin describes Luther's work as containing the most important elements of Christian doctrine that we need to know to be saved, to believe, and to live a godly life. These elements are three in number: the law, the gospel, and the "table of duties" (*Haustafel*) for the various members of the Christian community. The law shows us our sin, much like a doctor who diagnoses an illness. The gospel, comprising the creed, prayer, and the sacraments, contains the medication we need. And the "table of duties" near the end of the catechism provides a specific regimen by which a person can live righteously before God in his or her station in life.[56] The deeper threefold structure that Mörlin detected here, therefore, also foreshadows the misery-deliverance-gratitude organization of the HC, but as in the *Loci,* it does not form the surface structure of the Small Catechism and nowhere designates gratitude as the theme of the third part.[57]

Luther's "Short Form of the Ten Commandments . . ." has more to commend it as a possible source text than Melanchthon's *Loci* or his own Small Catechism, since it is clearly organized into three parts that are explicitly introduced at the beginning. Furthermore, the medical metaphor that Luther employed to illustrate the roles of the law and the gospel recurs in the instructions for preaching in the Palatinate Church Order of 1563 in an application to the threefold division of the HC.[58] When sermons lead people to know their misery, how they are delivered from it, and how they should live in gratitude for such deliverance, such preaching becomes "medicine for relieving the wounded conscience."[59] And Ursinus himself asserted in his commentary on the HC years later that "a knowledge of our misery is necessary for our comfort . . . because it excites in us the desire of deliverance, just as a knowledge of disease awakens a desire of medicine on the part of the sick."[60]

Nevertheless, the third part of Luther's schema makes no mention of gratitude and is not really even about the place of good works in the Christian life. For the roots of the connection between gratitude and good works that is introduced in HC 86, one must look back not to Luther or even to the Reformed tradition, as Lang claimed, but very likely to another Lutheran source, a 1535 catechism by Johannes Brenz:

> Q. **Why ought we to do good works?**
> A. Not because we pay for sin and earn eternal life with our deeds—for Christ alone has paid for sin and earned eternal life—but rather because we ought to bear witness to our faith with good works and be thankful to our Lord God for his good deeds.[61]

The parallels in language between this question and answer and HC 86 are too striking to be just a coincidence.

What Hollweg suggested as another possible source for the HC's organization, namely, Beza's "Second Brief Confession," is also attractive at first glance. Unlike Melanchthon's *Loci* it contains an explicit threefold design, and unlike Luther's "Short Form" it makes a clear connection between the third part of that design and the Christian life of sanctification. What militates against Hollweg's thesis, however, is that Beza's doctrine of the threefold work of the Holy Spirit, on which the HC's triadic structure was allegedly based, is embedded in the middle of the confession, comprises only five articles out of thirty-three, and has no bearing on the organization of the document as a whole. In addition, it never mentions gratitude in relation to the sanctifying work of the Holy Spirit.

Of the four possibilities before us, the 1558 Heidelberg edition of the Regensburg "Summary" would seem the most likely because of its explicit organization around the three themes that anticipate the divisions of the HC and because of the appearance in the text, albeit very rarely, of the terminology that the HC would later use to label these divisions. We might even say that gratitude plays a thematic role in the "Summary" if one takes the third part of the simple confession at the end ("for such great grace and goodness I should be truly thankful to God") as a condensation of the third section of the document as a whole.

What gives one pause, however, is that this same triad of law/sin, gospel/faith, and good works appears also in other literature from the first half of the sixteenth century, sometimes even in a structural role and/or with accompanying references to gratitude. We find versions of it, for example, in Melanchthon's Visitation Articles of 1527–28[62] and in the combination of contrition, faith, and fruits of repentance in article XII ("Repentance") of the AC (1530):

> Now properly speaking, true repentance is nothing else than to have contrition and sorrow, or terror about sin, and yet at the same time to believe in the gospel and absolution that sin is forgiven and grace is obtained through Christ. Such faith, in turn, comforts the heart and puts it at peace. Then improvement should also follow, and a person should refrain from sins. For these should be the fruits of repentance.[63]

Moreover, according to AC article XX (1531, *editio princeps*) on faith and good works, the Holy Spirit produces in us a knowledge of sin and then faith, so that we may derive eternal comfort (!) and life from the great mercy promised us in Christ. After that, the Spirit also produces in us the virtues that God requires in the Ten Commandments: to fear, love, thank (!), call upon, and honor God, and to love our neighbor.[64] We hear echoes of this also in the Apology of the AC (1531).[65]

Yet another pre-HC source in which the threefold division appears is the 1533 Brandenburg-Nürnberg Church Order, in which the Lutheran reformers Johannes Brenz and Andreas Osiander had a major hand.[66] In the section on the sacrament of baptism, the church order states:

> In order that we might regard this work of God [in baptism] in a more heartfelt and orderly way, we should first of all diligently consider how great the misery [German: *elend*] and wretchedness are into which, according to Scripture, all of us have been plunged; second, how great the grace of God through our Lord Jesus Christ is, shown to us by freeing us from our misery and wretchedness through baptism; and third, how we should remember this grace of baptism always, but especially in time of need, and should praise and honor God in it.[67]

The document goes on to explain this threefold perspective in greater detail and even exhorts us in its exposition of the third point not only to find "comfort" in our baptism but to do so with "gratitude [German: *danckbarkeyt*] to God."[68]

Deciding the question, then, of the exact source of the HC's tripartite structure is next to impossible. From the 1520s on, various forms of the misery-deliverance-gratitude triad made their appearance in an array of theological resources in Germany—in catechisms, church orders, prayer books, summaries of doctrine, and confessions. The influences that came to bear upon Ursinus in the structuring of the SC and HC could have followed any number of these textual pathways to the Palatinate. What is significant for our study here, however, is that this triadic structure was given its earliest and widest expression not in the Reformed but in the Lutheran tradition, especially the works of its founders Luther and Melanchthon. Reu probably went too far in claiming that the configuration of the HC originated in a particular Lutheran catechism, but he was certainly right that it had a Lutheran background. Even if the threefold division was actually inspired by a Bezan Reformed confession, as Hollweg alleged, Beza himself was simply drawing on a construct with a long Lutheran pedigree. Like the theme of comfort to which it is attached, the triad of misery, deliverance, and gratitude provides a framework for the HC that is deeply rooted in the Lutheran tradition.

3

LAW AND GOSPEL

Q/A 3–19

In the previous chapter we noted the Lutheran, especially Melanchthonian-Lutheran, background to the theme and structure of the HC, with strands of Lutheran and Reformed texts woven into the pivotal first question and answer of the catechism. In HC 3–19, we find further evidence of a Lutheran-Reformed synthesis in the contrast between law and gospel that is wedded to the catechism's first two sections on misery and deliverance. What we encounter this time, however, is a basic Lutheran skeleton that is sometimes fleshed out with material that appears dependent on Reformed sources or at least reflects a Reformed theological slant.

The first major division of the HC opens with the question and answer:

> **3 Q. How do you come to know your *misery*?**
> A. The *law* of God tells me.

And early in part 2 we have a parallel question and answer:

> **19 Q. How do you come to know this [your *deliverance*]?**
> A. The holy *gospel* tells me.

To understand this connection of misery to law and deliverance to gospel, we should remember that the HC is not simply a manual on Christian comfort that was organized into these three sections on misery, deliverance, and gratitude. Like Christian catechisms for hundreds of years before and after it, the HC is essentially an explanation of the basic elements of the Christian faith: the Ten Commandments, the Apostles' Creed, the Lord's Prayer, and the sacraments. Therefore, beneath the theme and threefold structure introduced in HC 1 and 2, we also find a fivefold substructure in the following sequence: the Law (in summary), the Creed, the sacraments, the Law again (individual Ten Commandments), and the Lord's Prayer.

There is, of course, nothing distinctively Lutheran or Reformed about the ordering of these substructural elements in the HC. A simple comparison with the patterns of some of the major source catechisms for the HC bears this out:

Luther's Small Catechism (1529):
  Law-Creed-Prayer-Sacraments
Brenz's Smaller Catechism (1535):
  Baptism-Creed-Prayer-Law-Lord's Supper

Jud's Shorter Catechism (1541):
  Law-Creed-Prayer-Sacraments
Calvin's Genevan Catechism (1545):
  Creed-Law-Prayer-Sacraments
Lasco's (Large) Emden Catechism (1546):
  Law-Creed-Sacraments-Prayer
Lasco's Small Emden Catechism (1554):
  Law-Creed-Sacraments-Prayer
Ursinus's Smaller Catechism (1561/62):
  Law (summary)-Creed-Sacraments-Law-Prayer
Ursinus's Larger Catechism (1562):
  Law (summary)-Creed-Law-Prayer-Sacraments
Heidelberg Catechism (1563):
  Law (summary)-Creed-Sacraments-Law-Prayer

As we can see, the opening law-creed sequence of the SC and the HC can be found earlier not only in Luther's Small Catechism but also in Reformed works by Jud and Lasco. And both Brenz's and Calvin's catechisms, the one Lutheran and the other Reformed, lead off with different patterns altogether.

What distinguishes the HC and SC from their predecessors is first of all the way they divide their exposition of the law into two parts: (1) the summary of the law, which functions as a mirror of human sin, and (2) the individual Ten Commandments, which function as a pattern for grateful living. What further distinguishes these catechisms is how they then connect their five substructural elements—law (summary), creed, sacraments, law (commandments), and prayer—to the threefold division of misery, deliverance, and gratitude, and ultimately to the theme of comfort itself. In outline form the HC, for example, looks like this:

INTRODUCTION: Theme and Structure (HC 1–2)
- I. **HUMAN MISERY**
  - A. **Exposition of the Law (summary)** (3–5)
  - B. Creation and Fall of Humanity (6–11)
- II. **HUMAN DELIVERANCE**
  - A. Christ the Mediator (12–19)
  - B. Faith and the Creed (20–25)
  - C. **Exposition of the Apostles' Creed**
    - 1. God the Father (26–28)
    - 2. God the Son (29–52)
    - 3. God the Holy Spirit (53–58)
  - D. Justification (59–64)
  - E. **Exposition of the Sacraments**

1. Introduction to the Sacraments (65–68)
2. Baptism (69–74)
3. The Lord's Supper (75–80)
4. The Keys of the Kingdom: Preaching and Church Discipline (81–85)

III. **GRATITUDE**

A. Good Works & Repentance/Conversion/Sanctification (86–91)
B. **Exposition of the Law (Ten Commandments)** (92–115)
C. **Exposition of the Lord's Prayer** (116–129)

The law (in summary), therefore, is located in the first section on human misery, and the creed, which is really a summary of the gospel (HC 22), is treated under human deliverance. In fact, as we saw in the HC's two questions and answers quoted at the beginning of this chapter, it is *through* (the summary of) the law that we come to know our misery (HC 3) and *through* (the creedal summary of) the gospel that we come to know our deliverance (HC 19).

This structural linkage in the HC between law and misery in part 1 and gospel and deliverance in part 2 creates a dialectic between law and gospel with a very Lutheran flavor.[1] Luther had taught that the Word of God addresses us in Scripture and preaching as both law and gospel. The law is an expression of the perfect and holy will of God, but as a way of salvation it becomes devilish and tyrannical. It wags a finger at us, saying, "This is what you must do to live," and in the process it exposes our sin and prepares us to receive grace. The gospel, by contrast, is not God's command but God's gift to us. "This is what God has done for you in Christ so that you may live," it declares. The gospel promises us what the law cannot provide: grace, righteousness, and life.[2]

Calvin, as a representative of the Reformed tradition more generally, also recognized this polarity between law and gospel but only in a narrow sense. In its broader and more common meaning, the law is not mere precept that threatens condemnation and death but the whole covenantal law of the Old Testament, containing God's promises of grace as well. And the gospel in its broader sense is not just the proclamation of grace by the incarnate Christ but all the testimonies of God's mercy and favor found already in the Old Testament. In this broader or fuller sense, gospel differs from law only in the clarity of its manifestation.[3]

The first two parts of the HC, then, clearly reflect in their structure and substructure a more Lutheran than Reformed view of the relationship between law and gospel. The law reveals our misery (part 1); the gospel reveals our deliverance from that misery (part 2). Nevertheless, we must not draw this law-gospel distinction in the HC too sharply, for sometimes the Lutheran structure of parts 1 and 2 is mitigated by subtle Reformed accents or fleshed out with Reformed content.[4] This is probably not so surprising when we consider that much of the wording of HC 3–19 is dependent on texts from the Reformed tradition, particularly the "Second Brief Confession of Faith" (SBC) by Theodore Beza. Hollweg has identified the following verbal parallels between the two documents:[5]

HC 4 Q. **What does God's law require of us?**

A. Christ teaches us this in summary in Matthew 22:37–40: "'You shall love the Lord your God with all your heart, and with all your soul, and with all your mind.' This is the greatest and first commandment. And a second is like it: 'You shall love your neighbor as yourself.' On these two commandments hang all the law and the prophets."

SBC III And after it is found in the law that we are obligated to love the Lord our God with all our heart and our neighbor as ourselves, we see clearly enough what it is that we owe: perfect love toward God and our neighbor.[6]

HC 5 Q. **Can you live up to all this perfectly?**

A. No. I have a natural tendency to hate God and my neighbor.

SBC IV But how can someone accomplish such a thing if one is not first of all equipped for it by nature? For experience teaches us that our nature is inclined to do just the opposite; hence all people . . . are hateful toward God and neighbor.[7]

HC 12 Q. **According to God's righteous judgment, we deserve punishment both now and in eternity: how then can we escape this punishment and return to God's favor?**

A. God requires that his justice be satisfied. Therefore the claims of this justice must be paid in full, either by ourselves or another.

SBC I, V They do not fully satisfy the justice of God . . . Therefore, it necessarily follows either that all people without exception must be damned or that they must find someone to pay the debt for them.[8]

HC 13 Q. **Can we make this payment ourselves?**

A. Certainly not. Actually, we increase our debt every day.

SBC V Through further transgression, they become more and more guilty every day.[9]

HC 14 Q. **Can another creature—any at all—pay this debt for us?**

A. No. To begin with, God will not punish any other creature for what a human is guilty of. Furthermore, no mere creature can bear the weight of God's eternal wrath against sin and deliver others from it.

SBC VI Where does one find such a surety who can do this? Certainly nowhere among creatures. . . . The justice of God does not allow angels to be liable for what humans are guilty of. Moreover, since this is a matter of bearing the anger of God, there is no doubt that even the angels are not strong enough to bear such a heavy weight.[10]

HC 15 Q. What kind of mediator and deliverer should we look for then?

A. One who is a true and righteous human, yet more powerful than all creatures, that is, one who is also true God.

SBC VII It is absolutely necessary, therefore, that we find refuge in someone who is stronger and more powerful than all creatures, and yet at the same time is truly human.[11]

HC 18 Q. Then who is this mediator—true God and at the same time a true and righteous human?

A. Our Lord Jesus Christ, who was given to us to completely deliver us and make us right with God.

SBC VII Thus it is necessary that one find a mediator who is both God and human. The only such mediator is the Lord Jesus Christ.[12]

This Bezan confession, therefore, in all likelihood provided the textual foundation for parts of HC 3–19. The parallels in language and flow of the argument are simply too striking to be coincidental. But is there anything Reformed also about the way the HC's teaching on law and gospel is actually organized and explained? Or is Cornelius Graafland correct in his claim that Ursinus's arrangement of the material in the HC and in his subsequent commentary on the catechism represented a "striking deviation" from Calvin in the 1559 *Institutes*?[13] Graafland argues that the *Institutes*, like the HC, places the treatment of the law immediately before the discussion of redemption through Christ the Mediator, but it does so in book 2, titled "The Knowledge of God the Redeemer in Christ, First Disclosed to the Fathers under the Law, and Then to us in the Gospel." That means that Calvin's treatment of deliverance or redemption begins not, as in the HC, with the doctrine of the Mediator but with the doctrines of sin and law. In other words, Graafland concludes, the *Institutes* place both law and gospel within the framework of redemption, whereas the HC treats law apart from and prior to redemption.[14]

This interpretation of the HC, however, is not borne out by a closer examination of the text. The contrast between law and gospel is not as rigid as the outline of the catechism might imply, for there is already a hint of gospel in part 1 on the law and much more than a hint of law in part 2 on the gospel. To begin with, it is worth looking at the wording of HC 4 in the context of HC 3:

3 Q. How do you come to know your misery?
A. The law of God tells me.

4 Q. What does God's law require of us?
A. Christ teaches us this in summary in Matthew 22:37–40: "'You shall love the Lord your God with all your heart, and with all your soul, and with all your mind.' This is the greatest and first commandment. And a second is like it: 'You shall love your neighbor as yourself.' On these two commandments hang all the law and the prophets."

The law that reveals our misery requires of us something that "*Christ* teaches us" in summary form in the *Gospel* of Matthew. It is Christ, the end of the law, the fulfillment of the law, indeed the one who fulfilled the gospel proclaimed already in the Old Testament (HC 19), who teaches us what God's law requires of us. What the law demands is first that we love God with all our heart, something that, according to HC 6, God created us in his image to do and that, according to part 3 of the HC, Christ is restoring us in his image to do as we respond to the gospel in faith and obedience to the law (HC 86, 92, 114). By placing law on the lips of Christ in part 1, the HC is hinting already in this section on human misery that law can really be understood only within the broader context of gospel.[15]

If in good Reformed fashion, then, there is already a hint of gospel in part 1 of the HC on the law, there is an even stronger presence of law at the beginning of part 2 on the gospel. For one thing, some of the language from HC 10 and 11 at the end of part 1 is repeated almost verbatim in HC 12:

Part 1: Human Misery

10 Q. Does God permit such disobedience and rebellion to go unpunished?
A. Certainly not. God is terribly angry with the sin we are born with as well as the sins we personally commit. As a just judge, God will punish them both now and in eternity, having declared: "Cursed is everyone who does not observe and obey all the things written in the book of the law."

11 Q. But isn't God also merciful?
A. God is certainly merciful, but also just. God's justice demands that sin, committed against his supreme majesty, be punished with the supreme penalty—eternal punishment of body and soul.

Part 2: Human Deliverance

12 Q. According to God's righteous judgment we deserve punishment both now and in eternity: how then can we escape this punishment and return to God's favor?

A. God requires that his justice be satisfied. Therefore the claims of this justice must be paid in full, either by ourselves or by another.

The first lines of both Q 12 and A 12, which introduce the HC's second section on deliverance and gospel, pick up some of the phrases of HC 10 and 11, which conclude the first section on misery and law. "God's righteous judgment" (Q 12) echoes "As a just judge, God ..." (A 10) and "God's justice" (A 11). "We deserve punishment both now and in eternity" (Q 12) harks back to "God will punish them both now and in eternity" (A10). And "God requires that his justice be satisfied" (A 12) evokes the line in A 11, "God's justice demands that sin . . . be punished with the supreme penalty." The righteous judgment of God, the demand for satisfaction, and the temporal and eternal punishment to which we are liable are all themes that bridge the first two sections of the HC. The first thing we encounter in the section on the gospel, therefore, is a reiteration of our condemnation under the law.[16]

Ursinus proceeds at the end of A 12 to lay out two ways in which the demands of the law can be satisfied: "either by ourselves or by another." The first of these options is what Goeters calls the *modus legalis* ("the method revealed in the law"), that is, the satisfaction of God's justice by perfectly obeying the law and paying its penalty.[17] That option, however, is ruled out as a possibility in HC 13:

Q. Can we make this payment ourselves?

A. Certainly not. Actually, we increase our debt every day.

The second option, that our debt be paid "by another," is the *modus evangelicus* ("the method revealed in the gospel").[18] The "another" who can satisfy the justice of God is not any mere creature (Q 14), since "God will not punish any other creature for what a human is guilty of," and "no mere creature can bear the weight of God's eternal wrath against sin and deliver others from it" (A 14). The "another" must be "a mediator and deliverer" (Q 15) who is "a true and righteous human, yet more powerful than all creatures, that is, one who is also true God" (A 15). The rationale for the true humanity and divinity of this mediator is given in HC 16 and 17, respectively, and then comes the climactic question and answer in HC 18:

Q. Then who is this mediator—true God and at the same time a true and righteous human?

A. Our Lord Jesus Christ, who was given to us to completely deliver us and make us right with God.

This doctrine of the Mediator, framed against the background of the law, is something we come to know from the gospel:

19 A. God began to reveal the gospel already in Paradise; later God proclaimed it by the holy patriarchs and prophets and foreshadowed it by the sacrifices and other ceremonies of the law; and finally God fulfilled it through his own beloved Son.

This is a remarkable answer because, in typically Reformed fashion, it places the gospel of redemption through Christ the Mediator squarely at the center of the entire biblical message, in Old and New Testament alike.[19] The revelation of the gospel begins in Genesis, is proclaimed and adumbrated in various forms in Israel's history, and is finally fulfilled in the ministry of the incarnate Son of God. Particularly striking is the assertion that the gospel is foreshadowed even "by the sacrifices and other ceremonies of the *law*" (A 19). "Law" here could be simply be a reference to the ceremonial law of the Old Testament, but it could also refer to the entire framework of religious life or the entire period of salvation history of which that ceremonial system was a part. In any case, HC 19 explicitly and closely connects gospel and law.[20]

The opening questions and answers of part 2 of the HC, therefore, are not just about gospel, but about gospel and law, or gospel as it relates to law in both a moral and ceremonial sense. Once again, the sharp distinction between law and gospel suggested by the Lutheran structure of the HC is mitigated by a more typically Reformed discussion of the interconnection between the two and, as in Calvin, by the placement of that discussion under the doctrine of deliverance through Christ the Mediator.

If we should not exaggerate the distinction between law and gospel in the HC, however, we should not minimize it either. Neuser has argued that the Calvinistic view of the law embedded in HC 3–4 represents a significant revision of Ursinus's SC 4–7, which, in Neuser's view, portrays a sharp Melanchthonian contrast between law and gospel:[21] The text of SC 4–7 reads as follows:

3 Q. How do we come to know our misery?
A. From the divine law, which is summarized in the Decalogue.

4 Q. How do we learn the way of deliverance?
A. From the gospel, that is, the articles of the Christian faith, and the sacraments.

5 Q. **Where are we taught the gratitude that we owe to God?**
A. In the Decalogue, and in the doctrine of the invocation of God.

6 Q. **What is the summary of the Decalogue?**
A. Christ summarized it with these words in Matthew 22: "You shall love the Lord your God with all your heart, and with all your soul, and with all your mind. This is the first and great commandment. And a second is like it—You shall love your neighbor as yourself. On these two commandments all the law and the prophets depend." Concerning these commandments God said: "Cursed be everyone who does not abide by all the things written in the book of the law and do them."

Neuser notes first of all that HC 3–4 refers to the summary of the "law" as a teacher of sin. The HC here no longer speaks, in what he regards as more typically Melanchthonian fashion, of the "Decalogue" as a summary of the law that shows us our misery (SC 4) or of the double commandment of love as the "summary of the *Decalogue*" (SC 7; italics added). Direct reference to the Decalogue in the HC is reserved, in more Calvinian fashion, for the treatment of the third use of the law in part 3.[22]

What this argument fails to recognize, however, is that the law *is* explicitly equated with the Decalogue in part 3 (HC 92), and that one of the functions of the Ten Commandments in part 3 is to expose in an ongoing way the sinfulness of those who have been regenerated (HC 115). The Decalogue as such, therefore, clearly has a pedagogical or exposure function also in the HC.[23] Furthermore, the quotation in HC 4 of Christ's double command of love as the requirement of the law does not represent a mitigation of the contrast between law and gospel in the SC, as Neuser suggests.[24] Both the SC and HC build this contrast into their basic structure, both underscore it by quoting words of imprecation from the *Old* Testament ("Cursed be everyone who does not abide by all the things written in the book of the law and do them."), and both take some of the edge off the contrast by quoting Christ's summary of the law. This subtle Reformed accent inside a Lutheran structure was not an innovation by the HC, therefore, but already a feature of one of its major sources.

It is not just this interplay between law and gospel, however, that gives the Lutheran structure of parts 1 and 2 a Reformed slant. Woven through the HC's section on misery and the beginning of the section on deliverance are several other Reformed emphases as well. First, there is a stress on human depravity and the bondage of the will in a couple of the questions and answers that immediately follow the introduction of the law:

5 Q. Can you live up to all this [summary of the law] perfectly?
A. No. I have a natural tendency to hate God and my neighbor.

8 Q. But are we so corrupt that we are totally unable to do any good and inclined toward all evil?
A. Yes, unless we are born again by the Spirit of God.

The law calls us to *love* God and neighbor with our whole being (HC 4), but our fallen nature is inclined to do just the opposite, to *hate* them (HC 5). This inclination is so deeply rooted in our corruption that it cannot be undone apart from a miraculous rebirth by the Holy Spirit (HC 8). In these questions and answers, the HC may simply be espousing a general Protestant doctrine of total inability over against the more optimistic view of fallen humanity in medieval Catholicism. HC 8 may also reflect the general Protestant notion of salvation as a sovereign work of God over against the Catholic emphasis on human cooperation. But the catechism might also be displaying here the Reformed instincts of Ursinus and others on the writing team by taking a firm stand against any kind of *Lutheran* synergism.[25] The view of conversion as a joint operation between God and the human convert had first been intimated by Melanchthon in the mid-1530s, and by the time the HC was being composed, it had become the subject of a raging controversy in Lutheran circles.[26] Even though the HC presents the doctrines of depravity and regeneration in what Couard calls a "decisive but gentle and inoffensive way,"[27] the catechism could be seen here as injecting itself into the synergistic debate and actually aligning itself with the Gnesio-Lutherans. This could serve to enhance its claim as a confession within the framework of Lutheran orthodoxy.[28]

Second, the opening questions and answers of part 2 likely reflect a Reformed (or perhaps a Reformed-Philippist) view of the integrity of the two natures of Christ that anticipates the polemic against ubiquitarian Lutheranism in HC 47–48.[29] This is not just an abstract christological point in the HC but one that is intimately connected with the redemptive work of the mediator on which our salvation, and thus our comfort, depend. The kind of mediator and deliverer that we should look for is one who is at the same time a true human and true God (HC 15)—true human because a human must pay for human sin (HC 16), and true God "so that the mediator, by the power of his divinity, might bear the weight of God's wrath in his humanity and *earn for us and restore to us righteousness and life*" (HC 17; italics added). It is the Lord Jesus Christ, sinless and truly human and divine, "who was given to us to completely deliver us and make us right with God" (HC 18).[30] Deliverance through Christ the Mediator is at the heart of the gospel that is introduced here in part 2, and the repeated references to "*true* human" and "*true* God" in HC 15–18 suggest that the properties of each of the natures of the mediator must remain intact to ensure the efficacy of the work he came to do.

Finally, the view of atonement reflected in these early questions on the gospel has more of a Reformed than Lutheran flavor to them. In Luther we find something of a balance between, and even a blending of, the emphasis in the ancient church on the triumph of Christ over Satan and the evil powers (Christus Victor theory of atonement), on the one hand, and the doctrine of penal substitution developed during the Protestant Reformation, on the other.[31] Calvin and the Reformed tradition did not neglect the victory dimension of the atonement, but they gave greater prominence to the themes of substitution, satisfaction of divine justice, propitiation, and sacrifice.[32] The HC begins with a Luther-like balance between the two motifs in the opening lines of A 1: "He [Jesus Christ] has fully paid for all my sins with his precious blood" (penal substitution), "and has delivered me from the tyranny of the devil" (Christus Victor). Such a balance is not surprising, since, as we saw in the previous chapter, the wording of the first part of A 1 follows very closely that of Luther's Small Catechism.

But in HC 12–18 the scales are tipped. To be sure, the victory motif is still there: the references to our need of a "deliverer" (HC 15) and to Christ being given "to completely deliver us" (HC 18) evoke the language of HC 1 that Christ has "delivered me from the tyranny of the devil." Even the requirement that the mediator and deliverer be "more *powerful* than all creatures" (HC 15; italics added) so that "by the *power* of his divinity" (HC 17; italics added) he might withstand the wrath of God and deliver us from it (HC 14) may be reminiscent of Luther's inclusion of divine wrath among the powers to be defeated by Christ on the cross.[33] Nonetheless, these hints at a victory motif in HC 12–18 are overshadowed by the legal language of penal substitution, which is introduced in the very first question of part 2 and carries through to the climactic answer on the identity of the mediator: "God's righteous judgment" (Q 12), "punishment" (Q 12), "justice" (A 12), "satisfied" (A 12), "paid in full" (A 12), "payment" (Q 13), "debt" (A 13), "pay this debt" (Q 14), "punish" (A 14), "guilty" (A 14), "God's justice" (A 16), "righteous" (Q 16, 18), "pay for sin" (A 16), "pay for others" (A 16), "earn for us" (A 17), "righteousness" (A 17), "make us right with God" (A 18).

Furthermore, in his later lectures on the HC, Ursinus makes very clear that the misery from which humanity is delivered consists, first, in the loss of righteousness and in inbred corruption, or sin; and secondly, in the punishment of sin. His deliverance, therefore, from this misery requires, first, the pardon and abolishing of sin, and a restoration of the righteousness lost; and secondly, a release from all punishment and misery.[34]

Even though Ursinus states at the beginning of this discussion of deliverance that "all men, by nature, are the slaves of sin, *satan*, and death," he concludes that "deliverance consists of *two* parts—a deliverance from sin and death."[35] He does not mention a deliverance from Satan. The emphasis here in Ursinus's commentary on the HC, therefore, is the same as in the text of HC 12–18 itself: the penal dimension of the atonement eclipses that of Christ as victor over Satan.

This perspective on the atonement is yet another instance of a Reformed emphasis inside the Lutheran law-gospel dialectic of HC 3–19. Here and with the other Reformed accents we have identified in this chapter—the hints of gospel in part 1 of the HC and of law in part 2, the firm statement in part 1 on human depravity, and the stress in part 2 on the integrity of the two natures of Christ—the HC appears to be drawing the two Protestant traditions together by staking out middle ground between them, a position that at once honors the sharp distinction between law and gospel of the Lutherans and softens that distinction somewhat with several Reformed emollients.

4

PROVIDENCE AND PREDESTINATION

Q/A 20–28

FAITH AND THE APOSTLES' CREED

Part 2 of the HC, titled "Human Deliverance" (German: *Von des Menschen Erlösung*), consists largely of expositions of the Apostles' Creed and of the sacraments of baptism and the Lord's Supper. The creed summarizes the promises of the gospel that we must believe to be grafted into Christ the Mediator and receive all his benefits (HC 20, 22), and the sacraments serve as signs and seals of those gospel promises (HC 66).

Introducing these explanations of the creed and the sacraments is one of the HC's best-known questions and answers: its definition of faith, which follows closely the content of Ursinus's two earlier catechisms:

HC 21 Q. What is true faith?
A. True faith is not only a sure knowledge by which I hold as true all that God has revealed to us in the Scripture; it is also a wholehearted trust, which the Holy Spirit creates in me by the gospel, that God has freely granted, not only to others but to me also, forgiveness of sins, eternal righteousness, and salvation. These are gifts of sheer grace, granted solely by Christ's merit.

SC 12 Q. What is faith?
A. It is a firm assent by which we know that everything related to us in God's Word is true, and a deep-rooted assurance created by the Holy Spirit in the hearts of God's elect, by which each person is convinced that God has graciously granted him remission of sins, righteousness, and eternal life because of Christ's merit alone.

LC 38 Q. What is faith?
A. It is to assent firmly to every word of God related to us, and a firm assurance by which each person is convinced that God has graciously granted him remission of sins, righteousness, and eternal life because of Christ's merit and through him; and which, having been awakened in the hearts of the elect by the Holy Spirit, makes us living members of Christ and produces in us true love and invocation of God.

Much of the text of these three versions appears to be based on Melanchthon's descriptions of faith in his *EO* ("Examination of Ordinands") of 1552 (German) and 1554 (Latin):

EO **(1552):** The faith by which a person obtains forgiveness of sins and is righteous is not only a knowledge of history like that found in devils and godless people. Rather, this genuine faith is to know and to hold as true all the articles of the faith, and thus also the promise of the grace of Christ, to which end, as it were, all the articles are directed. Faith, therefore, is a truly wholehearted trust in the Son of God, Jesus Christ the Mediator and Reconciler, that because of him and through him we have forgiveness of sins, grace, and salvation.[1]

EO **(1554):** Faith is to assent to every word of God related to us, and thus to the promise of grace, and it is a trust that approaches God, calls upon him, and cries out, "Abba, Father" . . . I believe that the forgiveness of sins is given not only to others but to me also.[2]

The similarity of vocabulary and phraseology between this portrayal of faith and that of HC 21 is unmistakable. Both speak of true faith as "knowledge" (1552 *EO*: *wissen, erkentnis*; HC: *erkandtnusz*) and "wholehearted trust" (1552 *EO*: *herzlich vertrawen*; HC: *hertzliches vertrawen*). Genuine faith is to "hold as true" (1552 *EO*: *fur war halten*; HC: *für war halte*) all the articles of the faith (1552 *EO*) or every word that comes from God (1554 *EO*; HC). And it is "because of [Christ]" (1552 *EO*: *umb seinet willen*) or "by Christ's merit" (HC: *umb des verdiensts Christi willen*) that "forgiveness of sins, grace, and salvation" (1552 *EO*) or "forgiveness of sins, eternal righteousness, and salvation" (HC) have been granted "not only to others but to me also" (1554 *EO*; HC). Furthermore, Melanchthon's assertion in the 1552 *EO* that the articles of the Apostles' Creed are really to be understood as promises of grace is echoed in HC 22, which immediately follows the HC's definition of faith:

Q. What then must a Christian believe?

A. All that is promised us in the gospel, a summary of which is taught us in the articles of our universal and undisputed Christian faith.

This definition of faith as both knowledge and trust goes back deep into the Lutheran tradition, appearing already in Luther's "Eyn kurcz form der zeehen gepott . . ." ("A Short Form of the Ten Commandments . . .") of 1520[3] and in Melanchthon's AC of 1530.[4] That is not to say, however, that it is an exclusively Lutheran conception.[5] The double aspect of faith can also be found in such early Reformed sources as Leo Jud's (Large) Catechism (1534) and Calvin's first edition of the *Institutes* (1536).[6] And the reference in HC 21 to faith as something "which the Holy Spirit creates in me" is found in similar form in earlier Reformed catechisms by Micronius and Lasco.[7] But the basic outline and phraseology of HC 21 and the interpretation of the creed in HC 22 as a summary of the promises of the gospel are rooted in Lutheran, especially Melanchthonian, sources. This is significant because Ursinus thus introduces the very heart of the catechism, the exposition of the creed and the sacraments, with language that is not only familiar to Lutheran ears but resonant with the authoritative text of the AC.

After quoting the Apostles' Creed in full in HC 23, the catechism goes on in HC 24 to outline the structure of the exposition to follow. Once again, Ursinus follows closely the wording of both of his earlier catechisms:

HC 24 Q. **How are these articles [of the Apostles' Creed] divided?**
A. Into three parts: God the Father and our creation; God the Son and our deliverance; and God the Holy Spirit and our sanctification.

SC 15 Q. **How many parts does this creed have?**
A. Three. The first has to do with the eternal Father and our creation; the second with the Son and our redemption; and the third with the Holy Spirit and our sanctification.

LC 40 Q. **How many main parts does this creed have?**
A. Three. The first has to do with creation and preservation; the second with redemption; and the third with our sanctification.

This threefold division and summary of the creed is very likely based on Luther's Small Catechism of 1529.[8] Already in his "A Short Form of the Ten Commandments . . ." (1520), Luther had abandoned the tradition developed during the previous millennium of organizing the creed into twelve articles and had adopted a trinitarian division instead.[9] Other catechisms before Ursinus's had also outlined the creed in this threefold fashion, but none of them went on to specify the *works* of the individual persons of the Trinity.[10] What distinguished Luther's Small (and Large) Catechism from the tradition before them was the way that they connected the three parts of the creed both with the individual persons of the Trinity and with their works of creation, redemption, and sanctification, respectively.[11] It is this double connection that is picked up in HC 24 in almost identical language:

Small Catechism: The First Article: On Creation (German: *Schöpfung*)

HC 24: God the Father and our creation (German: *erschöpffung*)

Small Catechism: The Second Article: On Redemption (*Erlösung*)

HC 24: God the Son and our deliverance (*erlösung*)

Small Catechism: The Third Article: On Being Made Holy (*Heiligung*)

HC 24: God the Holy Spirit and our sanctification (*heiligung*)[12]

This threefold structure, drawn from a Lutheran source widely used in the Palatinate, shapes the organization of the thirty-three questions and answers on the Apostles' Creed (HC 26–58), fully one-quarter of the entire document! But the influence of Luther's Small Catechism here is tonal as well as structural. The personal tone in Luther's exposition ("I believe that God has created *me* . . . I believe that Jesus Christ . . . has redeemed *me* . . . I believe that . . . the Holy Spirit has . . . made *me* holy."[13]) is echoed in HC 24 in the references to the Father and "*our* creation," the Son and "*our* deliverance," and the Spirit and "*our* sanctification." In addition, the HC follows Luther's lead here and in the explanation of the creed that follows by emphasizing the economic rather than the immanent Trinity and the threeness rather than the oneness of the Godhead—a tack that ran counter to the general tendency in early Reformed theology.[14] HC 25 does raise the question of the oneness of God ("Since there is only one divine being, why do you speak of three: Father, Son, and Holy Spirit?"), using language that may reflect Reformed sources,[15] but the response to the question is terse ("Because that is how God has revealed himself in his Word: these three distinct persons are one, true, eternal God."). The emphasis of the exposition of the creed as a whole will not be the essence or oneness of God but the three distinct persons of the Trinity and their work.

PROVIDENCE

The HC follows the lead of Luther's Small Catechism when it introduces the theme of the first article of the Apostles' Creed (HC 26–28) as "God the Father and our *creation*" (HC 24). Like many catechisms of the day, however, Ursinus's exposition of this article in both HC 26–28 and SC 17, its primary base text, focuses not on the act of creation at the beginning of time but on the preservation and governance of that creation by divine providence:

HC 26 Q. What do you believe when you say, "I believe in God the Father almighty, creator of heaven and earth"?

A. That the eternal Father of our Lord Jesus Christ, who out of nothing created heaven and earth and [together with] everything in them, who still upholds and rules them by his eternal counsel and providence, is my God and Father because of Christ the Son. I trust God so much that I do not doubt he will provide whatever I need for body and soul, and will turn to my good whatever adversity he sends upon me in this sad world. God is able to do this because he is almighty God, and desires to do this because he is a faithful Father.

HC 27 Q. **What do you understand by the providence of God?**
A. The almighty and ever present power by which God upholds, as with his hand, heaven and earth and all creatures, and so rules them that leaf and blade, rain and drought, fruitful and lean years, food and drink, health and sickness, prosperity and poverty—all things, in fact, come to us not by chance but by his fatherly hand.

HC 28 Q. **How does the knowledge of God's creation and providence help us?**
A. We can be patient when things go against us, thankful when things go well, and for the future we can have good confidence in our faithful God and Father that nothing in creation will separate us from his love. For all creatures are so completely in God's hand that without his will they can neither move nor be moved.

SC 17 Q. **What do you believe about the eternal Father?**
A. That the eternal Father is the first person of the Godhead, who from eternity generated the Son, his own image, through whom he made heaven and earth and all creatures out of nothing. He preserves and governs them according to the eternal decree of his will for his own glory and the salvation of his people, and works all good things in everything and through all creatures, even through the wicked when they sin out of their own corruption. Because of his only begotten Son, he has adopted me as his own child and takes care of my body and soul in such a way that nothing can happen to me apart from his fatherly will and in such a way that all things necessarily work together for my salvation.

Even though Luther's Small Catechism provides the framework for this short section of the HC, some scholars have identified Calvin, especially in his GC and *Institutes* (1536), as the inspiration for much of the content. Sudhoff, for example, detected the influence of the GC on HC A 27 and on both the question and answer of HC 28.[16] Jacobs also found parallels between the GC and HC 26,[17] and Lang found echoes of all three questions and answers in the HC in Calvin's treatment of the first article of the creed in the *Institutes* of 1536.[18]

There is certainly some truth to these claims when it comes to the wording of SC 17 and HC 26–28. The references, for example, to the fatherhood of God in both SC 17 ("Because of his only begotten Son, he has adopted me as his own child") and HC 26 ("the eternal Father of our Lord Jesus Christ . . . is my God and Father because of Christ the Son") are reminiscent of GC 22:

> **Q. Why do you call him Father?**
> A. Primarily with regard to Christ, who . . . was declared his Son. From this, however, we infer that, since God is the Father of Jesus Christ, he is also our Father.[19]

Furthermore, among the major source catechisms for the HC, the association of providence with God's "decree" (SC 17) or "counsel" (HC 26) is found only in GC 24.[20] The pairs of opposites that Calvin lays out in GC 27 (rain and drought, fertile and sterile earth, health and disease[21]) are also included in a similar, though longer, list in HC 27 ("rain and drought, fruitful and lean years, . . . health and sickness"). The metaphor of God's hand, which Calvin employs no fewer than five times in GC 23, 24, and 27,[22] also appears three times in HC 27 and 28 ("as with his hand," "by his fatherly hand," "in God's hand"). It is also in Calvin that we encounter the connection between providence and our "good" (see HC 26), and providence and our "salvation" (see HC 1).[23] Finally, only Calvin in GC 29 and Ursinus in HC 28 devote an entire question to the benefit of the doctrine of providence,[24] and HC 28's threefold answer echoes Calvin's language in the 1559 edition of the *Institutes* (1.17.7):

> HC 28: We can be patient when things go against us
>
> *Institutes* (1559): Patience in adversity
>
> HC 28: Thankful when things go well
>
> *Institutes* (1559): Gratitude of mind for the favorable outcome of things
>
> HC 28: And for the future we can have good confidence in our faithful God and Father
>
> *Institutes* (1559): And also incredible freedom from worry about the future[25]

There are, however, other Reformed sources that may have influenced the wording of SC 17 and HC 26–28 as well. Two pairs in the list of things under the rule of God in HC 27 also appear in Bucer's "Brief Written Explanation" of 1534: "leaf and blade" and "food and drink."[26]

Bullinger's catechism of 1559 contains the phrases "heaven and earth and everything in them" (see HC 26), "is willing and able to supply all that is needed for body and soul" (see HC 26), and "we receive from the hand of God all those benefits and gifts" (see HC 27).[27] In addition, much of the language in SC 17 and HC 26 is adumbrated in some of the north-German catechisms of Micronius and Lasco:

Micronius's Small Catechism (1552)

[48] Q. **What do you understand by the words that are said about the Father?**

A. That is, I believe that the eternal God is my God and Father—the creator, upholder, and ruler of heaven and earth and everything in them. I completely place my trust in him alone, being assured that he likes to and will help me, since he is almighty and my Father for that reason.[28]

Micronius's *A Brief Examination of the Faith* (1553)

[12] Q. **What do you believe about that first part that deals with God the Father?**

A. That is, I place my whole trust in the eternal and faithful God, being assured that he will help me in every need of soul and body, having seen that he is an almighty God and a benevolent Father to me.[29]

Lasco's Small Emden Catechism (1554)

[30] Q. **What do you believe about the first main article on God the Father?**

A. That the true, eternal, and living God has created and upholds us and all creatures, and that he has accepted us as children in Christ Jesus and is a gracious Father.[30]

A significant clause in SC 17 ("because of his only begotten Son, he has adopted me as his own child") and several key phrases and clauses in HC 26 ("heaven and earth and everything in them," "is my God and Father," "I trust God so much," "he will provide whatever I need for body and soul," "God is able to do this because he is almighty God, and desires to do this because he is a faithful Father") all bear the linguistic print of these Reformed catechisms from northern Europe.

That is not to say, however, that the textual influence on this portion of the HC is exclusively from Reformed sources. Ursinus's preposition "together with" (*sampt*) in HC 26 (translated as "and") is found in the same context only in Luther's Small Catechism,[31] which also included the phrase "food and drink" (HC 27) on its list of divine provisions five years before Bucer's "Brief Written Explanation."[32] Melanchthon, too, affirms that God both "is able . . . and desires" to help us (cf. HC 26) and that our lives are in God's providential "hand" (cf. HC 27, 28).[33] But the preponderance of sources employed by Ursinus and the drafting team appear to be Reformed works by Calvin and the Lasco circle.

How much, then, does this dependence on early Reformed texts affect the theological tone of HC 26–28? Gyenge has claimed, for example, that the HC interprets the first article of the creed entirely in the spirit of Calvin: it is Calvin's concept of faith as focused on Christ alone (1559 *Institutes* 3.2.1) that lies behind the confession in HC 26 that God "is my God and Father *because of Christ the Son*" (italics added).[34] For Latzel, however, the existential character of HC 26, seen especially in the eight first-person pronouns in the answer, are redolent of the personal tone of Luther's Small Catechism.[35] And Verboom finds in this section of the HC a harmonic combining of the personal and soteriological emphasis in early Lutheran sources with the more theologically oriented approach to providence among the Reformed.[36]

It must be said, first of all, that the christological motif in HC 26 and SC 17 is not unique to Calvin but can be found also in the catechisms of Lasco and Bullinger.[37] Moreover, the first-person language of Luther's Small Catechism ("I believe that God has created *me*"[38]) is also present in many early Reformed sources: Bucer's "Brief Written Explanation," Calvin's 1536 *Institutes*, Jud's (Large) Catechism, Bullinger's catechism for adults, Micronius's Small Catechism and *A Brief Examination of the Faith*, and Lasco's Small Emden Catechism.[39]

However, the christological-soteriological dimension to HC 26 ("The eternal Father of our Lord Jesus Christ . . . is my God and Father because of Christ the Son") does have a Lutheran ring to it if it is read against the background of the view of providence in HC 1: "I am not my own, but belong . . . to my faithful Savior, Jesus Christ. He . . . watches over me in such a way that not a hair can fall from my head without the will of my Father in heaven."[40] HC 1 here fuses two themes from Luther's Small Catechism: (1) salvation as the believer's "belonging" to Christ in Luther's exposition of article 2 of the creed, and (2) providence as God's "preserving" (Luther: *bewahret*) or "watching over" (HC: *bewaret*) the believer in Luther's exposition of article 1. To confess, therefore, that God is my Father "because of Christ the Son" (HC 26) is another way of stating that because I belong to Christ I am, among other things, in a filial relationship with the Father that results in the Father's special care for me through the Son (HC 1).[41] That, according to HC 1, is part of the comfort of the gospel, and it is rooted in Luther's doctrine of "possession": I belong not to myself but to my Savior Jesus Christ. True to its perspective in A 22, therefore, the HC presents the first article of the Apostles' Creed as one of the key promises of the *gospel*.

PREDESTINATION

We cannot leave this section of the HC without noting the absence of a topic that we might expect to find here in the context of the doctrines of God and providence, namely, predestination. Even in the lead-in to the exposition of the Apostles' Creed, the HC provides a perfect opportunity to address this issue when it asks in Q 20, "Are all people then saved through Christ just as they were lost through Adam?" Instead of responding with something like, "No. Only those are saved whom God has predestined to eternal life," the HC simply says, "No. Only those are saved who through true faith are grafted into Christ and accept all his benefits." The focus is on the salvation of believers in history and not on an eternal divine decision that lies behind their coming to faith. In fact, predestination is explicitly mentioned only twice in the entire catechism, both times in passing: When Christ returns to judge the living and the dead, he will "take me and all his chosen ones [*auszerwehlten*] to himself into the joy and glory of heaven" (HC 52), and the church is "a community chosen [*auszerwelte*] for eternal life" (HC 54).

How is this near silence on such an important theological issue to be explained? Some have suggested that it had to do with the genre and audience of the HC. Even though the main author and others on the drafting committee were themselves strong predestinarians, they thought it best not to address such a complex matter in a catechism intended for youth and lay adults.[42] Here they could have been following the lead of Calvin, who, despite the extensive treatment of predestination in so many of his works, did not devote a single question to it in his GC of 1545.[43]

This approach, however, is not entirely satisfactory for two reasons. First, the HC does not bypass other difficult or controversial theological topics, such as the Trinity or the relationship between Christ's divine and human natures (HC 46–49).[44] Second, Ursinus's SC, which served as the base text for so much of the HC and was also designed for a youthful and unlettered audience, has three whole questions on the subject, including a reference to reprobation:

50 Q. Why is it that this gift comes to you instead of to so many others who are lost forever?

A. Because God elected me in Christ for eternal life before the foundations of the world were laid, and he now regenerates me by the special grace of his Spirit. For unless this had happened, the corruption of my nature is such that I would have knowingly and willingly perished in my sins just like the many reprobate.

51 Q. **Doesn't this view, in which you declare that you were elected to eternal life, make you careless and more negligent in the daily exercises of obedience?**

A. Not at all. Rather it kindles in me even more a desire to persevere and advance in piety, since without true conversion to God I cannot comfort myself with the assurance of my election. And the more certain I am of my salvation, the more I wish to show God that I am thankful.

52 Q. **But aren't you inclined to doubt your salvation when you hear that none are saved except those elected by God?**

A. Certainly not. In fact, precisely because of this, I have a firm comfort in every temptation. For if I seriously desire with my heart to believe and obey God, I ought to be convinced by this most compelling evidence, as it were, that I am numbered among those who have been elected to eternal life and that therefore I can never be lost, no matter how weak my faith is.

None of these questions from the SC made its way into the HC. Furthermore, the other three references to election in SC 12 ("God's elect"), SC 39 ("all the elect"), and SC 43 ("all the elect") are also missing in their parallel answers in HC 21, 53, and 57, respectively.[45]

A more likely explanation for the HC's near silence on predestination is that the authors intentionally steered clear of it for the sake of doctrinal harmony.[46] Frederick III's consensus in the Palatinate had to embrace not just Calvinists but also followers of Melanchthon and Bullinger, neither of whom wished to probe the doctrine of predestination as deeply as Calvin had. It was a topic that "Melanchthon had, so to speak, declared off limits in the 1535 *Loci*" already,[47] and Calvin himself admitted that Melanchthon did not want "to give curious folk a reason for inquiring too deeply into the secrets of God."[48] Although Bullinger did not diverge substantially from Calvin's doctrine of predestination, he, too, seemed "uncomfortable with too speculative or thoroughgoing an analysis of the various aspects of the divine decree," including reprobation.[49] Given Frederick's own Melanchthonian predilections and his desire to unite the theological parties in his realm, his reluctance to grant confessional status to such a potentially divisive doctrine would certainly have been understandable.

There is, however, one more factor that may account for the HC's relative silence on predestination—the confessional framework of the AC. The AC never mentions predestination directly,[50] but it does include the following statement in the German text of article 5: "To obtain such faith God instituted the office of preaching, giving the gospel and the sacraments.

Through these, as through means, he gives the Holy Spirit who produces faith, where and when he wills [the Latin text reads: where and when it pleases God], in those who hear the gospel."[51] This is as close as the AC gets to an explicit reference to predestination; the acknowledgment that the Holy Spirit produces faith "when and where he wills" or "when and where it pleases God" implies that salvation is ultimately rooted in the sovereign will of God.[52] What is striking is that this is almost exactly how the HC answers the question about whether all people will be saved: "Only those are saved who through true faith are grafted into Christ" (HC 20), a faith that "the Holy Spirit produces . . . in our hearts by the preaching of the holy gospel, and confirms by the use of the holy sacraments" (HC 65). In language that not only respects the boundaries of the AC but echoes its very language, the HC puts in place of the doctrine of predestination a doctrine of the Holy Spirit who works faith in believers.[53]

Since not only the production of faith but also its preservation (perseverance of the saints) is a fruit of predestination to salvation, we find implicit references to election in several other places in the HC as well:[54]

A 1: Christ, by his Holy Spirit, assures me of *eternal* life and makes me wholeheartedly willing and ready *from now on* to live for him (italics added).

A 21: True faith is . . . a wholehearted trust . . . that God has freely granted . . . to me also . . . *eternal* righteousness and salvation (italics added).

A 31: [Christ has been ordained] to be . . . our eternal king who governs us by his Word and Spirit, and who guards us and keeps us in the freedom he has won for us."

A 32: And afterward to reign with Christ over all creation for eternity.

A 52: [Christ is] the very judge who has already offered himself to the judgment of God in my place and removed the whole curse from me. Christ will cast all his enemies and mine into everlasting condemnation, but will take me and all his chosen ones to himself into the joy and glory of heaven.

A 53: [The Holy Spirit] . . . will remain with me forever.

A 54: The Son of God through his Spirit and Word . . . gathers, protects, and preserves for himself a community chosen for eternal life and united in true faith. And of this community I am and always will be a living member.

A 56: I believe that God . . . will no longer remember any of my sins or my sinful nature . . . . Rather, by grace God grants me the righteousness of Christ to free me forever from judgment.

A 57: My soul [will] be taken immediately after this life to Christ its head.

A 58: I already now experience in my heart the beginning of *eternal* joy . . . (italics added).

A 59: In Christ I am . . . heir to *everlasting* life (italics added).

With this rather muted treatment of predestination in the background, the fact that God upholds and rules the entire creation by his eternal "counsel" (decree) and providence and "will turn to my good whatever adversity he sends upon me in this sad world" (HC 26) should probably be understood as broad enough to include God's decision of election.[55] After all, not even "a hair can fall from my head without the *will* of my Father in heaven; in fact, all things must work together for my *salvation*" (HC 1; italics added). And "nothing in creation will separate us from his love. For all creatures are so completely in God's hand that without his will they can neither move nor be moved" (HC 28). Indeed, as Neuser has suggested, all the "I" references in the HC's twenty-eight questions and answers in the first person singular could really be read as "I as one of the elect."[56]

What we find in this first part of the HC's exposition of the Apostles' Creed, then, is once again a Lutheran framework fleshed out with language and subthemes from both Lutheran and Reformed sources. At the forefront is a Melanchthonian definition of faith (HC 21) and a division and thematization of the creed that goes back to Luthers's Small Catechism (HC 24). The explanation of providence in HC 26–28, under Luther's heading "God the Father and our creation," draws largely on Reformed sources and language but with a soteriological slant that again reflects the influence of Luther's catechism. Finally, the HC's near silence on predestination follows the pattern of the AC: not a single question is devoted specifically to election, and there is no mention at all of double predestination, reprobation, or limited atonement. Nevertheless, the AC's portrayal of faith as the work of the Holy Spirit in those in whom God pleases to effect it creates an opening for the HC to include at least an implicit doctrine of election and perseverance that usually found its most explicit expression in the Calvinist tradition.

5

CHRIST AND THE HOLY SPIRIT

Q/A 29–64

THE WORK AND PERSON OF CHRIST

At the center of the center of the center of the HC is the doctrine of Christ. The catechism is divided, of course, into three major parts: "Human Misery" (HC 3–11), "Human Deliverance" (HC 12–85), and "Gratitude" (HC 86–129). Situated in the middle of the second part, between the doctrines of the mediator and the sacraments, is the exposition of the three articles of the Apostles' Creed (HC 26–58). And at the heart of this exposition of the creed is the explanation of article 2 on "God the Son" (HC 29–52). The focus in this subsection, however, is not on the doctrine of the Son in general but on "God the Son *and our deliverance*" (HC 24; italics added). As we have already seen, the person and redemptive work of the Son provide the christological foundation for the theme of the entire catechism, the comfort of the believer. Hence the twenty-four questions and answers on the second person of the Trinity form not only the structural center of the catechism but also its theological core.

What exactly is the deliverance through Christ that lies at the heart of the catechism? The HC uses some form of the word *deliverance* a total of seventeen times—seven as a noun (German: *Erlösung*), nine as a verb (*erlösen*), and once as a title for the Mediator (*Erlöser*: "Deliverer"). Not surprisingly, twelve of these usages appear in the second major division of the catechism ("Human *Deliverance*"). The various contexts in which they appear show that the authors of the HC understood deliverance broadly enough to include several dimensions of the work of Christ, including some aspects of the application of that work. Already, in the opening question and answer of the catechism, we learn that Jesus Christ "has *delivered* me from the tyranny of the devil" (HC 1; italics added). HC 34 states, in addition, that he has delivered us "from *sin* and from the tyranny of the devil" (italics added). As the Mediator, he also delivers people from "God's eternal *wrath* against sin" (HC 14; italics added) and "from eternal *condemnation*" (HC 37; italics added). How? As "our only high priest who has delivered us by the one sacrifice of his body" (HC 31), "with his precious blood" (HC 34), and "by his suffering as the only atoning sacrifice" (HC 37). Furthermore, "by suffering unspeakable anguish, pain, and terror of soul, on the cross but also earlier, [Christ my Lord] has delivered me from hellish anguish and torment" (HC 44).

But this deliverance is even broader than liberation from the devil, sin, divine wrath, eternal condemnation, and the anguish and torment of hell. It also includes the kingly work of Christ, who now and in the future "guards us and keeps us in the freedom [*erlösung*] he has won for us" (HC 31). The German verb for "keep" here (*erhalten*) is also used later in the HC's explanations of the second and sixth petitions of the Lord's Prayer:

HC 123 Q. What does the second petition mean?
A. "Your kingdom come" means: Rule us by your Word and Spirit in such a way that more and more we submit to you. Preserve [*erhalte*] your church and make it grow. Destroy the devil's work; destroy every force which revolts against you and every conspiracy against your holy Word. Do this until your kingdom fully comes, when you will be all in all.

HC 127 Q. What does the sixth petition mean?
A. "And do not bring us to the time of trial, but rescue [*erlöse*] us from the evil one" means: By ourselves we are too weak to hold our own even for a moment. And our sworn enemies—the devil, the world, and our own flesh—never stop attacking us. And so, Lord, uphold [*erhalten*] us and make us strong with the strength of your Holy Spirit, so that we may not go down to defeat in this spiritual struggle, but may firmly resist our enemies until we finally win the complete victory.

God helps to preserve the church by destroying the work of the devil. And our prayer for rescue or deliverance from evil is that the Lord uphold us in our spiritual struggle against the devil and other enemies. The fact that Christ "keeps us in the freedom he has won for us" (HC 31), therefore, suggests that although we have been delivered from the *tyranny* of the devil (HC 1, 34), we have not yet been delivered from every devilish threat. Part of Christ's work of deliverance is ongoing, namely, fending off the attacks of the devil against those already rescued from his clutches.

There is one other occurrence of the term *deliverance* in the catechism that also suggests it is not simply something that Christ has completed in the past. HC 74 on infant baptism reads as follows:

Q. Should infants also be baptized?
A. Yes. Infants as well as adults are included in God's covenant and people, and they, no less than adults, are promised *deliverance* from sin through Christ's blood and the

> Holy Spirit who produces faith. Therefore, by baptism, the sign of the covenant, they too should be incorporated into the Christian church and distinguished from the children of unbelievers. This was done in the Old Testament by circumcision, which was replaced in the New Testament by baptism (italics added).

Infants no less than adults "are promised deliverance from sin through Christ's blood." We have encountered a form of the phrase "deliverance from sin" before (HC 34), but there it referred to something that Christ did in his ministry on the cross ("with his precious blood . . . he has delivered us from sin"). In HC 74 it seems to be used more in the sense of the application of Christ's work to individuals—in this case the forgiveness of sins whose promise is signified and sealed in baptism to covenant children. Deliverance from sin, therefore, can refer in the HC to both redemption accomplished and redemption applied.

The scope of this concept is even broader when one considers that all of part 2, HC 12–85, is placed under the heading of "Deliverance." Although the term itself appears only twelve times in part 2, the entire section is actually governed by this theme and contributes to its overall meaning. Included in this deliverance through Christ is his assumption of the role of mediator (HC 12–18), his payment for human sin (HC 16), and his restoring us to righteousness and life (HC 17). We are grafted into Christ through faith (HC 20), receive all his benefits (HC 20), and are assured by the Holy Spirit that God has given us "forgiveness of sins, eternal righteousness, and salvation . . . [as] gifts of sheer grace, granted solely by Christ's merit" (HC 21). God the Father is our God and Father "because of Christ the Son" (HC 26). By grace through Christ we become "adopted children" of God (HC 33), and by his innocence and perfect holiness "he covers . . . my sinfulness in which I was conceived" (HC 36). Standing condemned before an earthly judge, he "free[d] us from the severe judgment of God that was to fall on us" (HC 38). On the cross "he shouldered the curse" that lay on us (HC 39), and "by Christ's power our old selves are crucified, put to death, and buried with him" (HC 43). His resurrection accomplishes three things: it overcomes death so that "we might share in the righteousness he obtained for us by his death," it unleashes the power by which "we too are already raised to a new life," and it serves as a guarantee of our own future resurrection (HC 45). The ascended Lord remains in heaven "on our behalf" (HC 46), advocating for us in the presence of the Father and sending his Spirit to us on earth (HC 49). Through that Spirit "he pours out gifts from heaven upon us his members" and by his power he "defends and keeps [*erhält*] us safe from all enemies" (HC 51). Finally, he will return someday to "cast all his enemies and mine into everlasting condemnation" and "take me and all his chosen ones to himself into the joy and glory of heaven" (HC 52). All of these salvific actions fall under the rubric of "deliverance." For the HC, *deliverance* is really an equivalent term for *salvation*.

That this comprehensive deliverance or salvation through Christ forms the theological core of the HC is signaled already in HC 1, where the believer's "only comfort in life and in death" is said to be found in belonging to "my faithful *Savior*, Jesus Christ" (italics added). The comfort of the gospel is that the Christ to whom we belong is the one who saves us: He has fully paid for our sins and delivered us from the tyranny of the devil. He watches over us in such a way that all that happens to us falls within the Father's will and works for our salvation. And by his Spirit he assures us of our salvation and enables us to live for him. Moreover, to live and die in the joy of that comfort, we must know the magnitude of the sin and misery from which we are delivered, the means by which we are delivered from such sin and misery, and the ways in which we can then thank God for such deliverance (HC 2). That is the message of the HC in a nutshell. Thus if HC 1 and the catechism as a whole are indeed christocentrically trinitarian,[1] they are also christocentrically soteriological in their summary of the Christian faith.[2] The entire catechism could really bear the title of the subsection on Christ: "God the Son and Our Deliverance" (HC 24).

This christological-soteriological motif is, once again, rooted in Luther's Small Catechism, whose heading for his exposition of the second article of the creed is "On Redemption [Deliverance]" (*Von der Erlösung*).[3] As in the case of the first article of the creed (God the Father), the authors of the HC follow Luther closely in their description of the second article in HC 24: "God the Son and Our Deliverance [*Erlösung*]." Already in HC 1, and again in HC 34, this theme is expressed in language that also bears a strong resemblance to Luther's catechism.[4] We have noted the similarities between the Small Catechism and the opening lines of HC 1[5]:

> I believe that Jesus Christ . . . is my Lord. He has redeemed me . . . He has purchased and freed me from all sins, from death, and from the power of the devil . . . with his . . . precious blood . . . in order that I may belong to him. (Small Catechism[6])

> That I am not my own, but belong—body and soul, in life and in death—to my faithful Savior, Jesus Christ. He has fully paid for all my sins with his precious blood, and has set me free from the tyranny of the devil. (HC A 1)

But the parallels to HC 34 ("Why do you call him 'our Lord'?") are also striking[7]:

> He has purchased and freed me from all sins, from death, and from the power of the devil, not with gold or silver but with his holy, precious blood . . . in order that I may belong to him. (Small Catechism[8])

> Because—not with gold or silver, but with his precious blood—he has set us free from sin and from the tyranny of the devil, and has bought us, body and soul, to be his very own. (HC A 34)

The similarities here in vocabulary and phrasing are obvious: "freed me/set me free," "from the power of the devil/from the tyranny of the devil," "purchased/bought," "not with gold or silver, but with his holy, precious blood/not with gold or silver but with his precious blood."

Perhaps the most significant influence of Luther's text, however, is found in the HC's language of mutual possession (I am Christ's, and he is mine): The Small Catechism's "in order that I may belong to him" is echoed in both HC 1 ("I belong . . . to my faithful Savior, Jesus Christ") and HC 34 ("to be his very own"). And Luther's affirmation that "Jesus Christ . . . is *my* Lord" is reflected in HC 1 in the phrase "*my* faithful Savior, Jesus Christ." This relational language, which forms the soteriological center of Luther's exposition of the creed, serves the same theological role in the HC as the basis for the overarching theme of comfort.[9]

As with other parts of the HC, this Lutheran framework for the interpretation of the second article of the Apostles' Creed is sometimes fleshed out with Reformed material. This is evident first of all in the remarkable linguistic parallels that scholars have noted between the HC and Calvin's treatment of this article in his GC.[10] Some of this language of the GC probably made its way into the HC via Ursinus's LC and SC,[11] but the similarities are still too numerous and too striking to be discounted. Here are a number of examples:

HC 31 Q. Why is he called "Christ," meaning "anointed"?
A. Because he has been ordained by God the Father and has been anointed with the Holy Spirit to be our chief prophet and teacher . . . ; our only high priest . . . ; and our eternal king.

GC 34 Q. What force then has the name Christ?
A. It signifies that he is anointed by his Father . . . to be King, Priest, and Prophet.[12]

GC 36 Q. But with what kind of oil was he anointed?
A. By the grace of the Holy Spirit.[13]

HC 32 Q. But why are you called a Christian?
A. I am anointed to . . . present myself to him as a living sacrifice of thanks, [and] to strive with a free conscience against sin and the devil in this life.

GC 43 Q. What is the purpose of his priestly office?
A. So that . . . we may . . . offer in sacrifice ourselves and all we have.[14]

GC 42 Q. **What does his Kingdom confer upon us?**
A. Just this, that by its benefit we are accorded freedom of conscience for pious and holy living . . . and also armed with strength sufficient to overcome the perpetual enemies of our souls, sin, the flesh, the devil, and the world.[15]

HC 38 Q. **Why did he suffer "under Pontius Pilate" as judge?**
A. So that he, though innocent, might be condemned by an earthly judge, and so free us from the severe judgment of God that was to fall on us.

GC 57 Q. **Explain this more clearly.**
A. In order to stand in our stead, he desired to be arraigned before an earthly judge . . . so that we might be acquitted before the heavenly tribunal of God.[16]

HC 39 Q. **Is it significant that he was "crucified" instead of dying some other way?**
A. Yes. By this I am convinced that he shouldered the curse which lay on me, since death by crucifixion was cursed by God.

GC 60 Q. **Is the fact that he was crucified of greater importance than if he suffered any other kind of death?**
A. Certainly, as even Paul reminds us (Gal. 3:10), when he writes that he hung upon the tree to take our curse upon himself; and by this we are absolved from it. For this kind of death was regarded with execration (Deut. 21:23).[17]

HC 42 Q. **Since Christ has died for us, why do we still have to die?**
A. Our death does not pay the debt of our sins. Rather, it . . . is our entrance into eternal life.

GC 63 Q. **But we seem to gain nothing from this victory, since we still have to die.**
A. That is no obstacle. For death for believers is now nothing but the passage to a better life.[18]

HC 43 Q. **What further benefit do we receive from Christ's sacrifice and death on the cross?**
A. By Christ's power our old selves are crucified, put to death, and buried with him, so that the evil desires of the flesh may no longer rule us.

GC 72 Q. **Does it [the death of Christ] not offer us any other advantage besides?**
A. Yes indeed. For by his benefit, if we are true members of

Christ, our old nature is crucified, and the body of sin is destroyed, so that the lusts of perverse flesh no longer rule in us.[19]

HC 44 Q. Why does the creed add, "He descended to hell"?

A. To assure me during attacks of deepest dread and temptation that Christ my Lord, by suffering unspeakable anguish, pain, and terror of soul, on the cross but also earlier, has delivered me from hellish anguish and torment.

GC 65 Q. As for what immediately follows, that he descended into hell, what does this mean?

A. That he endured not only common death . . . but also the pains of death, as Peter calls them (Acts 2:24). By this word I understand the fearful agonies with which his soul was tormented.[20]

HC 45 Q. How does Christ's resurrection benefit us?

A. First, by his resurrection he has overcome death, so that he might make us share in the righteousness he obtained for us by his death. Second, by his power, we too are already raised to a new life. Third, Christ's resurrection is a sure pledge to us of our blessed resurrection.

GC 73 Q. Proceed with the remaining articles.

A. There follows: the third day he rose again from the dead. By this he shows himself to be conqueror over sin and death.[21]

GC 74 Q. What are the manifold benefits that come to us from his resurrection?

A. Three. For by it righteousness is obtained for us (Rom. 4:24); it is a sure pledge of our future immortality (1 Cor. 15); and even now by its virtue we are raised to newness of life.[22]

HC 49 Q. How does Christ's ascension to heaven benefit us?

A. First, he is our advocate in heaven in the presence of his Father. Second, we have our own flesh in heaven as a sure pledge that Christ our head will also take us, his members, up to himself.

GC 77 Q. What good do we obtain from the ascension?

A. There is a double benefit. For since Christ is entered into heaven in our name . . . he opens up for us a way there . . . Then, too, he appears before God as intercessor and advocate on our behalf (Heb. 7:25).[23]

These are just some of the linguistic parallels between the two catechisms' explanations of the second article of the Apostles' Creed.[24] In addition, the HC, like the GC, discusses the doctrine of justification immediately after its exposition of the creed (HC 59–64),[25] and HC 59, 62, and 63 even echo some of Calvin's language in GC 114–16, 118, 121–22, and 125.

There also appears to be a Bezan provenance to the form and some of the language of the Heidelberger's definition of justification in HC 60. There the authors of the catechism lay out a threefold accusation of the conscience, a threefold remedy to these attacks found in the person and work of Jesus Christ, and a threefold state of justification for the believer that ensues:[26]

Accusation of Conscience	Remedy	State of Justification
1. I have grievously sinned against all God's commandments	Christ's Satisfaction	It is as if I had never sinned.
2. I have never kept any of the commandments.	Christ's Righteousness	It is as if I had been as perfectly obedient as Christ was.
3. I am still inclined toward all evil.	Christ's Holiness	It is as if I had never been a sinner.

These three accusations and three antidotes in Christ are virtually identical to those proposed by Beza in his *Confessio christianae fidei* ("Confession of the Christian Faith") of 1560[27]:

Accusation of Conscience	Remedy
1. We have committed innumerable sins.	Christ's Satisfaction
2. Nowhere within us can be found the righteousness that God requires of us.	Christ's Righteousness
3. By nature we are corrupt and thus hateful toward God.	Christ's Holiness

The HC's exposition of article 2, however, derives its Reformed character from more than just the language it employs from Reformed texts. There are several doctrines in this section of the catechism that are either unique to the Reformed tradition or presented in a characteristically Reformed manner. The threefold office of Christ, for example, which appears in HC 31–32, was a distinctively Calvinian contribution to Reformation theology. There are no references at all to these offices in Luther's Small and Large Catechisms or the AC, and even some of the early Reformed literature mentions only a kingly office (Bucer) or a double role as priest and king (Jud, Bullinger, and Calvin before the 1539 *Institutes* and 1545 GC).[28] This Calvinian-Reformed distinctive is woven into the general Lutheran theme of the catechism, for in HC 31 each of the three offices is explicitly connected to Christ's work of deliverance:

> **Q. Why is he called "Christ," meaning "anointed"?**
> A. Because he has been ordained by God the Father and has been anointed with the Holy Spirit to be our chief prophet and teacher who fully reveals to us the secret counsel and will of God concerning our deliverance [*erlösung*]; our only high priest who has delivered [*erlöset*] us by the one sacrifice of his body, and who continually pleads our cause with the Father; and our eternal king who governs us by his Word and Spirit, and who guards us and keeps us in the freedom [*erlösung*] he has won for us (italics added).

The Lutheran framework of the HC's subsection on God the Son also contains what we might call a more Reformed view of the atonement. As we saw in chapter 3, Luther and the Lutheran tradition maintained something of a balance between the Christus Victor theory of atonement of the ancient church and the penal substitution view developed during the Protestant Reformation. Calvin and the Reformed tradition certainly acknowledged Christ's victory on the cross over Satan, but they placed greater emphasis on the themes of substitution, satisfaction, propitiation, and sacrifice.[29] The HC begins with a Luther-like juxtaposition of the two motifs in A 1: "He [Jesus Christ] has fully paid for all my sins with his precious blood" (penal substitution) "and has delivered me from the tyranny of the devil" (Christus Victor). But as we indicated earlier, in the opening questions and answers of part 2 (HC 12–18), the work of Christ the Mediator is described largely in terms of punishment and satisfaction.

This imbalance is carried over to the exposition of the second article of the creed in HC 29–52. To be sure, the Christus Victor motif is not wholly obscured. We are assured that Christ "guards [*schützet*] us and keeps [*erhält*] us in the freedom he has *won* for us" (HC 31; italics added) and that he "defends [*schützet*] and keeps us safe [*erhält*] from all enemies" (HC 51). Since this deliverance that Christ has won for us is in part his triumph as "Lord" over the tyranny of the devil (HC 34[30]; see also HC 1), he now assists us in our own kingly calling to strive against "sin and the devil in this life" (HC 32).[31] That is why we continue to pray, "Preserve (*erhalte*) your church. . . . Destroy the devil's work" (HC 123), and "Uphold (*erhalten*) us and make us strong with the strength of your Holy Spirit, so that we may not go down to defeat in this spiritual struggle, but may firmly resist our enemies [the devil, the world, and our own flesh] until we finally win the complete victory" (HC 127). And we can have every confidence that someday Christ will return as judge and "cast all his enemies and mine into everlasting condemnation" (HC 52).

Nevertheless, the language of substitutionary sacrifice and satisfaction still dominates this part of the catechism. Christ the high priest has delivered us "by the one sacrifice of his body" (HC 31). He "sustained in body and soul the wrath of God against sin," so that "by his suffering as the only atoning sacrifice, he might deliver us, body and soul, from eternal condemnation" (HC 37). By being "condemned by an earthly judge," he "frees us from the severe judgment of God that was to fall on us" (HC 38). In his crucifixion, he "shouldered the curse which lay on me" (HC 39), thereby meeting the demands of "God's justice and truth" (HC 40) and paying "the debt of our sins" (HC 42). The "unspeakable anguish, pain, and terror of soul" that he suffered on the cross but also earlier assures me that he "has delivered me from hellish anguish and torment" (HC 44). In his resurrection, "he has overcome death, so that he might make us share in the righteousness he obtained for us by his death" (HC 45). Even in our expectation of his return, we "await the very judge who has already offered himself to the judgment of God in [our] place and removed the whole curse from [us]" (HC 52).[32]

In addition to the doctrines of the threefold office and atonement, it has also been argued that "the catechism gives us the Reformed view of the descent [into hell] clause, the view developed by John Calvin."[33] In wording that echoes Calvin's GC, HC 44 does indeed present a figurative interpretation of Christ's descent into hell in the suffering he experienced prior to his death on the cross. To call this understanding "*the* Reformed view," however, and to claim that it is "entirely opposed to the Lutheran view,"[34] is more than the evidence will allow. At the time the HC was written, no unified Reformed view yet existed,[35] and there was no consensus among the Lutherans either.[36] As a matter of fact, Luther himself taught a descent of Christ into hell both before and after Christ's death, the former of which anticipated Calvin's focus on the "hell" of Gethsemane and the cross.[37] When the Formula of Concord finally settled the issue in 1577, it followed Luther's other line of thought that "the entire person [of Christ], God and human being, descended to hell after his burial, conquered the devil, destroyed the power of hell, and took from the devil all his power."[38] But even the Formula of Concord acknowledged that "among the teachers of the ancient church, as well as among some of us, different explanations of the article on Christ's descent into hell may be found."[39] This fluidity of interpretation in both the early Lutheran and Reformed traditions may help to explain why the writers of the HC had no compunctions about including within the Lutheran framework of the catechism a view of the descent that only later would come to be identified as Reformed.[40]

Another allegedly Reformed accent in the HC is its response in HC 47–48 to the challenges presented by the Lutheran doctrine of the ubiquity (omnipresence) of Christ's human nature.[41] This doctrine, which Luther had employed already in the 1520s to support his belief in the real presence of Christ's humanity in the Lord's Supper, had recently achieved confessional status in the nearby territory of Württemberg in Johannes Brenz's Stuttgart Confession of 1559.[42] The HC tackles the doctrine of ubiquity in the course of four questions (46–49) on Christ's ascension into heaven, the obvious place in an exposition of the creed to discuss the present makeup and whereabouts of Christ's human nature. According to HC 46, when we recite the clause in the Apostles' Creed "He ascended to heaven," we mean that Christ "was taken up from the earth into heaven and remains there on our behalf until he comes again to judge the living and the dead." But that raises a difficult question: if Christ is now "there" in heaven, how can he fulfill his promise to be *here* with us until the end of the world (Q 47)? At this point the catechism explicitly rejects the ubiquity doctrine by stating that "in his human nature Christ is not now on earth"; he is present with us only by his "divinity, majesty, grace, and Spirit" (A 47). Q 48 then anticipates the charge that this is tantamount to voicing the ancient Nestorian heresy, which tended to divide the two natures of Christ: "If his humanity is not present wherever his divinity is, then aren't the two natures of Christ separated from each other?" A 48 responds with the so-called *extra Calvinisticum* doctrine that "Christ's divinity is surely beyond the bounds [Latin: *extra*] of the humanity that has been taken on" but that "at the same time his divinity is in and remains personally united to his humanity." This does not present a barrier to our eating and drinking the body and blood of Christ at the Lord's Supper, as Luther might think, for "although he is in heaven and we are on the earth," at the Supper "we are united more and more to Christ's blessed body through the Holy Spirit" (HC 76).

To claim, however, that the HC is engaging here in a Reformed polemic against all Lutheran teaching is not entirely correct. In point of fact, the dividing line on the doctrine of the omnipresence of Christ's human nature was not between Lutherans and Reformed but between ubiquitarian (usually Gnesio-) Lutherans, on the one hand, and Philippist Lutherans, Calvinists, and Zwinglians, on the other. The latter followed Melanchthon, Calvin, and Zwingli in affirming the local presence in heaven of the ascended body of Christ.[43] Given Frederick III's long affection for

Melanchthon, Frederick's new interest in Reformed theology, and his increasing disillusionment with Gnesio-Lutheranism, it is hardly surprising that on the issue of ubiquity, the HC sides with the Melanchthonians and Reformed and stresses the common ground on which these parties stood.

That still leaves the question of whether the HC's anti-ubiquitarian stance remains within the bounds of the AC. As Winter has noted, however, the AC says no more than that the two natures of Christ are "inseparably united in one person" (art. 3). Whatever ubiquitarian suppositions may lie beneath that text, the affirmation in HC 48 that Christ's "divinity is in and remains personally united to his humanity" is, on the surface at least, in full compliance with the wording of AC art. 3, and Ursinus never considered his Christology here to be at odds with the AC.[44] Indeed, when Frederick III had to defend his allegiance to the HC before the emperor at the Diet of Augsburg in 1566, Elector August of Saxony supported him by arguing that on this point the HC had no more strayed from the AC than Brenz's ubiquitarian Stuttgart Confession had in 1559.[45] Both could be regarded as legitimate interpretations of the same confessional text.

What the HC has done in its exposition of the creedal article on the Son, therefore, is once again incorporate a variety of Reformed elements into a Lutheran framework. The framework is an overarching christological-soteriological motif drawn from Luther's own treatment of this article in his Small Catechism—deliverance through Christ the Son to whom the believer belongs. This skeletal structure is then filled out with language from Calvinian and Bezan sources and with the Reformed emphases on the threefold office of Christ and penal substitutionary atonement. In the doctrines of the descent of Christ into hell and ascension into heaven, however, there is less of a Reformed accent than is often supposed. Here the HC seems to point to a consensus by identifying common ground between the two traditions: common in the first case because the Lutheran and Reformed positions were not yet clearly enough defined for the Lutherans to rule out the interpretation in HC 44, and common in the second case because on the matter of ubiquity the Melanchthonian Lutherans and Reformed had reached similar conclusions in their debates with the Gnesio-Lutherans.

THE WORK OF THE HOLY SPIRIT

The HC's exposition of the third article of the Apostles' Creed, "God the Holy Spirit" (HC 53–58), is similar to the previous subsections on "God the Father" (HC 26–28) and "God the Son" (HC 29–52) in one important respect: its overarching theme, "God the Holy Spirit and our sanctification [*Heiligung*]" (HC 24) comes straight out of Luther's Small Catechism.[46]

Some of the content of this subsection also appears to be indebted to Luther's catechism. The identification of the believer as part of a larger Christian community, which is implied in HC 53 ("the Spirit is given also to me") and made explicit in HC 54 ("of this community I am and always will be a living member") and HC 55 ("believers one and all, as members of this community, share in Christ and in all his treasures and gifts"), echoes a similar emphasis in Luther's exposition of the third article of the creed:

> The Holy Spirit has called *me* . . . , enlightened *me* . . . , made *me* holy and kept *me* in the true faith, just as he calls, gathers, enlightens, and makes holy *the whole Christian church* . . . . Daily . . . the Holy Spirit abundantly forgives all sins—*mine and those of all believers*. On the Last Day the Holy Spirit will raise *me and all the dead* and will give to *me and all believers in Christ* eternal life.[47]

Even more striking, however, are the parallels between HC 53 and Melanchthon's treatment of the Holy Spirit in AC art. 3:

HC 53 Q. **What do you believe concerning "the Holy Spirit"?**
A. First, that the Spirit, with the Father and the Son, is eternal God. Second, that the Spirit is given also to me, so that, through true faith, he makes me share in Christ and all his benefits, comforts me, and will remain with me forever.

AC 3 Moreover, the same Christ "descended into hell, truly rose from the dead on the third day, ascended into heaven, is sitting at the right hand of God" in order to rule and reign forever over all creatures, so that through the Holy Spirit he may make holy, purify, strengthen, and comfort all who believe in him, also distribute to them life and various gifts and benefits, and shield and protect them against the devil and sin.[48]

What one notices immediately is several common aspects to the Spirit's work in both documents: both talk about the comfort,[49] distribution of spiritual gifts, and abiding presence (HC 53: "remain with me forever"; AC 3: "shield and protect them") of the Holy Spirit.

It is also worth noting, however, that AC 3 portrays the work of the Holy Spirit as really the work of Christ through the Spirit. It is Christ who makes holy, purifies, strengthens, comforts, distributes life and gifts, and protects against the devil and sin—through the agency of the Holy Spirit. This perspective on the Spirit as the Son's agent par excellence is also present in HC 53, though not as explicitly. The Spirit who comforts me, makes me share in Christ and his benefits, and remains with me forever "is *given* also to me" (italics added). The one who does this giving is not named here, but he was identified earlier in HC 49: it is Christ who "sends his Spirit to us on earth."[50]

In addition, the HC is replete with other references to the assisting role of the Spirit in the work of Christ.[51] "Christ, by his Holy Spirit, assures me of eternal life and makes me wholeheartedly willing and ready from now on to live for him" (HC 1). As our eternal king, he "governs us by his Word and Spirit" (HC 31). "In his divinity, majesty, grace, and Spirit he is never absent from us" (HC 47) but "sends his Spirit to us on earth as a corresponding pledge [that he will also take us, his members, up to himself]" (HC 49). "Through his Holy Spirit he pours out gifts from heaven upon us his members" (HC 51). "The Son of God through his Spirit and Word . . . gathers, protects, and preserves for himself a community chosen for eternal life" (HC 54). The Spirit teaches us in the gospel and confirms in the sacraments that our entire salvation rests in the one sacrifice of Christ on the cross (HC 67). In the institution of the outward washing of baptism, Christ promises "that . . . his blood and his Spirit wash away my soul's impurity" (HC 69; see also HC 73). "To be washed with Christ's Spirit means that the Holy Spirit has renewed and sanctified us to be members of Christ" (HC 70). "To eat the crucified body of Christ and to drink his poured-out blood" means that "through the Holy Spirit . . . we are united more and more to Christ's blessed body " (HC 76; see also HC 79). "The Lord's Supper declares to us . . . that the Holy Spirit grafts us into Christ" (HC 80). "Christ, having redeemed us by his blood, is also restoring us by his Spirit into his image" (HC 86). In almost every case here, Christ is the subject of the action and the Holy Spirit the object of an instrumental preposition (e.g., "*by* his Spirit," "*through* the Holy Spirit"). This emphasis in the HC on the Spirit's work on behalf of Christ may take its cue from Luther's Small Catechism ("By my own understanding or strength I cannot believe in Jesus Christ my Lord or come to him, but instead the Holy Spirit has called me"),[52] but it more likely follows the lead of the AC.

Once again, however, what appears at first to be a Lutheran theme and flavor is modified by Reformed influences. Some of this influence is linguistic. Several of the questions and answers in HC 53–58, for example, reflect the wording of Calvin's GC:

HC 53 Q. **What do you believe concerning "the Holy Spirit"?**
A. First, that the Spirit, with the Father and the Son, is eternal God. Second, that the Spirit is given also to me, so that, through true faith, he makes me share in Christ and all his benefits, comforts me, and will remain with me forever.

GC 91 Q. **This needs a rather clearer explanation.**
A. I mean that the Spirit of God, while he dwells in our hearts, operates so that we feel the virtue of Christ (Rom. 5:5). For when we conceive the benefits of Christ with the mind, this happens by the illumination of the Holy Spirit. . . .

Hence whatever gifts are offered us in Christ, we receive them by virtue of the Spirit.[53]

HC 54 Q. **What do you believe concerning "the holy catholic church"?**
A. I believe that the Son of God through his Spirit and Word, out of the entire human race, from the beginning of the world to its end, gathers, protects, and preserves for himself a community chosen for eternal life and united in true faith. And of this community I am and always will be a living member.

GC 93 Q. **What is the Church?**
A. The body and society of believers whom God has predestined to eternal life.[54]

HC 55 Q. **What do you understand by "the communion of saints"?**
A. First, that believers one and all, as members of this community, share in Christ and in all his treasures and gifts. Second, that each member should consider it a duty to use these gifts readily and joyfully for the service and enrichment of the other members.

GC 98 Q. **But what is the force of adding forthwith the Communion of Saints?**
A. This is put here to express more clearly that unity which exists between the members of the Church. At the same time it is indicated that whatever benefits God bestows upon the Church serve the common good of all, since all have communion with each other.[55]

HC 56 Q. **What do you believe concerning "the forgiveness of sins"?**
A. I believe that God, because of Christ's satisfaction, will no longer remember any of my sins or my sinful nature which I need to struggle against all my life. Rather, by grace God grants me the righteousness of Christ to free me forever from judgment.

GC 102 Q. **What do you mean by the word forgiveness?**
A. I mean that God by his gratuitous goodness forgives and pardons the faithful their sins, so that they are not summoned to judgment nor is punishment exacted from them.[56]

In the case of HC 54–55 (and the nearly identical earlier versions in SC 40–41 and LC 125 and 116), a more likely Reformed textual source might have been Lasco's Small Emden Catechism of 1554[57]:

HC 54 Q. What do you believe concerning "the holy catholic church"?

A. I believe that the Son of God through his Spirit and Word, out of the entire human race, from the beginning of the world to its end, gathers, protects, and preserves for himself a community chosen for eternal life and united in true faith. And of this community I am and always will be a living member.

Em [45] Q. What do you believe in the next article: A holy Christian church or community?

A. I believe that my Lord Jesus Christ through the Holy Spirit and the voice of the holy gospel, out of this corrupt and evil race from the beginning of the world, gathers and preserves for himself an eternal, holy, and lasting church or community of the elect, of which I confess myself to be a member.[58]

HC 55 Q. What do you understand by "the communion of saints"?

A. First, that believers one and all, as members of this community, share in Christ and in all his treasures and gifts. Second, that each member should consider it a duty to use these gifts readily and joyfully for the service and enrichment of the other members.

Em [47] Q. How do you understand the words, "the communion of saints"?

A. I understand them as follows: that just as the true members of the community of Christ, united with their Head and all his benefits, have communion among themselves, so also they share their gifts in love for the building up of the community.[59]

However, the Reformed influences here are more than linguistic. One of the striking features of Luther's paragraph on the Holy Spirit in the Small Catechism is that he not only titles the third article of the creed "On Sanctification [Being Made Holy[60]]" but explicitly connects this work of the Spirit to the remaining lines of the Apostles' Creed—the holy, catholic church; the communion of saints; the forgiveness of sins; the resurrection of the body; and the life everlasting:

> I believe that . . . the Holy Spirit has called me through the gospel, enlightened me with his gifts, made me holy and kept me in the true faith, just as he calls, gathers, enlightens, and makes holy the whole Christian church on earth and keeps it with Jesus Christ in the one common, true faith. Daily in this Christian church the Holy Spirit abundantly forgives all sins—mine and those of all believers. On the Last Day the Holy Spirit will raise me and all the dead and will give to me and all believers in Christ eternal life.[61]

The Holy Spirit gathers and sanctifies the church, forgives us, resurrects us, and bestows upon us everlasting life.

This link between the work of the Spirit and the final lines of the creed is missing, however, in the HC and its immediate sources, the SC and LC. After HC 53, the Holy Spirit is mentioned again only once in this section (HC 54). That could reflect the influence of Calvin's GC, which actually divides the last third of the creed into two parts, the Holy Spirit and the Church.[62] Calvin, too, makes only one reference to the Spirit in his fourth section on the church.[63] In the case of the SC and, even more so, the HC, it could also be because the entire third division of these catechisms ("Gratitude") is already devoted to the Spirit's work of sanctification. HC 86, for example, which introduces part 3 of the HC, states that "Christ . . . is also restoring us by his Spirit into his image, so that with our whole lives we may show that we are thankful to God for his benefits." This "rising-to-life of the new self . . . is . . . a love and delight to live according to the will of God by doing every kind of good work" (HC 90) as described for us in God's law. Therefore, even though the HC places Luther's heading of "sanctification" over HC 53–58, it is, in more typically Reformed fashion, in the exposition of the Ten Commandments and the Lord's Prayer in part 3 that the sanctifying work of the Holy Spirit comes to its clearest and most detailed expression.

The identification of the believer as part of a larger Christian community, which we encountered in Luther's Small Catechism and again in HC 53–55, may also have a subtle Reformed twist to it. As Verboom suggests, the reference in HC 53 to the Spirit's being "*also* given to me" could be an allusion to the Reformed doctrine of the covenant.[64] Since the HC was intended first of all as a catechism for the youth of the Palatinate, and since, according to HC 74, infants, "no less than adults, are promised deliverance from sin through Christ's blood *and the Holy Spirit* who produces faith" (italics added), HC 53–55 could be construed as a series of testimonies from the lips of a baptized covenant child: "I, no less than an adult, am given the Holy Spirit" (53); "I, also, am a living member of this community" (54); "I, too, share in Christ and in all his treasures and gifts" (55).

We must be careful, however, not to overemphasize the Reformed accents in this section of the HC. There is, of course, a reference to election here, but it appears only in passing in HC 54's definition of the church, and it is one of only two such references in the entire catechism.[65] The combination in HC 54 of "Spirit and Word" is also sometimes identified as a special mark of Calvinism,[66] but the connection is just as strong, if not stronger in the Lutheran tradition.[67] Finally, it has been suggested that the allusions in HC 53 and 55 to the believer's spiritual union with Christ and his benefits also have their roots in Calvin's theology.[68] It should be remembered, however, that the close tie between "Christ and all his benefits," which occurs here and three other times in the HC (HC 20, 65, and 75), is probably rooted in Melanchthon.[69] And even though Melanchthon may not have had a fully developed doctrine of union with Christ,[70] Luther certainly did—one that was not only similar to Calvin's but may also have influenced it.[71] At the same time, as Goeters has noted, the HC's doctrine of union with Christ through the Holy Spirit may also reflect a subtle Reformed polemic against the Gnesio-Lutheran doctrine of Christ's omnipresent human nature. Since the body of the ascended Lord is not ubiquitous but localized in heaven, the benefits he obtained for us in his body on earth can only be communicated to us through the Holy Spirit, "who lives both in Christ and in us. And so, although [Christ] is in heaven and we are on earth, we are flesh of his flesh and bone of his bone" (HC 76).[72]

The HC's exposition of "God the Holy Spirit," therefore, is formally very much like the earlier subsections on law and gospel, providence, and Christology. HC 53–58 is introduced with a title right out of Luther's Small Catechism, and the emphasis throughout the HC on the Holy Spirit as the agent through whom the work of Christ is applied (the reason we are treating Christ and the Holy Spirit in the same chapter) appears to follow the script of AC 3. Reformed accents can be detected, but for the most part they are rather subtle. The result is an intricate blend of language from both traditions that focuses not on the fault lines between them but on common ground. In that regard, the exposition of the third article of the creed nicely anticipates the next subsection of the HC on the sacraments.

6
THE SACRAMENTS

Q/A 65–85

THE DEBATE

Probably no ecclesiastical issue created more controversy in the sixteenth century than the doctrine and practice of the sacraments. The theological battles it incited were not just between Catholics and Protestants, but between and among Lutherans, Anabaptists, Reformed, and Anglicans as well. And little wonder: at stake were the very means by which people believed that they received the grace of salvation, and how one viewed these means of grace was often related to their understandings of sin, Christ, the Holy Spirit, the church, and the Christian life.

As we saw in chapter 1, the Palatinate experienced its own share of these sacramental battles, especially over the Lord's Supper, in the years leading up to the HC. In the centuries since, however, the debate has centered on the view of the sacraments in the HC itself. The modern phase of this debate began in the mid-1800s, and by the end of the nineteenth century at least five positions had surfaced. The HC's sacramental doctrine was presented as either (1) Melanchthonian-Calvinist (Johannes Ebrard, John Nevin), (2) strictly Melanchthonian (Heinrich Heppe), (3) strictly Calvinist (Karl Sudhoff), (4) Zwinglian/Bullingerian (Maurits Gooszen), or (5) a compromise between the Calvinist and Zwinglian views (Charles Hodge).[1] As the debate moved into the twentieth century, the number of positions actually declined while the number of individuals joining the discussion significantly increased. The argument now focused largely on whether the HC's doctrine of the sacraments was Calvinist, Zwinglian (usually "neo-Zwinglian" or "late-Zwinglian," i.e., Bullingerian[2]), or some blend of the two. Melanchthon was rarely mentioned anymore.[3]

Those promoting a purely Calvinist interpretation in the past century included E. F. Karl Müller, Jan Bavinck, Hermann Hesse, Hendrikus Berkhof, and Fred Klooster.[4] Jan Rohls is probably the best representative of the "modified Zwinglian" or Bullingerian interpretation.[5] Several twentieth-century studies, however, concluded that the HC's sacramental teaching contains elements of both traditions, although in various admixtures. George Richards, for example, maintained that the sacramental teaching in the HC is "clearly Calvinistic," yet acknowledged that in the doctrine of the Lord's Supper, at least, "the views of Zwingli and of Calvin are blended."[6] James Good, too, held that the treatment of the sacraments throughout the HC is Calvinistic, but he was willing to grant that the catechism might be intentionally indefinite in some respects so as to accommodate both high and low sacramentarians.[7] G. P. Hartvelt, by contrast, did not rule out Calvin's paternity altogether, but he did find real differences with Calvin there and insisted that one must look also to the considerable influence of Bullinger, and perhaps even Boquinus.[8] For Brian Gerrish also, the sacramental theology of the HC owes more to Zwingli, and especially to Bullinger, than to Calvin.[9] Neuser, finally, drew a sharp line between the HC's second and third sections on the sacraments: the introduction to the sacraments (HC 65–68) and treatment of baptism (HC 69–74) are more Calvinistic, whereas the doctrine of the Lord's Supper (HC 75–82) reflects the neo-Zwinglian position of Heinrich Bullinger.[10]

These different labels have been applied not simply to the HC's general perspective on the sacraments but also to the details of its sacramental teaching. For example, the HC's claim that nothing is communicated to the participant in a sacrament apart from faith was identified as a Calvinist feature by Sudhoff but as Bullingerian by Gooszen.[11] Gerrish and (implicitly) Rorem both considered as Bullingerian the parallelism between sign and signified in the HC's questions on baptism and the Lord's Supper ("as surely as . . . so surely"), whereas Berkhof termed it Calvinist.[12] The spiritual presence of Christ in the Lord's Supper, too, was alleged to be Bullingerian by some (e.g., Gooszen) and Calvinist by others (e.g., Good).[13] And Sudhoff and Rohls viewed as Calvinist and Bullingerian, respectively, the treatment of the sacraments as pledges or assurances of the certainty of Christ's death for the believer.[14]

At the beginning of the twenty-first century, therefore, there is no more consensus on the theological orientation of the HC's doctrine of the sacraments than there was at the end of the nineteenth. The only difference is that Melanchthon's role has practically disappeared from the discussion. It is our contention, however, that the HC's view of the sacraments, like the catechism as a whole, reflects the general pattern of the Palatinate Reformation and must be interpreted in that light. Once again, we encounter a synthesis of textual and doctrinal elements from both the Lutheran and Reformed traditions. And here, perhaps more than in any other part of the HC, we see the "ecumenical" strategies of Frederick III and his team of authors in play. Since sacramental theology was the issue that most sharply divided the Protestant parties in the Palatinate, the authors seem to have tried especially hard at this point in the catechism to reflect what Verboom has called "maximal consensus" and "minimal dissensus."[15]

LUTHERAN ELEMENTS

What constitutes the Lutheran dimension of the doctrine of the sacraments in the HC? Part of it might be detected already in the definition of the sacraments in HC 66:

> **Q. What are sacraments?**
> A. Sacraments are visible, holy signs and seals. They were instituted by God so that by our use of them he might make us understand more clearly the promise of the gospel, and seal that promise. And this is God's gospel promise: to grant us forgiveness of sins and eternal life by grace because of Christ's one sacrifice accomplished on the cross.

The first half of the answer follows closely the structure and wording of the corresponding material in Ursinus's two earlier catechisms:

> **SC 54 Q. What are sacraments?**
> A. They are ceremonies instituted by God, so that by these visible pledges and public testimonies, as it were, he might remind and assure all believers of the grace promised them in the gospel; and so that they, on their part, might obligate themselves to faith and a holy life and distinguish themselves from unbelievers.

> **LC 275 Q. Say [what sacraments are] more clearly.**
> A. Sacraments are ceremonies instituted by God and added to the promise of grace, so that he might represent to them the grace promised in the gospel, that is, the communication of Christ and all his benefits; and so that, by these visible pledges and public testimonies, as it were, he might assure all those who use these ceremonies in true faith that this promise most certainly belongs to them and will be valid for them forever; and so that those using them might, on their part, bind themselves to perseverance in true faith and piety toward God.

All three answers above include a brief description of sacraments ("sacraments/they are"); an identification of their origin ("instituted by God"); a twofold purpose (to "make us understand more clearly/remind/represent," and to "seal/assure"); and a focus on what is signified and sealed ("the promise of the gospel/the grace promised in the gospel"). According to Gooszen and Neuser,[16] LC 275, in turn, was based on Melanchthon's definition in his *EO* (1554): "A sacrament . . . is a divinely instituted rite, added to the promise related in the gospel, to be a testimony and pledge of the promise of the grace that is presented and applied."[17] This is certainly a possibility, since Ursinus had used the *EO* as a textbook while teaching in Breslau and had also referred to and even quoted its definition of a sacrament in a defense of Melanchthon's position that he had composed in 1559.[18] The pattern and much of the language of this definition appear not only in LC 275 but also earlier in SC 54 and then again in HC 66.

Another aspect of the definition in HC 66 may also reflect Melanchthon's influence. God's double purpose in instituting the sacraments, namely, to make us understand the promise of the gospel more clearly and to put his seal on that promise, is summarized in subsequent questions and answers in two verb combinations: "remind and assure" (HC 69, 75), and "teach" and "assure" (HC 73, 79). Ursinus had also employed the compound verb "remind and assure" three times in his treatment of the sacraments in the SC a year earlier (SC 54, 57, 64). This usage may again go back to his teacher Melanchthon, who as early as the 1521 *Loci* had insisted that the sacraments have a dual function: not only to "remind" (*admonent*) believers of the promises of God but also to "render certain" or "give assurance" (*certa reddatur*) to persons with troubled consciences that God applies those promises to them personally.[19] In fact, the very Latin verbs that Melanchthon uses throughout the passage to summarize this point (*admonere* and *confirmare*) reappear in tandem in both the SC (54, 57, 64) and the Latin translation of the HC (69, 75).[20]

Still another part of the definition, HC 66's reference to a double promise of the gospel that is signified and sealed in the sacraments, may have been inspired by Luther's Small Catechism.[21] The assertion that "God's gospel promise [is] to grant us forgiveness of sins and eternal life" (HC 66; see also HC 70, 74, 76) echoes Luther's statements that baptism "brings about forgiveness of sins . . . and gives eternal salvation" and that in the Lord's Supper we are also given "forgiveness of sin, life, and salvation."[22]

Finally, the Lutheran context in which the HC arose may be reflected also in what is *not* included in the definition in HC 66 or in the introductory questions on baptism (HC 69) and the Lord's Supper (HC 75)—any reference to human responsibility. According to Ursinus's two earlier catechisms, one of the reasons that God instituted the sacraments was "so that [believers], on their part, might obligate themselves to faith and a holy life" (SC 54) and "bind themselves to persevere in true faith and piety toward God" (LC 275; see also LC 277). Baptism reminds and assures us "that we, on our part, might be obligated to advance each day in true conversion" (SC 57), and the Lord's Supper "that we, on our part, will be obligated to seek life in him alone, to live in a way befitting his members, and to love one another" (SC 64). However, as closely as HC 66, 69, and 75 follow the structure and wording of their counterparts in the SC and LC, they contain no such reference to the sacraments as signs of human obligation. At first this may seem odd, since Melanchthon, Calvin, and Bullinger had all included such language in their own definitions of sacraments.[23]

Nevertheless, the early Zwinglian tradition had *stressed* this meaning of the sacraments, and the HC may have excluded the language of human responsibility to keep from sounding too Zwinglian to the Philippists and Calvinists in the Palatinate and to the Lutheran princes in other territories in the empire.[24]

Even though the structure and some of the wording may go back to Luther and Melanchthon, there is nothing exclusively Lutheran or Melanchthonian about the definition in HC 66. Parts of it can be found also or only in earlier Reformed catechisms. For one thing, the fourfold structure (description, origin, purpose, focus) that we observed in the definitions in HC 66, SC 54, LC 275, and Melanchthon's *EO* (1554) is present also in Bullinger's definition in his 1559 catechism for adults:

> **Q. Explain to me what you mean by a sacrament.**
> A. A sacrament is a holy symbol or holy rite, or rather a holy action, instituted . . . by God, . . . by which he also seals and represents what he offers to us.[25]

The same is true of some of the details of the HC's definition. For example, the compound verb in HC 66, "make us understand . . . and seal," is found in various forms in Melanchthon's and Ursinus's earlier works but also in Calvin's 1545 GC ("represents . . . to seal")[26] and Bullinger's catechism for adults ("seals and represents").[27] Likewise, the double promise of the gospel, "forgiveness and new life" (HC 66), appears in a baptismal context not only in HC 70, Luther, and Melanchthon, but also in Bullinger and Calvin.[28] The reference in HC 66 to the sacraments as "*visible* . . . signs" is missing in the earlier definitions of Melanchthon and Ursinus but is present in Leo Jud's Zwinglian Shorter Catechism (1541)[29] and in the GC.[30] Finally, the repetition of the adjective "holy" in HC 65 and 66 ("*Holy* Spirit," "*holy* gospel," "*holy* sacraments," "*holy* signs and seals"), also absent in Melanchthon's and Ursinus's earlier works, does appear in the corresponding questions and answers in the Zurich catechisms of Jud[31] and Bullinger[32] and in the north-German Reformed catechisms of Micronius and Lasco.[33] Thus, whatever Lutheran or Melanchthonian sources may lie beneath the definition of sacraments in HC 66, the structure and some of the phraseology of the definition resonate with sources from the Reformed tradition as well. It seems that the HC is trying to set the tone for its discussion of the sacraments with a simple definition that is constructed from, and is broad enough to include, all perspectives in the Palatinate—Philippist, Calvinist, and Bullingerian.

A more significant part of the Lutheran influence on HC 65–85, however, may have been the presence of two documents in the background, Melanchthon's AC and his "Responsio" to Frederick III in 1559. The AC, of course, served as the confessional norm for the Palatinate at the time of the HC, and the "Responsio" provided some welcome advice to Frederick from Melanchthon in the aftermath of a bitter Palatinate debate on the Lord's Supper. These documents may have helped to guide the way the catechism deals with the most controversial question in sixteenth-century sacramental theology: how exactly the material signs of the sacraments are related to the spiritual blessings they signify.

Most of the scholarly discussion over the past century has paid little attention to Melanchthon on this point and has focused instead on whether the HC follows Calvin or Bullinger. Calvin defended a position that Gerrish has termed "symbolic instrumentalism," which holds that the signs or elements of a sacrament are the instruments through which or by which God's Spirit conveys the spiritual reality that they symbolize.[34] Sacramental signs can be distinguished from that which they signify, but they cannot be separated. The sign is joined with the signified in such a way that the latter is offered to and received by the believer simultaneously with the former.[35] Sacraments are, in the strictest sense of the term, "means of grace."

Bullinger, on the other hand, held a position that Gerrish has called "symbolic parallelism." Bullinger was concerned that Calvin's uses of the noun *instrumentum*, the verb *exhibere*, and the preposition *per* ascribe more efficacy to the sacramental signs than to the Holy Spirit. The sacraments are not "instruments" that "confer" grace "through" the signs. Rather, the elements provide only a symbolic parallel or visual analogy in which God testifies to the inner working of divine grace *independently* of the signs. The Spirit may operate simultaneously with the signs, as in the case of the Lord's Supper, but the signs remain separate from the blessings to which they point. They only resemble grace, not confer it.[36]

As Rorem has recently shown, these differences between Calvin and Bullinger endured beyond their compromise in the *Consensus Tigurinus* of 1549, both in the two men themselves and in the confessional traditions they inspired. With respect to the doctrine of the Lord's Supper, Rorem concludes:

> In any case, the two views of the Lord's Supper have managed to live side by side within the Reformed tradition for centuries. Does a given Reformed statement of faith consider the Lord's Supper as a testimony, an analogy, a parallel, even a simultaneous parallel to the internal workings of God's grace in granting communion with Christ? If so, the actual ancestor may be Heinrich Bullinger, Zwingli's successor in Zurich. Or does it explicitly identify the Supper as the very instrument or means through which God offers and confers the grace of full communion with Christ's body? The lineage would then go back to John Calvin (and to Martin Bucer).[37]

The question, then, that so many have debated is what the orientation of the HC is on this point. Is the catechism Calvinist or Bullingerian in its view of the relation between sign and signified? Neuser argued that we may have a clue already in HC 65:

> **Q. It is through faith alone that we share in Christ and all his benefits: where then does that faith come from?**
>
> A. The Holy Spirit produces it in our hearts by the preaching of the holy gospel, and confirms it by the use of the holy sacraments.

According to Neuser, the reference here to the Spirit's confirmation of one's faith through the use of the sacraments reflects Calvin's view that the sacraments help a weak faith to grow (see also HC 66: "make us understand . . . better") rather than Zwingli's position that they merely confirm those blessings that faith already possesses. In other words, for the HC the Holy Spirit does not simply reinforce something that the believer already has, but actually gives something *through* the sacraments. Like Calvin, the HC treats the sacraments as *Heilsmittel*, means by which the blessings of salvation are communicated to the believer.[38]

Gerrish and Rohls maintained, however, that the HC stops short of a full Calvinistic depiction of the sacraments as means of grace. For Gerrish the sacraments in the HC are signs and pledges of God's grace, but they do not themselves convey the grace that they signify. They only remind and assure us that we have it independently of the sacraments.[39] Indeed, according to Rohls, HC 73 leaves the impression that baptism is a divine sign and pledge of grace *already* given.[40] And the Lord's Supper in the HC is only a means of *assurance* that we spiritually feed on Christ, not a means by which that feeding itself takes place.[41] Both Gerrish and Rohls conclude that the HC is much closer to Bullinger here than to Calvin.

At first glance, it would seem that Gerrish and Rohls have the better of this argument. Although it is true that Calvin, like HC 65, regards the sacraments as means by which the Spirit confirms and nourishes faith,[42] this emphasis is not unique to him; Bullinger makes the very same point.[43] Furthermore, HC 65 does not teach that the sacraments possess what Neuser calls a *Gabecharakter*, that is, that believers are actually *given* something *through* the signs. It does say, of course, that the Holy Spirit confirms our faith through our use of the sacraments, but that does not necessarily mean that they are instruments through which the spiritual benefits signified by the elements are conveyed. Indeed, the HC drafting committee never employed the terms "means" and "instruments" that were available to it in parallel statements in SC 53 (*mediis et instrumentis*) and in LC 266 and 267 (*instrumentum*)—perhaps in an attempt to prevent the very reading of this question that some have since given it.

The same is true of the HC's individual treatments of baptism (HC 69–74) and the Lord's Supper (HC 75–85). According to HC 69, baptism reminds and assures us that "as surely as water washes away the dirt from the body, so certainly his blood and Spirit wash away my soul's impurity," but nowhere in the HC is it stated, as it is in Calvin's GC, that "reality is attached to [the water]" in such a way that "both pardon for sins and newness of life are certainly offered to us and received by us in baptism."[44] Similarly, the Lord's Supper reminds and assures us that "as surely as I receive from the hand of the one who serves and taste with my mouth the bread and cup of the Lord, . . . so surely he nourishes and refreshes my soul for eternal life with his crucified body and poured-out blood" (HC 75). But nowhere does the catechism teach, as Calvin does in his *Short Treatise on the Holy Supper*, that the terms *body* and *blood* are attributed to the bread and wine "because they are as instruments [French: *instrumens*] by which our Lord Jesus Christ distributes them to us."[45] One might say that the HC portrays the sacraments as means of confirmation or assurance, but not, in the strict Calvinist sense of the term, as means of grace, by or through which the Spirit communicates to the believer the divine benefits represented in the external signs and seals.[46]

However, although the HC does not echo Calvin in its treatment of the relationship between sign and signified, it cannot be characterized as distinctively Bullingerian either. To be sure, the HC, like Bullinger, places sign and signified together in a kind of "symbolic parallelism," but as the following comparisons show, so did Calvin:

HC 73 Q. **Why then does the Holy Spirit call baptism the water of rebirth and the washing away of sins?**

A. God wants to teach us that the blood and Spirit of Christ take away our sins *just as* water removes dirt from the body. But more important, God wants to assure us . . . that we are *as truly* washed of our sins spiritually *as* our bodies are washed with water physically (italics added).

HC 79 Q. **Why then does Christ call the bread his body and the cup his blood?**

A. He wants to teach us that *just as* bread and wine nourish the temporal life, *so too* his crucified body and poured-out blood are the true food and drink of our souls for eternal life. But more important, he wants to assure us . . . that we . . . share in his true body and blood *as surely as* our mouths receive these holy signs in his remembrance (italics added).

In the same way that . . . people's bodies are cleansed with water [in baptism], God works in our souls with the blood of Christ by his Spirit. (Bullinger; italics added)[47]

> Now in the Lord's Supper bread and wine represent the very body and blood of Christ. . . . *As* bread nourisheth and strengtheneth man, . . . *so* the body of Christ, eaten by faith, feedeth and satisfieth the soul of man . . . *As* wine is drink to the thirsty, . . . *so* the blood of our Lord Jesus, drunken by faith, doth quench the thirst of the burning conscience (Bullinger; italics added).[48]

> **GC 325 Q. What similarity has water to these things, that it represents them?**
>
> A. Forgiveness of sins is a kind of washing, by which our souls are cleansed from all their stains, *just as* bodily defilements are washed away by water[49] (italics added).
>
> **GC 341 Q. But why is the body symbolized by bread and the blood by wine?**
>
> A. By this we are taught that the body of our Lord has *the same* virtue spiritually to nourish our souls *as* bread has in nourishing our bodies for the sustenance of this present life. *As* wine exhilarates the heart of men, refreshes their strength, and fortifies the whole body, *so* from the blood of our Lord the very same benefits are received by our souls[50] (italics added).

Calvin, therefore, fully as much as Bullinger and the HC, portrays the outward signs of physical washing in baptism and physical eating and drinking in the Lord's Supper as "symbolic parallels"[51] to an inner spiritual washing and nourishment. Where Calvin and Bullinger parted ways was not on whether the sign and signified are parallel but on whether they are *merely* parallel. Are sacramental signs and actions only visual analogies to the grace that the Holy Spirit bestows apart from them (Bullinger), or are they more than analogies, namely, the very means or instruments through which that grace is communicated to believers (Calvin)? That is a question that the HC does not address. It neither affirms nor denies one position or the other. On this point, the catechism goes as far as the two reformers might agree, but then it is silent.

The only reference to the sign-signified relation that might be construed as distinctively Zwinglian or Bullingerian is, according to Rohls, a part of the answer in HC 73:

> **Q. Why then does the Holy Spirit call baptism the water of rebirth and the washing away of sins?**
>
> A. God wants to assure us, by this divine pledge and sign, that we are as truly washed [*gewaschen sind*] of our sins spiritually as our bodies are washed [*gewaschen werden*] with water physically.

Rohls's thinking seems to be that the first use of "washed" here expresses a current *state* or condition, whereas the second expresses a current *process* or action. The English translation, therefore, could better read, "God wants to assure us . . . that we are as truly *already* washed of our sins spiritually as our bodies are *being* washed with water physcially." In other words, water baptism is an assurance of a spiritual baptism that has previously taken place; it signifies a grace already given.[52]

This temporal separation of sign and signified has a definite Zwinglian ring to it[53] and is strongly implied also in Bullinger's treatment of baptism.[54] However, the HC does not necessarily betray a debt to Zurich here, for a similar approach to baptism can be found earlier in Ursinus, Melanchthon, and even Calvin. In his discussion of the sacraments in his 1559 "Theses," for example, Ursinus had emphasized that it is the function of sacraments not to confer (*conferre*) grace and its gifts but to seal in us the grace and gifts already conferred (*collata*). It is only after the sacramental reality (*res*) has been received, whether before or during the ceremony, that the sacrament becomes a testimony to that bestowal of grace.[55] Ursinus then reiterates this point in the next section on baptism.[56] That he should describe baptism in this way is understandable when we recall that he had composed these "Theses" in defense of Melanchthon's view of the sacraments and that Melanchthon had also referred to baptism in this way. In a relatively brief treatment of baptism in his 1521 *Loci*, for example, Melanchthon characterizes post-Pentecost baptism as a sign of grace "already bestowed" (*iam donatae*), a pledge and seal of grace "already conferred" (*iam collatae*), a testimony of "bestowed grace" (*donatae gratiae*), and an assurance of grace "already conferred" (*iam collatam*).[57]

Calvin, too, was willing to grant in the 1549 *Consensus Tigurinus* ("Zurich Consensus") with Bullinger that the reality signified in the sacrament can also be received by the faithful outside of the sacrament. According to the *Consensus* (XIX[58]), the apostle Paul had been granted remission of sins and Cornelius had received the Holy Spirit already *before* their baptisms. Water baptism was still a washing away of sins for Paul and a laver of regeneration for Cornelius but only insofar as it confirmed and increased the faith by which these benefits were appropriated in greater measure.[59] However, this common approach to baptism as a sign and seal of grace already conferred is not tied to a uniform understanding of the relationship between sign and signified in the sacrament itself. In his commentary on Acts in 1552, Calvin could still describe the remission of sins as "annexed" (*annectitur*) to baptism (a verb that would have made Bullinger uncomfortable), even though this benefit is only being granted in greater measure to a faith that is being strengthened in baptism.[60]

Ursinus, meanwhile, took a position between that of Calvin and Bullinger. In the case of those who come to baptism already regenerated, he, like Calvin, speaks of a certain concurrence of sign and signified as the gifts to which water baptism testifies are increased in the believer.[61] At the same time, Ursinus is more cautious than Calvin when it comes to describing the conferral of grace *through* the sacraments. The preposition *per* may be used in this context but only if it is understood that the benefits of the sacrament are communicated simultaneously with the sign or in greater abundance than before.[62] Like his mentor Melanchthon,[63] Ursinus believed that the expressions "with the sacraments" or "in the sacraments" (that is, in the use of the sacraments) are more precise.[64]

In short, followers of Calvin, Bullinger, and Melanchthon could all affirm HC 73's parallelism between inner and outer baptism and still hold to different understandings of the union between sign and signified. In HC 73 the sign of water baptism can testify to a grace already given regardless of whether the additional grace of assurance and strengthened faith is given *along with* the sacrament or *through* it. In this respect, HC 73 is typical of the catechism's entire section on the sacraments: it does not take a position on the precise relationship between sign and signified.

How might we account for this silence? Leaving this question open was probably a way for the HC as a union catechism to accommodate a range of viewpoints. And Frederick III and his team of authors might have gotten a cue here from the two Lutheran documents mentioned earlier, Melanchthon's AC and his "Responsio" to Frederick in 1559. First of all, the AC, whose doctrinal norms the HC was obligated to honor, is itself noncommittal on the relationship between sign and signified in the sacraments. On the Lord's Supper, for example, the 1530 German and Latin editions of AC art. 10 read as follows:

> **German text:** Concerning the Lord's Supper it is taught that the true body and blood of Christ are truly present under the form of bread and wine in the Lord's Supper and are distributed and received there.[65]

> **Latin text:** Concerning the Lord's Supper they teach that the body and blood of Christ are truly present and are distributed to those who eat the Lord's Supper.[66]

In 1540, however, Melanchthon produced an altered version of the Latin edition (the "Variata"), which Frederick III persuaded the German Protestant princes to recognize as an acceptable interpretation of the unaltered 1530 version (the "Invariata") at the Naumburg Conference in 1561. In the altered version, art. 10 now read: Concerning the Lord's Supper, they teach that with the bread and wine the body and blood of Christ are truly offered to those who eat in the Lord's Supper.[67]

To assert here that the body and blood of Christ are "offered" or "presented" (*exhibeantur*) "with" (*cum*) the bread and wine is ambiguous, perhaps intentionally so. It affirms a true feeding on Christ without resolving the questions of how exactly Christ is present in the Supper or whether he is received through the elements or only alongside of them.[68] The wording is indefinite enough to allow Lutherans (Philippists *and* Gnesio-Lutherans) and Reformed (Calvinists *and* Bullingerians) to interpret it in their own ways.[69] This ambiguity seems to have been preserved in the HC. To receive Christ in the Lord's Supper "as surely" as one receives the bread and the cup (HC 75) sounds little different than to receive Christ "with" the bread and the wine (AC 10). In neither case is there a clear indication of how Christ and the material elements are related.

Surprisingly, Ursinus even saw agreement here between the HC and the 1530 "Invariata" version of the AC. The HC insists that although the signs of bread and wine do not become the "real" (*wesentlich)* body and blood of Christ (HC 78) and that Christ is not "bodily [*leiblich*] present under the form of bread and wine" (HC 80), believers at the Lord's table still "truly" (*wahrhafftig*) share in Christ's "true [*waren*] body and blood" (HC 79). In a defense of the HC in 1564, Ursinus argued that this is fully consistent with the German and Latin texts of the 1530 AC.[70] According to Ursinus, the AC never states that Christ is "essentially" (*wesentlich*) or "bodily" (*leiblich*) present in the Lord's Supper. All it says is that the "true" (*warer*) body and blood of Christ are "truly" (*wahrhafftig*) present. We indeed receive that true body and blood, but we do so only "sacramentally" (*sacramentsweise*) and "spiritually" (*geistlich*).[71]

The authors of the HC, therefore, consciously sought to operate within the framework of the AC's doctrine of the Lord's Supper and even followed the AC in leaving ambiguous the relationship between sign and signified. But Melanchthon's influence did not stop there. In 1559, Frederick III had intervened in the contentious debate on the Lord's Supper in Heidelberg between Tilemann Heshusius, a Gnesio-Lutheran, and William Klebitz, a Calvinist. Shortly thereafter, Frederick asked Melanchthon for his opinion on the affair, and Melanchthon composed a short "Responsio" with some advice for Frederick: rather than try to solve the mystery of the mode of Christ's presence in the Lord's Supper, the Palatinate should unite around the Pauline formula in 1 Corinthians 10:16 that the bread of the Supper is a *koinonia* (communion, participation, fellowship) with the body of Christ. All we need to say is that in the Lord's Supper we are indeed united with Christ's body and blood.[72]

Frederick and the authors of the HC seem to have followed that advice in HC 75–80. In response to the question about where Christ promises "to nourish and refresh believers with his body and blood as surely as they eat this broken bread and drink this cup," HC 77 quotes Paul's summary in 1 Corinthians 11 of Jesus' institution of the sacrament. It then goes on, however, to cite the text suggested by Melanchthon: "This promise is repeated by Paul in these words: 'The cup of blessing that we bless, is it not a sharing in the blood of Christ? The bread that we break, is it not a sharing in the body of Christ? Because there is one bread, we who are many are one body, for we all partake of the one bread.'"[73] The Melanchthonian formula appears again in HC 79: "Why then does Christ call the bread his body and the cup his blood, or the new covenant in his blood, and Paul use the words, a participation in Christ's body and blood?" The answer is because Christ wants to teach us that "just as bread and wine nourish the temporal life, so too his crucified body and poured-out blood are the true food and drink of our souls for eternal life" and to assure us that "that we . . . share in his true body and blood as surely as our mouths receive these holy signs in his remembrance." This emphasis on communion with Christ in the Lord's Supper is present also in HC 75, 76, and 80. In every case, the HC follows Melanchthon's lead by focusing not on how Christ is joined to the elements but on how we are joined to Christ.

REFORMED ELEMENTS

The Lutheran influence on this section of the HC is provided, then, by some of the wording of Melanchthon's *EO* (and possibly Luther's Small Catechism), by the doctrinal boundaries of Melanchthon's AC, and by the advice in Melanchthon's "Responsio." Once again, however, the HC seeks to hold together the coalition of Philippist Lutherans, Bullingerians, and Calvinists in the Palatinate by weaving Reformed language and emphases into the text as well. This can be illustrated with six examples:

(1) Some of the wording of HC 65–85 may have been influenced by or even drawn from Reformed sources. The HC begins its sequence of questions on baptism, for example, by introducing a double washing that is promised in baptism (HC 69), explaining the two parts of this washing (HC 70), and providing the biblical basis for it (HC 71). Then comes the question,

> **HC 72 Q. Does this outward washing with water itself wash away sins?**
> A. No, only Jesus Christ's blood and the Holy Spirit cleanse us from all sins.

This follows quite closely the pattern and language of Calvin's GC of 1545. The GC also begins its series of questions on baptism by introducing the double meaning of the sacrament (GC 324) and explaining each of the two parts (GC 325–26). Then comes the question (with echoes in HC 72),

> **GC 327 Q. Do you regard the water as the washing of the soul?**
> A. Not at all. For it is wrong to snatch this honour from the blood of Christ. . . . And we perceive the fruit of this

cleansing when the Holy Spirit sprinkles our conscience with that sacred blood.[74]

The language of HC 76 on the Lord's Supper also sounds very much like Calvin:

HC 76 Q. What does it mean to eat the crucified body of Christ and to drink his poured-out blood?

A. It means to accept with a believing heart the entire suffering and death of Christ and thereby to receive forgiveness of sins and eternal life. But it means more. Through the Holy Spirit, who lives both in Christ and in us, we are united more and more to Christ's blessed body.

***Institutes*:** There are some who define the eating of Christ's flesh and the drinking of his blood as, in one word, nothing but to believe in Christ. But it seems to me that Christ meant to teach something more definite, and more elevated. . . . It is that we are quickened by the true partaking of him. . . . In this way, the Lord intended, by calling himself the "bread of life" [John 6:51], to teach not only that salvation for us rests on faith in his death and resurrection, but also that, by true partaking of him, his life passes into us and is made ours.[75]

In the context of this passage from the 1559 *Institutes*, Calvin is criticizing the Zwinglian tradition for showing too little regard for the signs of the Lord's Supper, but "good ecumenical theologian that he was, . . . Calvin doesn't anathematize the opposition, or even identify them by name."[76] Instead, he highlights common ground with the Zwinglians and then takes his own position a step beyond it. HC 76 does much the same thing, distancing itself from a purely Zwinglian position (a move toward the Lutherans?) while at the same time affirming what the Zwinglian and Calvinist views have in common (a move toward the Bullingerians?).

Finally, there are some striking parallels between the HC's treatment of the Lord's Supper and an earlier work on the same subject by Thomas Erastus—court physician in Heidelberg, member of the Palatinate consistory, lay theologian, and a disciple of Bullinger. The parallels are most vivid when we lay the German texts side by side:

HC 75: *allen seinen gütern gemeinshafft habest* ("share . . . in all his benefits")

Erastus: *in die gemeinschafft aller seine güter angenommen*[77]

HC 75: *er selbst meine seel mit seinem gecreutizigten Leib vnnd vergossnen Blut, so gewisz zum ewigen leben speise und trencke . . . als ich . . . empfange . . . das brod vnnd den Kelch des HERRN* ("as surely as I receive . . . the bread and cup of the Lord, . . . so surely he nourishes and refreshes my soul for eternal life with his crucified body and poured-out blood")

Erastus: *er speise und träncke uns so gewiss mit der gemainschafft seines gekreutzigten leibs und vergossnen Blüts zum ewigen leben als gewiss wir brot und wein empfahen*[78]

HC 79: *gleich wie brod vnnd wein das zeitliche leben erhalten, also sey auch sein gecreutzigter leib vnd vergossen blut . . . zum ewigen leben* ("just as bread and wine nourish the temporal life")

Erastus: *wie mit brot und wein sich der mensch zu disem zeitlichen leben zu erhalten pflegt, also muss er sich mit der gemainschafft des leibs und bluts Christi . . . auffenthalten zum ewigen leben*[79]

HC 79: *zeichen vnd pfand* ("sign and pledge")

Erastus: *warzaichen oder pfand*[80]

These are just some of the parallels that show the likely influence of Erastus's language on this part of the HC. It may be going too far to attribute the HC's whole doctrine of the Lord's Supper to Erastus on this basis[81] or to cite this as evidence of his extensive involvement in the preparation of the entire catechism,[82] but it does suggest that he played more than a minimal role as a Reformed representative on the drafting committee.

(2) A second Reformed element is the repeated connection in HC 66 and 67, 69, 70, 75, and 80 between the sacraments and Christ's sacrificial death on the cross. Sturm argued that this reflects a distinctive Zurich tradition going back through Bullinger, Erastus, and Lasco to Zwingli,[83] and Neuser and Rohls made the same observation with respect to the HC's doctrine of the Lord's Supper.[84] It should be noted, however, that at several points in the GC, Calvin too links the sacraments to Christ's sacrifice on the cross. For example, he maintains that neither one of the benefits of baptism inheres in the baptismal water itself: rather, the washing of the soul is rooted in "the blood of Christ, which was poured out," and regeneration comes "from both the death and resurrection of Christ."[85] He makes the connection between Christ's sacrificial death and the Lord's Supper even more explicit:

GC 347 Q. What then do we have in the symbol of bread?
A. The body of Christ, as it was once sacrificed for us to reconcile us to God, is now thus also given to us.

GC 348 Q. What is the symbol of wine?
A. Christ, as he poured out his blood once for satisfaction for sins and as the price of our redemption, so now holds it forth for us to drink, that we may feel the benefit which ought to accrue to us from it.

GC 349 Q. According to those replies of yours, the Holy Supper of

our Lord refers us to his death, in order that we may partake of its virtue.

A. Quite so: for then the one and perpetual sacrifice, which suffices for our salvation, was made. There remains nothing further, except to enjoy it.[86]

This sounds little different from HC 75's claim that the bread and cup of the Lord's Supper remind and assure believers that they share in the broken body and poured-out blood of Christ's one sacrifice on the cross. The HC's links between sacrament and sacrifice, therefore, can be identified as a Reformed emphasis, but not a purely Zwinglian one.

(3) The doctrine of the covenant is yet another Reformed element in the HC. The term *covenant* occurs fairly often in Ursinus's LC, especially in the section on sacraments (see LC 274, 276–77, 279, 284, 288, 293–96, 306), but curiously it is found in only three questions in the SC (55, 63, 71) and only two in the HC (74, 82). We will examine this anomaly more closely in the next chapter, but for now we can say that it is related in part to the different purposes and audiences of these documents. Furthermore, the doctrine of covenant might have posed a theological stumbling block to Lutherans both inside and outside of the Palatinate and thus may have been intentionally muted in the drafting of the HC. But the fact remains that the term itself does appear in the catechism, and, as we will also see in the next chapter, there is more to this Reformed covenantal element than what appears on the surface.

(4) It was not just Lutheran toes, however, on which the HC sought not to tread. As far back as the "Apology of the AC" in 1531, Melanchthon had declared that Christ's body and blood are "truly and substantially [*substantialiter*] present" in the Lord's Supper,[87] and Calvin had even asserted in the GC that believers are made "partakers of his substance [*substantia*]" as they partake of the elements.[88] Both of these expressions appeared again in Ursinus. In his 1559 "Theses," he states that Christ is "truly and substantially present" (*vere et substantialiter adest*) to believers in the Lord's Supper[89] and in LC 300 that the "eating of Christ" is not just a sharing in his merits but also a communication of the person and *substantia* of Christ himself.[90] Bullinger, however, had strongly opposed the use of the words *substance* or *essence* to describe the presence and communication of the body of Christ at the Lord's Supper,[91] and remarkably the term is not found in the SC or the HC either. Gooszen and Neuser saw this as evidence of a more general Zurich-oriented view of the Lord's Supper in the HC,[92] but given the political-theological situation in the Palatinate and the consensus nature of the catechism, it seems more likely that the omission of such terminology was intentional. As with the Lutherans and the term *covenant*, the authors of the HC may also have sought to avoid language that would have been a stumbling block to the Bullingerian party. We

should probably not call this a Reformed element *in* the HC, but it does represent a Reformed influence *on* the catechism.

(5) HC 75 asserts that Christ commanded us in the Lord's Supper to eat the "broken" bread in remembrance of him. In so doing, he promised that "as surely as I see with my eyes the bread of the Lord *broken* for me, . . . so surely his body was offered and *broken* for me." The references to "broken" here are to that moment in the Lord's Supper in which the administrant breaks the eucharistic bread before it is distributed to the congregation. Lutheran and Catholic churches did not practice this *fractio panis* ("breaking of the bread"); Reformed churches did, not just because, in their view, Christ commanded it but also as a symbolic rejection of any notion of Christ's bodily presence in the bread or as the bread.[93]

According to Sturm, the *fractio* was a late-Zwinglian element, never mentioned in the GC but introduced by Ursinus into the SC (64) and LC (297) under the influence of Zurich.[94] There is indeed reference to it in the Zurich confessional tradition as far back as Bullinger's *Warhaffte Bekanntnus* of 1545.[95] And what some have considered the classic Reformed statement on the practice, *Das Büchlein vom Brodbrechen* ("Booklet on the Breaking of the Bread") by the late-Zwinglian Thomas Erastus, was issued simultaneously with the HC in early 1563.[96] Sturm himself acknowledges, however, that the two confessions by the Calvinist Beza in the late 1550s may also have influenced Ursinus in this regard.[97] Considering that Olevianus, one of the drafters of the HC, was in all likelihood the translator of Beza's smaller confession into German in 1562, we have a possible Genevan source for the emphasis on the *fractio* in the HC as well.[98] In any case, the *fractio panis* is another distinctively Reformed element that has been integrated into the catechism.

(6) The final Reformed accent in the HC's treatment of the sacraments is its view of the Holy Spirit as the bond of the union between Christ and the believer in the Lord's Supper. HC 76 and 79 read in part:

HC 76 Q. What does it mean to eat the crucified body of Christ and to drink his poured-out blood?

A. But it means more. *Through the Holy Spirit,* who lives both in Christ and in us, we are united more and more to Christ's blessed body. And so, although he is in heaven and we are on earth, we are flesh of his flesh and bone of his bone (italics added).

HC 79 Q. Why then does Christ call the bread his body and the cup his blood?

A. He wants to assure us, by this visible sign and pledge, that we, *through the Holy Spirit's work,* share in his true body and blood as surely as our mouths receive these holy signs in his remembrance (italics added).

This feature of the HC is often alleged to be a distinctively Calvinist trademark.[99] It is indeed a key theme in Calvin and one that distinguished him from Melanchthon, who felt that such language could too easily be misconstrued in the Zwinglian sense of *limiting* Christ's presence in the Supper to his Spirit.[100] But references to the Spirit's binding of believers to Christ in the Lord's Supper appear also in the *Consensus Tigurinus* ("Zurich Consensus") between Bullinger and Calvin in 1549 and in Bullinger's subsequent writings. In the *Consensus Tigurinus,* the two reformers profess that it is only as believers are engrafted into Christ that they acquire and enjoy the blessings of salvation (III, V, VI, VIII). All who come to the sacraments in faith, therefore, receive what the sacraments represent to the senses, namely, Christ and his benefits (VIII, IX). Since Christ's finite body is contained in heaven (XXI, XXV), however, one's spiritual communion with him at the Lord's Supper is achieved through the Holy Spirit: Christ feeds the soul through faith by virtue of his Spirit's dwelling within the believer (III, VI, VIII, XII, XIV, XXIII).[101]

Bullinger makes much the same point in the Second Helvetic Confession. The body of Christ is in heaven at the right hand of God. Therefore we must not fix our attention on the sacramental bread but lift our hearts upward. Like the sun, which is far away in the heavens yet present among us "in its effects" (*efficaciter*), Christ, the Sun of Righteousness, is absent from us in body but present among us "spiritually" (*spiritualiter*) through his life-giving activity in the Lord's Supper.[102] For Bullinger, this spiritual presence of Christ in the Supper is not limited to the presence of his divine nature or, as the analogy of the sun suggests, to the *power* of his body. Rather it is the Holy Spirit who serves as the instrument by which Christ communicates his body and blood to the believing celebrant.[103] As Bullinger states in another place in the Second Helvetic Confession, believers receive the body and blood of Christ "not in a corporeal but in a spiritual mode, through the Holy Spirit." These benefits are "communicated to us spiritually by the Spirit of God."[104] When the HC states, therefore, that "we, through the Holy Spirit's work, share in [Christ's] true body and blood," it does so in the spirit of Calvin but not in a manner unique to Calvin. It was actually part of a broader Reformed emphasis.

In sum, identifying the approach to the sacraments in the HC as distinctively Calvinist or Bullingerian, or even some mixture of the two, is not warranted by the evidence. The HC's goal in this most controversial area of doctrine appears to have been "maximal consensus"[105] between the Lutherans and Reformed in the Palatinate, and, on the Reformed side, between the Calvinists and Bullingerians.[106] To ensure a common platform, the HC begins with an apparent nod to Melanchthon, drawing from Melanchthonian sources, honoring Melanchthonian boundaries (the AC), and following Melanchthonian advice. It then incorporates language and emphases from the Reformed tradition that are not found in the AC but, at the same time, do not directly contradict it. Along the way the HC employs multiple "ecumenical" strategies: use of source texts from all three parties, emphasis on views held in common, total or near silence on disputed topics, and positive statements of doctrine without explicit rejection of alternatives. The result was a position on the sacraments broad enough to encompass a range of views that lay between Zwingli on the left and the Gnesio-Lutherans on the right. If we must attach a label to this position, we could best describe it, like the Palatinate reformation itself, as Melanchthonian-Reformed.

7
COVENANT

Q/A 65–85

As we pointed out in the previous chapter, one of the distinctively Reformed elements in the HC's treatment of the sacraments is the doctrine of the covenant. Curiously, however, the word *covenant* (German: *Bund*) appears only three times in the entire catechism—twice in HC 74 in the explanation of infant baptism, and once in HC 82 in the answer to a question about admitting the unbelieving and ungodly to the Lord's table. The total reaches five if one includes the two citations of Jesus' reference to the eucharistic cup as the "new covenant [German: *Testament*] in my blood" in HC 77 and 79.

Nevertheless, a few scholars have argued for a broader doctrine of covenant in the HC than what only three or five occurrences of the term might suggest. The first was Heinrich Heppe, who 150 years ago argued that the HC and Ursinus's commentary on it were part of the rise of a new form of dogmatic theology in Germany in the mid-sixteenth century. At the foundation of this new "German Reformed" dogmatics was the concept of a covenant of grace between God and the elect that was joined to a doctrine of mystical union with Christ. The covenant idea could be found in the HC in its central motif of the believer's belonging to Christ, introduced already in its famous question and answer 1: "What is your only comfort in life and in death? I am not my own, but belong . . . to my faithful Savior, Jesus Christ." The rest of the material in the catechism is then presented from this perspective of the consciousness of the believer in covenant or union with Christ.[1]

Since the quadricentennial of the HC in 1963, at least three other scholars have followed Heppe's lead. In an essay on covenant and election in the HC, Lothar Coenen expanded on Heppe's notion that at the center of the catechism is an emphasis on God's placement of humanity in relation to himself. The language of covenant is not used, but the idea is certainly there, particularly in the HC's doctrine of the mediator (HC 15–18), which points to the restoration of a relationship between God and his people. Indeed, Coenen noted, it is precisely at this point in his later commentary on the HC that Ursinus introduced an excursus or locus on the covenant. But this covenant relationship can also be detected in the language of our being "grafted into Christ" (HC 20), God as "a faithful Father" (HC 26), our adoption as "children of God" (HC 33), our being delivered and bought as "his [Christ's] very own" (HC 34), and our sharing or participating in Christ (HC 32, 53, 65, 79).[2]

J. F. G. Goeters, too, found the covenant idea in the HC's doctrine of the mediator but only because, in his estimation, covenant theology informs the entire context in which the mediating work of Christ is treated, namely, the relationship between law and gospel. In support of this, Goeters pointed to questions 30–36 in the earlier LC, where Ursinus explicitly discusses the differences and connections between law and gospel within the framework of a doctrine of covenant.[3]

The most recent scholar to argue for a covenantal shape to the HC is Derk Visser. He claimed that the very arrangement of the catechism, the threefold structure of misery, deliverance, and gratitude, "can easily be read as a sequence resulting from God's covenant, which God, after man's willful fall, re-established and which was fulfilled by Christ, the Mediator."[4] Though not citing Heppe, Coenen, or Goeters, he too found in HC 1 a summary of the doctrine of the covenant of grace and, like them, appealed to the covenant language of Ursinus's LC and commentary on the HC as the context in which the HC's own covenant doctrine must be understood.[5]

How legitimate are these claims? May we really speak of the HC as covenantal in character when the word itself appears only five times in 129 questions and answers? It is our contention that many of these claims are indeed valid but that earlier scholarship falls short in two ways. First, it has not sufficiently developed the criterion by which to determine the presence of covenant in the HC, and second, it has not gone far enough in applying that criterion. Heppe, Coenen, Goeters, and Visser all insisted that the HC must be read in the context of those parallel passages in the LC and commentary on the HC where covenant is explicitly mentioned. But they did not make clear how exactly the HC is related to these other works by Ursinus or why such comparisons with them are even in order. Indeed, as we shall see, most scholarship in the past has concluded that Ursinus virtually abandoned the covenant idea of the LC when he composed the SC and HC a short while later, and that covenant reappeared in only a couple of contexts in his later commentary on the HC. If covenant plays a significant role in just a single early work by Ursinus and resurfaces in a later commentary in only a limited way, can it really be appropriate to use these documents to support a doctrine of covenant in the HC? What we need to do first, therefore, is take another look at the place of covenant in Ursinus's theological corpus as a whole.

THE PLACE OF COVENANT IN URSINUS'S WORKS

The conventional understanding of Ursinus's catechetical output is that he wrote the LC and its abridgment, the SC, as preliminary drafts for the new Palatine catechism (the HC) mandated in the early 1560s by Elector

Frederick III. The covenant theme dominated the LC, suddenly and mysteriously receded in the SC and HC, and then resurfaced in Ursinus's commentary on the HC in an excursus on the covenant and the sections on the sacraments.[6]

The question of why the covenant idea faded so quickly in Ursinus's shorter catechisms after featuring so prominently in the longer one has led to a good deal of speculation. Maurits Gooszen postulated over a century ago that the frequent references to covenant in the LC were omitted in the SC and HC under pressure from Lutheran theologians in the Palatinate who thought they sounded too sacramentarian (Zwinglian). Especially problematic would have been references to the sacraments as "signs" of the covenant, which to Lutheran ears tuned to the AC might have the ring of the "bare signs" or "mere signs" that they associated with Zwinglianism.[7] August Lang also considered this abrupt change as a concession to Lutheran critics of the LC, but he suggested that it was the concept of the natural covenant in the LC that became the stumbling block that led Ursinus to eliminate nearly all mention of covenant in the catechisms that followed.[8]

These early theories, however, are not fully satisfactory. For one thing, Gooszen and Lang both assumed that the LC was composed before the SC and that Ursinus was under pressure from critics of the first document to keep the covenant idea out of the second. As Erdmann Sturm has shown, however, there is stronger evidence that the SC was written first; hence Ursinus must have *added* covenant references to the LC, not *omitted* them from the SC under pressure.[9] Furthermore, the argument that a Zwinglian ring to the phrase "signs of the covenant" led to the suppression of all but a few references to the term *covenant* in the SC and HC is less than convincing. Would nonsacramental uses of the term need to be sacrificed just to avoid confusion about the sacramental use? And how then do we explain the fact that the phrase "sign of the covenant" still appeared in HC 74 or that the Palatinate Church Order of 1563 did not shy away from the terms *covenant* and *covenant signs* in its liturgical forms for baptism and the Lord's Supper?[10] Finally, if Ursinus had to forego practically all mention of covenant in the SC and HC because he could no longer employ the offending term *natural covenant*, why, when he was free to return to the covenant theme in his commentary on the HC, did he do so without any mention of the natural covenant?[11]

More recently, both Sturm and Cornelis Graafland have suggested that the presence or absence of the covenant theme in Ursinus's writings had to do with the different genres, purposes, and audiences of his works. The SC and its close relative, the HC, were confessions written for a general audience, whereas both the LC and commentary (lectures) on the HC were more technical works designed for theological instruction at the Sapience College and Heidelberg University. A relatively new and complex topic like covenant, therefore, might be appropriate study material for students of theology, but it was hardly fitting for a lay catechism.[12]

This may be a more promising line of argument, but it requires some refinement. Above all, we need to recognize that whereas the LC and the catechetical lectures might have been suitable genres for a subject like covenant, they also placed limits on how a doctrine of covenant could function within their structure as a whole. Ursinus's commentary on the HC, for example, is really a set of lectures on the *loci communes*, or major topics of theology, arranged in the order that these topics arise in the text of the HC. Since covenant is hardly mentioned in the HC and Ursinus still wished to devote a locus to it, he had to insert an excursus on covenant where he believed it fit most naturally, namely, between the loci on the mediator (HC 18) and the gospel (HC 19).[13] He also referred to the concept again periodically in his comments on the sacraments.[14]

This addition to his lectures of a locus on covenant and the placement of it in a carefully chosen context is not greatly different from the way he had dealt with covenant earlier in the LC, itself a kind of *loci communes*. As Sturm has noted, upon assuming the post of Professor of Loci Communes (Dogmatics) at the University of Heidelberg in September 1562, Ursinus reported that his first course of lectures would offer "a summary of doctrine" (*summam doctrinae*) that fell somewhere between a rudimentary catechism and a detailed exposition of the traditional theological loci. None of his extant writings fits the description of this "summary of doctrine" better than his "Catechesis, Summa Theologiae," the so-called *Catechesis maior* or LC.[15]

The question for Ursinus, however, seems to have been where to put a locus on covenant in a catechetical *loci communes* that consisted of several hundred questions and answers and was governed by the structure of a traditional catechism (creed, law, prayer, sacraments). Lang claims that Ursinus placed the covenant idea at the very foundation of the LC and wedded it to each major division of the material.[16] According to Graafland, Ursinus even gave it a "structurally determinative" role.[17] But these claims are not borne out by the text. The word *covenant* appears in only 40 of the 323 questions and answers of the LC, just 12 percent of the total number. Furthermore, at the point where Ursinus introduces the structure and major headings of the catechism (LC 8–9), he does not mention covenant at all:

LC 8 Q. How many parts are there to the summary of Christian doctrine?
A. Four.

LC 9 Q. What are they?
A. The summary of the divine law, or Decalogue; the summary of the gospel or Apostles' Creed; the invocation of God, or the Lord's Prayer; and the institution of the ministry of the church.

To be sure, Ursinus does refer to covenant in the introductory questions or answers that later lead off each of these sections of the LC (10 and 148 on law, 30 on gospel, 224 on invocation, and 265 on ministry), but he then proceeds, sometimes through long stretches of text, with no further mention of the topic. In his detailed explanation of the Ten Commandments, for example, he begins by asking whether "Christians, who have already been received into God's covenant, also need the teaching of the Decalogue" (LC 148), and two questions later he identifies the converted as "covenant partners." After that, however, the word *covenant* never appears again until a final transitional question just before the next section on prayer (LC 223)—73 questions and answers and an entire exposition of the Decalogue later! The same is true of that next section on prayer. Ursinus mentions covenant four times in the answer to the introductory question (LC 224), but in the next 39 questions and answers explaining the content of the Lord's Prayer, he never refers to it again. Covenant is connected to these sections of the LC in a general and sometimes even superficial way; it is not carefully integrated into the more detailed reflection on each topic.

The large majority of the references to covenant in the LC are found in the same two contexts in which it would later appear in the HC commentary: the doctrines of the gospel-mediator and the sacraments. Of the 40 questions and answers where Ursinus uses the term *covenant,* 33 are found in these two parts of the text—17 in the section on the gospel (LC 30–147), and 16 in the explanation of the ministry of the church (264–323), which comprises subsections on ministry in general, the Word, the sacraments in general, baptism, the Lord's Supper, and church discipline. Like the adjoining loci on covenant and gospel in the later commentary, the first of these two contexts in the LC treats the definition of covenant (31), its relation to the term *testament* (32), the differences between the Old and New Testaments (33), covenant as the essence of the gospel (34, 35), the difference between law and gospel (36), and the role of Christ the Mediator in the covenant (72–74). Once again, however, the LC seldom connects the covenant theme directly to the core material in this division of the catechism, in this case an exposition of the Apostles' Creed. Covenant does find a home in this subsection on gospel, but it is still something of a stranger there.

The picture that emerges here, then, is not that of a doctrine of covenant that dominates Ursinus's early thought, suddenly fades into the background, and then reappears in a more limited way in his mature theology. Not only were his three catechisms of the early 1560s probably composed in a different order than has traditionally been thought (SC-LC-HC rather than LC-SC-HC), but they belonged to different genres and served different purposes. In several respects, the LC had more in common with the later commentary on the HC than with the smaller catechisms with which it is usually compared. The LC and commentary were both a kind of a catechetical dogmatics or dogmatic catechesis designed for upper-level theological instruction.[18] It is true that the LC employs a question and answer format from beginning to end, whereas the commentary intersperses discussions of the loci among the questions and answers of the HC. But in both documents Ursinus seemed to regard covenant as a discrete theological topic, not the foundational or organizing principle of a system of theology. Moreover, his search for a place for this new topic in the system led him to the same theological contexts both times—the gospel of reconciliation through the Mediator, and the sacraments. Finally, with the exception of three references to a "covenant in creation" in the LC, which do not reappear in the commentary,[19] Ursinus invested the covenant locus with similar content in both documents. The same material that is spread over several questions and answers in the gospel section of the LC is brought together in expanded form in an excursus on covenant in the commentary. What this suggests is that once Ursinus introduced the covenant concept into his theological lectures in 1562, he never abandoned it or fundamentally altered it in the years that followed. Covenant played a permanent and consistent, albeit restricted, role as one locus in his system of theology.[20]

It is against this background, then, that the covenantal teaching of the HC must be assessed. The dearth of explicit references to covenant in the text (and in the earlier SC) can probably be explained by the genre of the HC as an official lay catechism that sought to cover only the basics of the Christian faith and to reflect as much as possible what the Protestant factions of the Palatinate held in common. Because of the novelty of the doctrine and its potential for offense in a territory that was still officially Lutheran, it is understandable that Ursinus would choose to give it, or was compelled to give it, a relatively low profile.[21] Nevertheless, Ursinus's inclusion of covenant in the LC around the time that he was working on the HC and his ongoing employment of the idea over a lifetime of lecturing on the HC suggest that one may also look for covenantal content in the HC even if the political and theological realities of the day kept covenantal language to a minimum.

COVENANT IN THE HEIDELBERG CATECHISM

An important consideration in evaluating claims for covenantal content in the HC has been whether Ursinus treats parallel material covenantally in his other works. Judged by this standard, many of the claims by past scholars are indeed legitimate. Heppe's assertion, for example, that the covenant idea can be found already in the HC's opening question and answer on the believer's belonging to Christ[22] is supported by the wording of LC 1. Both catechisms begin with similar questions: "What is your only comfort in life and in death?" (HC 1), and "What firm comfort do you have in life and in death?" (LC 1). In the answers, however, the LC's parallel to the HC's "That I am not my own, but belong . . . to my faithful Savior, Jesus Christ," is framed in explicit covenantal language: my firm comfort is "that . . . God received me into his covenant of grace." The HC's further response that "Christ, by his Holy Spirit, assures me of eternal life and makes me wholeheartedly willing and ready to live for him" also has a covenantal parallel in LC 1: "Christ sealed his covenant in my heart by his Spirit, who renews me in the image of God."

The same is true of the HC's treatment of the doctrine of the mediator, which, according to earlier scholarship, Ursinus discussed in covenantal language in both the LC and his commentary on the HC. HC 12–18 on the mediator never mentions the word *covenant*, but the LC's three main questions and answers on the mediator use it every time: the function of the mediator is "to restore the covenant between God and humanity" (LC 72); "this covenant" could not have been ratified without a mediator (LC 73); and "Why did this mediator of the covenant have to be truly human?" (LC 74; cf. the question in HC 16, "Why must the mediator be a true and righteous human?"). Furthermore, as Coenen pointed out, the commentary on the HC inserts the locus on covenant immediately after the locus on the mediator.[23] Ursinus's reasoning there is that because a mediator reconciles two parties at variance, and because in Scripture the reconciliation between God and humanity through Christ is called a covenant, "the doctrine of the Covenant which God made with man is closely connected with the doctrine of the Mediator."[24]

Finally, as Goeters noted, the HC places its questions on the mediator in the context of the relationship between law and gospel (HC 3–19), a topic that Ursinus discusses covenantally in LC 30–36.[25] His treatment of law and gospel is less explicitly covenantal in the commentary, although the locus on gospel in which he deals with its relation to law does immediately follow the locus on covenant. In his words, the gospel is, "with great propriety, made to follow the doctrine of the Mediator and the covenant . . . because the gospel is a part of the covenant; and is often taken for the new covenant."[26]

Heppe and others were right to conclude, therefore, that the theology of the HC can, in some respects, be characterized as covenantal. Nevertheless, there is at least one major dimension of covenantal teaching in the HC that earlier scholarship has not identified. For that we need to take another look at HC 74, which contains two of the catechism's five references to covenant:

> Q. **Should infants also be baptized?**
> A. Yes. Infants as well as adults are included in God's *covenant* and people, and they, no less than adults, are promised deliverance from sin through Christ's blood and the Holy Spirit who produces faith. Therefore, by baptism, the

> sign of the *covenant*, they too should be incorporated into the Christian church and distinguished from the children of unbelievers. This was done in the Old Testament by circumcision, which was replaced in the New Testament by baptism (italics added).

As with other parts of the HC, some of the phrasing here may have its origins in Melanchthon's "Examination of Ordinands," whose question on infant baptism is almost identical to HC 74's: "Should small children also be baptized?"[27] Melanchthon's response is that they should indeed be baptized because "the promise of grace, the Holy Spirit, and salvation belongs also to small children . . . who are incorporated into the church."[28] Twice in this answer he quotes Matthew 19:14 ("for it is to such as these that the kingdom of heaven belongs"), which HC 74 also cites as a source text, and at the end he defines "kingdom of heaven" as "forgiveness of sins, righteousness, the Holy Spirit, and the inheritance of eternal salvation."[29]

Ursinus appears to take this answer by Melanchthon and weave into it explicit Reformed covenantal language, thus making HC 74 a kind of lens through which other parts of the HC can be viewed as implicitly covenantal. For example, the assertion that infants belong to "God's covenant and people [*gemein*]" in HC 74 adds a covenantal overtone to the theme of belonging to Christ introduced in HC 1[30] and to the doctrine of the church in HC 54. As we saw in chapter 5, since the HC was designed primarily for the instruction of youth, HC 54 could be read as a testimony on the lips of a baptized covenant child: "Of this community [*gemein*] I am and always will be a living member" (54).[31] Furthermore, the reference at the end of HC 74 to the replacement of circumcision by baptism as a sign of the covenant alludes to the essential unity of the Old and New Testaments and identifies an explicit covenantal thread to the history of redemption outlined earlier in HC 19.[32] This perspective is reinforced by the fact that HC 66 on sacraments and HC 70 on baptism cite, respectively, Genesis 17:11 ("[Circumcision] shall be a sign of the covenant between me and you") and Hebrews 12:24 ("Jesus, the mediator of a new covenant") as source texts.[33]

Perhaps the most significant covenantal dimension of HC 74, however, is that forgiveness of sins and the Holy Spirit are promised to baptized children by virtue of their being part of the covenant; the two benefits identified here are benefits of the covenant. Baptism itself is called "the sign of the covenant," but it is a sign not just of covenantal membership but of the double benefit of the covenant that this sacrament signifies and seals. In baptism we are reminded and assured that we are forgiven of our sins and renewed by the Holy Spirit (HC 69, 70)—in other words, that we are justified and sanctified.

Previous studies have failed to notice both the connection of this double benefit theme to Ursinus's doctrine of covenant and its prominence in the rest of the HC. In addition to the explicit link between the twofold promise and covenant in HC 74, there are several passages in the HC where such a connection is also implicit, that is, where only the twofold benefit is mentioned but the parallel in the LC places it in a covenantal context. It is quite likely that we see this already in HC 1, where the double blessing of Christ's paying for our sin (1st benefit) and delivering us from the tyranny of the devil (2nd benefit) finds its parallel in LC 1 as the covenantal benefits of "righteousness and eternal life." Even clearer is HC 17, which states that the mediator must be true God so as to obtain for us "righteousness and life." The parallel answer in LC 75 also maintains that the divine mediator adorns us with "righteousness and eternal life," but this answer does so in the context of the three previous questions and answers (72–74), which, as we have seen, establish a clear connection between the mediator and the covenant.[34]

The double benefit of the covenant is also evident in the HC's exposition of the Apostles' Creed, where the suffering of Christ is said to have gained for us "righteousness and eternal life" (HC 37). In the parallel LC 87 ("What benefit accrues to us from the suffering and death of Christ?"), these same blessings of "remission of sins, the gift of the Holy Spirit, righteousness, and eternal life"[35] define what it means to be received "into the covenant of divine grace." LC 286–88, too, make clear that the twofold cleansing signified and sealed in baptism, namely, remission of sins and renewal by the Holy Spirit (HC 69, 70), assures us "of the *covenant* established with God and of his spiritual washing that happens by the blood and Spirit of Christ" (LC 286).[36] Probably the clearest example of this linkage between the twofold blessing and covenant is in HC 59, where the benefit of believing the gospel summarized in the creed is described as being "righteous before God and heir to life everlasting." The parallel answer in LC 132 is striking: "That all the things that God promised believers in his *covenant* are valid for us, that is, that we are justified and heirs to eternal life."[37]

The HC also contains numerous references to the twofold benefit that have no covenantal counterparts in the LC. However, they too can probably be thought of as covenantal, considering the several connections that we have identified between the HC and parallel passages in the LC where covenant is explicitly mentioned. What follows is a partial list of such references:

HC 21: "eternal righteousness and salvation"[38]

HC 34: "set us free from sin and from the tyranny of the devil" (see also HC 1)

HC 40: "nothing else could pay for our sins except the death of the Son of God" (1st benefit)

HC 43: "By Christ's power our old selves are crucified"(2nd benefit)

HC 45: "righteousness . . . new life"

HC 49: "[the Holy Spirit] is our advocate in heaven" (1st benefit) "by the Spirit's power we seek . . . the things above" (2nd benefit)

HC 76: "forgiveness of sins and eternal life"

HC 80: "all our sins are completely forgiven" (1st benefit); "the Holy Spirit grafts us into Christ" (2nd benefit)

HC 81: "those who . . . trust that their sins are pardoned" (1st benefit); "and . . . desire more and more . . . to lead a better life" (2nd benefit)

HC 84: "God . . . truly forgives all their sins" (1st benefit)

HC 85: "when promising and demonstrating genuine reform" (2nd benefit)

HC 86: "Christ, having redeemed us by his blood" (1st benefit); "is also restoring us by his Spirit into his image" (2nd benefit)

HC 115: "look to Christ for forgiveness of sins and righteousness" (1st benefit); "striving . . . to be renewed more and more after God's image" (2nd benefit)

Even this list does not convey how pervasive the double benefit theme is in the HC. It does not include, for example, any of the HC's references to the twofold nature of sin as both guilt (HC 14) and corruption (HC 5, 7, 8), which anticipate the remedy of the twofold benefit of the covenant: justification and sanctification. Furthermore, a case could be made that the double benefit doctrine determines the structure of the entire second half of the catechism from HC 60 to 129. As we noted earlier, HC 59 declares that the advantage of believing all the promises explained in the Apostles' Creed is that "in Christ I am righteous before God and an heir to eternal life." HC 60–63 then immediately turn to a discussion of the first of these benefits, beginning with the question in HC 60, "How are you righteous before God?" HC 64 marks the transition to the treatment of the second benefit, looking back at justification in its question ("But doesn't this teaching make people indifferent and wicked?") and ahead to sanctification in its answer ("No. It is impossible for those grafted into Christ through true faith not to produce fruits of gratitude"). After a bridge section on the sacraments (HC 65–85), HC 86 leads off part 3 of the catechism by reiterating the transition introduced already in HC 64: Christ has redeemed us by his blood, the basis of our justification, and he is also restoring us by his Spirit into his image, the basis for our sanctification, so that in all our living we may show our gratitude to God for his benefits. This gratitude, the overarching theme of part 3, comes to expression in our doing good works according to the law (HC 91–115), especially that most important work of prayer (HC 116–129). Therefore, one way of viewing the catechism from HC 59 to the end is as an exposition of the two benefits of the covenant.

CONCLUSION

For a document that employs the word *covenant* in only two of its 129 questions and answers, the HC contains a remarkable amount of covenantal material—much more, certainly, than first meets the eye. The muting of the concept was likely due to the original purpose and audience of the HC and to the circumstances under which it was composed. An official doctrinal standard designed for the instruction of youth and uneducated adults was no place to unveil a relatively new Reformed doctrine, especially one that could pose a stumbling block in a Lutheran territory still bound to the AC. In this respect, the Lutheran context of the HC once again helped to shape one of the Reformed elements in the text.

Nevertheless, Ursinus, the primary author of the HC, did not hesitate to expound on covenant in some of the more specialized theological works that he wrote alongside of and after the HC.[39] The contexts in these works where the covenant idea is developed provide a basis for interpreting parallel passages in the HC as also covenantal, even if the term itself is not used. By applying this method of analysis, the few scholars who claim to have found a doctrine of covenant in the HC were correct, particularly with respect to the HC's treatment of the believer as Christ's possession, the mediatorship of Christ, the definition of the gospel, and the sacraments. But these scholars were even more right than they realized, for they overlooked the fact that in HC 74 Ursinus also takes a Melanchthonian defense of infant baptism and recasts it in covenantal language, identifying forgiveness of sin and the gift of the Holy Spirit as a twofold benefit of the covenant. It is the frequency of this theme and the structural role it plays in the second half of the catechism that more than anything establish the HC as another place in Ursinus's corpus where his doctrine of covenant comes to expression. Covenant may be mentioned in the HC only rarely, but it is a significant Reformed accent in the catechism nonetheless.

8

GOOD WORKS AND GRATITUDE

Q/A 86–129

86 Q. Since we have been delivered from our misery by grace through Christ without any merit of our own, why then should we do good works?

A. Because Christ, having redeemed us by his blood, is also restoring us by his Spirit into his image, so that with our whole lives we may show that we are thankful to God for his benefits, so that he may be praised through us, so that we may be assured of our faith by its fruits, and so that by our godly living our neighbors may be won over to Christ.

HC 86 is a pivotal structural marker in the HC because it points back to the first two parts of the catechism ("*delivered* from our *misery*") and points ahead to the third and final section on gratitude ("*thankful* to God for his benefits"). However, it is not obvious from this question and answer that gratitude will serve as the theme of part 3, since the focus of HC 86 is not so much on gratitude as on the role of good works in the Christian life more broadly. This subject was raised already in HC 62–64 in the context of the doctrine of justification through faith alone:

62 Q. Why can't our good works be our righteousness before God, or at least a part of our righteousness?

A. Because the righteousness which can pass God's judgment must be entirely perfect and must in every way measure up to the divine law. But even our best works in this life are imperfect and stained with sin.

63 Q. How can our good works be said to merit nothing when God rewards them in this life and the next?

A. This reward is not earned; it is a gift of grace.

64 Q. But doesn't this teaching make people indifferent and wicked?

A. No. It is impossible for those grafted into Christ through true faith not to produce fruits of gratitude.

HC 86, then, picks up where HC 64 left off. If good works do not contribute to our justification or merit anything in the sight of God, why must we still do them? In part, as HC 64 already suggested, because they are a natural outgrowth of the restorative work in us by the Spirit of God. But also, HC 86 goes on to say, so that we may do four things: (1) by our good works ("with our whole lives") show our thankfulness to God; (2) by our good works ("through us") offer praise to God; (3) by our good works ("by its fruits") be assured of our faith; and by our good works ("by our godly living") win our neighbors over to Christ. Gratitude is just one of the stated reasons why we should still do good works, and there is no indication, other than that it is listed first, that it alone will constitute the theme of the 43 questions and answers to follow. For the thematic role that it plays, one must look to the explanation of the catechism's structure in HC 2; to the anticipatory references to gratitude in HC 28 ("thankful when things go well"), 32 ("a living sacrifice of thanks"), 43 ("a sacrifice of gratitude"), and 64 ("fruits of gratitude"); to the heading above part 3; and to HC 116, which introduces the subsection on prayer ("prayer is the most important part of the thankfulness God requires of us"). Surprisingly, after the term *gratitude* appears in the heading, in HC 86, and in HC 116, it is never used again in part 3.

The connection between gratitude and the law in part 3 is also less explicit than we might expect, since in HC 86 gratitude is mentioned only in relation to good works, and the definition of good works as "those which . . . conform to God's *law*" does not surface until HC 91. The parallel lead questions and answers that we encounter in part 1 (HC 3: "How do you come to know your misery? The law of God tells me.") and part 2 (HC 19: "How do you come to know [your deliverance]? The holy gospel tells me.") have no further parallel in part 3, such as "How do you come to express your gratitude? The law of God (Ten Commandments) tells me." Even in HC 115, the closest the catechism gets to a description of the role of the commandments in the Christian life, there is no explicit reference to gratitude.

As muted as some of these connections might be, it is still often claimed that the theme of gratitude in part 3 and the emphasis there on the law as a norm for grateful living are among the most transparently Reformed, even Calvinistic, aspects of the catechism.[1] As we shall see, such claims cannot really be substantiated. Indeed, the evidence from both subsections of part 3, namely the expositions of the Ten Commandments and the Lord's Prayer, points once again either to a blending of elements from both the Reformed and Lutheran traditions or to common theological ground between them.

GOOD WORKS, GRATITUDE, AND THE LAW

We encounter such common ground and blending already at the very beginning of part 3 in HC 86 itself. The link in this question and answer between good works and gratitude can be found in a variety of Reformed texts prior to the HC, such as catechisms by Leo Jud and John à Lasco and Calvin's *Institutes*.[2] Furthermore, Jud's Shorter Catechism of 1541 includes in its list of seven purposes of good works all four of the reasons stated later in HC 86: praise to God, gratitude to God, winning our neighbors, and assurance of our faith.[3] This last reason, "so that we may be assured of our faith by its fruits," as HC 86 puts it, is particularly worth noting, because implied there is a distinctive feature of Reformed theology and piety—a sixteenth-century version of Aristotle's practical syllogism:[4]

> Major premise: All good works come from true faith.
> Minor premise: I do good works.
> Conclusion: Therefore, I can be assured that I have true faith.

Nevertheless, as we have demonstrated elsewhere, the connection between gratitude and good works is a pervasive theme in early Reformation theology, in Lutheran as well as Reformed sources. Even before its appearance in Reformed texts in the 1540s and 1550s, we find it in Melanchthon's 1521 *Loci*, Luther's Small Catechism (1529), the AC (1530), the Apology of the Augsburg Confession (1531), Melanchthon's Scholia of 1534, Rhegius's handbook on Christian doctrine (1536), and the Lutheran "Summa" from Regensburg (1547).[5] In fact, as we saw in chapter 2, a good portion of the language of HC 86 appears to have been taken from a 1535 catechism by the Lutheran theologian Johannes Brenz:

> **Q. Why ought we to do good works?**
> A. Not because we pay for sin and earn eternal life with our deeds—for Christ alone has paid for sin and earned eternal life—but rather because we ought to bear witness to our faith with good works and be thankful to our Lord God for his good deeds.[6]

What some have identified as a uniquely Reformed emphasis on gratitude, therefore, is present also in a variety of earlier Lutheran sources, and HC 86 seems to have drawn its wording from catechisms in both the Reformed (Jud) and Lutheran (Brenz) traditions.

HC 88–91, which lead up to the exposition of the Ten Commandments (HC 92–113), also display a blend of Reformed and Lutheran textual influences. These four questions provide definitions of repentance or conversion, of each of its two parts, and of good works as a foundation for the HC's explanation of the law, which reveals the will of God to us and to which good works conform:

> **88 Q. What is involved in genuine repentance or conversion?**
> A. Two things: the dying-away of the old self, and the rising-to-life of the new.
>
> **89 Q. What is the dying-away of the old self?**
> A. To be genuinely sorry for sin and more and more to hate and run away from it.
>
> **90 Q. What is the rising-to-life of the new self?**
> A. Wholehearted joy in God through Christ and a love and delight to live according to the will of God by doing every kind of good work.
>
> **91 Q. What are good works?**
> A. Only those which are done out of true faith, conform to God's law, and are done for God's glory; and not those based on our own opinion or human tradition.

Parts of the first three of these questions and answers echo the following phrases in Calvin's definition of repentance in the GC:[7] "denial of self and mortification of the flesh" (cf. HC A88, Q89); "dissatisfaction and hatred of sin" (cf. HC A89); "love of righteousness" (cf. HC A90); and "obedience to the divine will" (cf. HC A90).[8] And the three elements that define good works in HC 91 ("out of true faith," "conform to God's law," "for God's glory") may have been patterned after similar criteria in Jud's Shorter Catechism[9] ("out of faith," "what is commanded us," "for God's glory"[10]) and/or Bullinger's *Hausbuch*[11] ("through faith," "according to the Word of God," "for God's glory"[12]). At the same time, HC 88–91 appears also to evoke the language of Melanchthon's *EO* (1552), which, like the HC, employs the terms *repentance* (*Buß*) and *conversion* (*Bekehrung*) synonymously (cf. HC Q 88), divides conversion into parts (cf. HC A88), describes the first part as "sorrow for sin" (cf. HC A89), and characterizes the second and third parts as including a "heartfelt joy" and an incipient obedience, respectively (cf. HC A 90 for both).[13]

The clearest indication of the HC's indebtedness to the Reformed tradition in part 3 is at the beginning of the exposition of the Decalogue, where the authors frame the biblical text of the Ten Commandments with a Reformed rather than Lutheran division and numbering

(HC 92). Whereas the Catholic and Lutheran traditions had combined "You shall have no other gods before me" and "You shall not make for yourself an idol" into the first commandment, the HC divides them into the first two. And whereas the Catholics and Lutherans had divided "You shall not covet your neighbor's house" and "You shall not covet your neighbor's wife . . ." into the ninth and tenth commandments, the HC holds them together as the tenth. Hence, for the HC, the first table of the law has only four commandments, and the second table has six (HC 93).

As the HC moves into the exposition of the individual commandments, the influence of Lasco's (Larger) Emden Catechism and especially Calvin's GC[14] can certainly be detected. As Rauhaus has noted, for example, a key phrase in Ursinus's SC 84 on the second commandment, "that we desire to worship God not by our own will but only by the prescription of God's Word, in spirit and in truth," which came over into HC 96 as "nor worship him in any other way than has been commanded in God's Word," appears to have its roots in the (Large) Emden Catechism ("and worship God alone according to his Word in spirit and in truth").[15] However, HC 97's broad application of the prohibition of images, which is typical of Reformed, not Lutheran, liturgical sensibilities at the time, echoes the language of Calvin's GC:

HC 97 Q. May we then not make any image at all?
A. God can not and may not be visibly portrayed in any way. Although creatures may be portrayed, yet God forbids making or having such images if one's intention is to worship them or to serve God through them.

GC 148 Q. We are not then to understand that these words simply condemn every picture and sculpture whatever. Rather we are forbidden to make images for the purpose of seeking or worshipping God in them . . .
A. Quite right.

A number of the HC's explanations of subsequent commandments also appear dependent on the GC (although sometimes by way of Ursinus's LC or SC):

3rd Commandment

HC 99: That we neither blaspheme nor misuse the name of God by cursing, perjury, or unnecessary oaths.

GC 160: He forbids us to abuse the name of God, either by perjury or by swearing unnecessarily.

HC 99: We should use the holy name of God only with reverence and awe, so that we may . . . glorify God in all our words and works.

GC 162: Never to bring forward the name of God except with fear and reverence and for the purpose of making his glory apparent.

4th Commandment

HC 103: That . . . I diligently attend the assembly of God's people to learn what God's Word teaches, to participate in the sacraments, to pray to God publicly, and to bring Christian offerings for the poor.

GC 183: To attend the sacred assemblies for the hearing of the Word of God, the celebration of the mysteries, and the regular prayers as they will be ordained.

HC 103: That every day of my life I rest from my evil ways, let the Lord work in me through his Spirit . . . [16]

GC 173: We renounce our own inclination, that we may be guided by the Spirit of God.

5th Commandment

HC 104: To my father and mother and all those in authority over me.

GC 194: Though the words refer to father and mother only, we must understand all who are over us.

6th Commandment

HC 106: By forbidding murder God teaches us that he hates the root of murder: envy, hatred, anger, vindictiveness. In God's sight all such are disguised forms of murder.[17]

GC 198: You appear to insinuate some kind of secret murder, from which God here prohibits us. That is so. For anger and hatred, and any kind of injurious desire, by which our neighbor may be harmed, is counted murder in the sight of God.

7th Commandment

HC 109: We are temples of the Holy Spirit, body and soul, and God wants both to be kept clean and holy. That is why God forbids all unchaste actions, looks, talk, thoughts, or desires, and whatever may incite someone to them.

GC 203: Since both our bodies and our souls are temples of the Holy Spirit . . . , we are to maintain a chaste purity in both, and accordingly, be chaste not only in abstaining from external licentiousness, but also in heart and speech, bodily gesture and action.[18]

8th Commandment

HC 110: In God's sight theft also includes all scheming and swindling in order to get our neighbor's goods for ourselves, whether by force or means that appear legitimate . . . or any other means forbidden by God.

GC 205: Under the name of theft, it includes all kinds of evil deeds, of defrauding and swindling, by which we hunt after other men's goods. We are therefore forbidden here either to raid the goods of our neighbors by violence, or by wiles and cunning to lay hands upon them, or by any other devious means to try to possess them.

Nevertheless, there are also textual parallels between the HC's exposition of the commandments and Luther's Small Catechism.[19] The phrase "love [*lieben*], fear [*förchten*], and honor God with all my heart" (HC 94; first commandment) echoes the Small Catechism's "fear [*fürchten*], love [*lieben*], and trust God above all things."[20] "Pray [*angeruffen*] to God, and glorify God" (HC 99; third commandment) parallels the Small Catechism's "call on [*anrufen*], pray, and give thanks to God."[21] HC 104's "honor [*ehre*], love [*liebe*], and be loyal to my father and mother and all those in authority over me" (fifth commandment) corresponds to the Small Catechism's "parents and others in authority, but instead honor [*in Ehre halten*], . . . love [*lieb . . . haben*], and respect them."[22] The sixth commandment calls us to "protect our neighbors from harm [*schaden*]" (HC 107) or not to "harm [*Schaden . . . thun*] the lives of our neighbors" (Small Catechism[23]). HC 108's "live decent and chaste lives" (seventh commandment) and Luther's "lead pure and decent lives" are identical in their original German texts (*keusch vnd züchtig leben*).[24] And the general outlines of the interpretation of the eighth and ninth commandments are also quite similar.[25]

Some of these linguistic parallels overlap, of course, with those we already found between the HC and Calvin's GC, but this could reflect the influence of Luther's catechism on both documents, either independently or on the HC by way of the GC. In any case, these parallels also point to a common hermeneutical approach by the three catechisms to the Ten Commandments as a whole. Luther's Small Catechism, the GC, and the HC all take the eight negatively formulated commandments in the Decalogue (first, second, and the fifth through tenth for Lutherans; first through third and sixth through tenth for the Reformed) and at some point turn the prohibitions into positive commands or guidelines. The intent of the first commandment, for example, is not only that we should have no other gods before God, but also that we are "to fear, love, and trust God above all things" (Luther's Small Catechism),[26] "to adore him, to place our trust in him, to call upon him" (GC 141),[27] and to "love, fear, and honor God with all my heart" (HC 94). This represents not just a linguistic similarity among the three catechisms but also a common way of interpreting the commandments beyond their literal meaning.[28]

Finally, the two transitional questions between the exposition of the Ten Commandments and the subsection on prayer also bring together linguistic and thematic elements from both Lutheran and Reformed traditions—more specifically, from Melanchthon and Calvin. The reference in HC 114 to "only a small beginning of this obedience" (*nur einen geringen anfang dieses gehorsams*) in the lives of the converted sounds very much like Melanchthon's contention in the *EO* (1552) that our works after regeneration represent only "an obedience that has begun."[29] Like Melanchthon, HC 115 raises the question of why the commandments then should be preached so "pointedly" (Melanchthon: "diligently"[30]), and both respond with what has often been called the "third use of the law." Melanchthon's twofold answer, "so that one . . . may know what sin is and . . . what works are pleasing to God,"[31] calls to mind the two aspects of the third use of the law that he had introduced already in his 1543 *Loci*: a pedagogical dimension by which ongoing sin in the believer's life is revealed, and a didactic dimension by which the believer is instructed in works of obedience.[32] The first of these dimensions, which is not found later in Calvin's treatment of the third use of the law, is reflected in HC 115's first reason for preaching the commandments: "so that the longer we live the more we may come to know our sinfulness and the more eagerly look to Christ." However, HC 115's second reason for preaching the commandments so pointedly ("so that we may never stop striving . . . to be renewed more and more after God's image") echoes Calvin's but not Melanchthon's view of the third use of the law.[33] What we have in HC 115, therefore, is yet another synthesis, this time a remarkable combination of "a Lutheran emphasis on the exposure of residual sin in the life of the believer with a Calvinistic emphasis on the exhortation to good works."[34]

GOOD WORKS, GRATITUDE, AND PRAYER

At first glance, the HC's lead question in the subsection on prayer may seem like a parallel to its earlier lead question in the subsection on the law: "Why then should we do good works? . . . So that . . . we may show that we are thankful to God for his benefits" (HC 86). "Why do Christians need to pray? Because prayer is the most important part of the thankfulness that God requires of us" (HC 116). In other words, there are two basic ways to show our thanks to God: do good works (that is, keep the law) and pray.

However, another way of interpreting the subsections on law and prayer is to understand HC 86 as the introductory question not simply to the exposition of the Ten Commandments but to the whole of part 3, including the exposition of the Lord's Prayer. In this view, prayer is not a second and separate way of showing thanks, alongside good works according to the law; it is itself a good work that we perform in gratitude as part of our fulfillment of the law. HC 86 states that we should do good works, in part, "so that with our whole lives we may show that we are thankful to God." Since good works are "those which conform to God's law" (HC 91), our whole lives are to be shaped according to the contours of the Ten Commandments. That includes, in obedience to the first commandment, that we "avoid and shun all . . . *prayer* to saints or to other creatures" (HC 94); that, in obedience to the third commandment, "we should use the holy name of God only with reverence and awe, so that we may properly . . . *pray* to God" (HC 99); and that, in obedience to the fourth commandment, we "diligently attend the assembly of God's people . . . to *pray* to God publicly" (HC 103, italics added). Furthermore, God wants the commandments preached so pointedly "so that we may . . . never stop *praying* to God for the grace of the Holy Spirit" (HC 115, italics added), by whom Christ is restoring us into his image so that we may keep those commandments in the first place (HC 86). To claim, therefore, that prayer is "the most important part of the thankfulness that God requires of us" (HC 116) is another way of saying that prayer is the greatest of the good works of gratitude that God expects of us. Gratitude through good works is given its highest expression in prayer, partly because, according to the HC, petitionary prayer should be focused on the Holy Spirit (HC 115, 116), whose work in us is fundamental to the performance of any deed of thankfulness.

This close connection between prayer and law in part 3 is further borne out by a remarkable overlap in the language the HC uses in its expositions of the Ten Commandments and Lord's Prayer.[35] The first commandment, for example, calls us to "rightly know [*recht erkennen*] the only true God" (HC 94) and the first petition then calls out to God, "Help us to truly know [*recht erkennen*] you" (HC 122). Also required in the first commandment is that we "trust [God] alone" (HC 94), something for which we then pray in the fourth petition: "And so help us to give up our trust in creatures and trust in you alone" (HC 125). Another implication of the first petition, "Help us to direct all our living—what we think, say, and do—so that your name will . . . always [be] honored and praised" (HC 122), undergirds our obedience to the third commandment: "We should use the holy name of God . . . so that we may properly . . . glorify God in all our words and works" (HC 99). And the sixth petition, "And so, Lord, uphold us and make us strong with the strength of your Holy Spirit, so that we may not go down to defeat in this spiritual struggle" (HC 127) supports the requirement of the fourth commandment "that every day of my life I rest from my evil ways [and] let the Lord work in me through his Spirit" (HC 103). Many more examples of this phenomenon could be cited,[36] but the pattern should be clear: in the HC, prayer to the Holy Spirit for grace to keep the law is not generic but specific to the contents of each commandment. The Ten Commandments teach us how we are to live; the Lord's Prayer teaches us to ask God for help in living that way. Doing the will of God and praying for grace to do the will of God are both works of gratitude, although the latter is "the most important part of the thankfulness that God requires of us" because it is foundational to all the rest.

This second way of reading the "Gratitude" section of the HC finds support in both Reformed and Lutheran sources that underlie the catechism. Beza, for example, in his treatment of good works in his larger confession of faith, speaks of prayer as the "first" or "chief" (*principatum*) among the fruits that faith produces in Christians, whether they be prayers of petition, praise, or thanks to God for the benefits that we have received. [37] This may well have inspired Ursinus's reference to prayer as "the most important part" of the gratitude that we express in good works.[38] Luther, too, connects prayer to the good works of the law.[39] In his introduction to the Lord's Prayer in the Large Catechism, he asserts that prayer is essential to our keeping of the commandments: "Nothing is so necessary as to call upon God incessantly and to drum into his ears our prayer that he may give, preserve, and increase in us faith and the fulfillment of the Ten Commandments."[40] Moreover, it is our duty to pray because God requires it in the second commandment as part of our not taking his name in vain.[41] This link is also found earlier in the Large Catechism's exposition of the second (Reformed: third) commandment: "All of this is what it means to call upon God's name. . . . In this way his name is hallowed, as we pray in the Lord's Prayer."[42] Later in the work, Luther takes the same tack in his explanation of the first petition of the Lord's Prayer: "So you see that in this petition we pray for exactly the same thing that God demands in the Second Commandment."[43]

The influence of earlier Lutheran and Reformed catechisms is also discernable in some of the other language and content of the HC's subsection on prayer. It may strike the reader as strange, for example, that HC 116 speaks of thankfulness as something that God "requires" (*erfordert*) of us, which is reminiscent of the language in HC 94: "What does the Lord require [*erfordert*] in the first commandment?"[44] However, in his *EO* (1552) Melanchthon makes a similar link between thankfulness and obligation: we should realize that God "requires" (*fordert*) thankfulness of us because "thankfulness comprises two great virtues, truth and justice. Truth professes where a benefit comes from; justice, on the other hand, obligates you to serve the benefactor."[45] HC 117 goes on to describe the kind of prayer that pleases God as that which is "from the heart" (*von hertzen*), is directed "to no other than the one true God, revealed to us in his Word," and rests on the foundation that "God will surely listen to our prayer because of Christ our Lord" (*er vnser Gebet . . . vmb des HERRN Christi willen gewiszlich wölle erhören*). All this may echo Melanchthon's characterization of true prayer in the *EO* (1552) as also "from the heart" (*hertzlich*), "to God alone," to God "as he has revealed himself," and with an assurance that God "will surely listen to them . . . because of Christ our Lord" (*wil sie gewislich erhören . . . umb des Herrn Christi willen*").[46] According to HC 118, we should pray for "everything we need, spiritually and physically" (*Alle geistliche vnd leibliche notturft*), a phrase that is found verbatim in Melanchthon's own definition of prayer (*geistlicher und lieblicher notdurfft*).[47] Finally, HC 122's list of the attributes that shine forth from God's works and elicit our prayers of praise is very similar to Melanchthon's own list in his call in the *EO* (1552) to consider the nature of the God to whom we pray:

> HC 122: your almighty power [*allmechtigkeyt*], wisdom [*weiszheyt*], kindness [*güte*], justice [*gerechtigkeyt*], mercy [*barmhertzigkeyt*], and truth [*warheyt*]

> *EO* (1552): almighty [*allmechtig*] . . . full of wisdom [*weisheit*], kindness [*gütikeit*], justice [*gerechtikeit*], mercy [*barmherzikeit*], truly pure [*wahrafft rein*][48]

There are also a number of parallels between Luther's Small Catechism and the text of the HC's exposition of the individual petitions:

	Small Catechism	Heidelberg Catechism
"Our Father"	"We may ask him boldly and with complete confidence, just as loving children ask their loving father."	"And that just as our parents do not refuse us the things of this life, even less will God our Father refuse to give us what we ask in faith." (A 120)
First Petition	"We ask in this prayer that . . . we . . . also live holy lives according to [the Word of God]."	"Help us to direct all our living . . . so that your name will . . . be . . . always honored and praised." (A 122)
Second Petition	"Whenever our heavenly Father gives us his Holy Spirit, so that through his grace we believe his Holy Word and live godly lives . . ."	"Rule us by your Word and Spirit in such a way that more and more we submit to you." (A 123)
Fourth Petition	"Everything included in the necessities and nourishment for our bodies . . ."	"Do take care of all our physical needs . . ." (A 125)
Sixth Petition	"Preserve and keep us, so that the devil, the world, and our flesh may not deceive us . . . and that, although we may be attacked by them, we may finally prevail and gain the victory."	"And our sworn enemies—the devil, the world, and our own flesh—never stop attacking us. And so, Lord, uphold us and make us strong . . . so that we may not go down to defeat . . . but firmly resist our enemies until we finally win the complete victory." (A 127)
"Amen"	"That I should be certain that such petitions are . . . heard by our Father in heaven, for he himself . . . has promised to hear us."	"It is . . . sure that God listens to my prayer . . ." (A 129)

There are even stronger correspondences, however, between the HC's exposition of the Lord's Prayer and the earlier Reformed catechetical tradition. For one thing, whereas Luther's catechisms divided the prayer into seven petitions, the HC follows the GC's division into only six, though not the GC's further organization into subgroups of three each.[49] Furthermore, composing each answer in HC 122–28 as a short prayer itself had precedents in the Lasco catechisms of northern Germany.[50] What is most striking, however, is the similarity in content and sometimes even language between the GC and HC in much of the commentary on the Lord's Prayer:

	Genevan Catechism	Heidelberg Catechism
"Our Father"	"If we who are evil are unable to deny good things to our children . . . , how much more beneficence is to be expected from the heavenly father . . ." (A 261)	"And that just as our parents do not refuse us the things of this life, even less will God our Father refuse to give us what we ask in faith." (A 120)
"in heaven"	"By this means we are taught to raise our minds upwards . . . lest we should think carnally or materially of . . . his glorious majesty." (A 265)	"These words teach us not to think of God's heavenly majesty as something earthly . . ." (A 121)
First Petition	"We rightly pray that . . . whatever God does, all his works may appear glorious as they indeed are, and thus he himself be glorified." (A 267)	"Help us to . . . honor, glorify, and praise you for all your works and for all that shines forth from them." (A 122)
Second Petition	"That he would govern the elect by his Spirit . . ." (A 268)	"Rule us by your Word and Spirit." (A 123)
Second Petition	"That he would prostrate and destroy the reprobate who decline to submit themselves to his obedience . . ." (A 268)	"Destroy every force which revolts against you." (A 123)
Second Petition	"That the Lord may daily increase the number of the faithful . . ." (A 269)	"Preserve your church and make it grow." (A 123)
Second Petition	"We pray that he assiduously increase and advance [the kingdom], until it reach the summit of its power . . . when God . . . will be all in all." (A 270)	"Do this until your kingdom fully comes, when you will be all in all." (A 123)

Third Petition	"We pray. . . that . . . he may subject the wills of all to his own will and direct them to his obedience." (A 272)	"Help us and all people to reject our own wills and to obey your will without any back talk." (A 124)
Third Petition	"As the holy angels . . . have this one intention, that they obey him in all things . . . and are prepared voluntarily to do him service." (A 274)	"Help us . . . to carry out the work we are called to, as willingly and faithfully as the angels in heaven." (A 124)
Fourth Petition	"Whatever contributes to the preservation of the present life . . . by which the needs of external life are met . . ." (A 275)	"Do take care of all our physical needs." (A 125)
Fourth Petition	"Although we are to work and even sweat to provide food, nevertheless we are not nourished by our labour or industry or diligence, but by God's blessing only." (A 276)	"So that we come to know that you are the only source of everything good, and that neither our work and worry nor your gifts can do us any good without your blessing." (A 125)
Sixth Petition	"That he would rather supply us with his strength to resist . . . When governed by his Spirit we are imbued with such love of righteousness . . . that we overcome sin, the flesh, and the devil." (A 289–90)	"And our sworn enemies—the devil, the world, and our own flesh—never stop attacking us. And so, Lord, uphold and make us strong with the strength of your Holy Spirit, so that we may . . . firmly resist our enemies." (A 127)
Sixth Petition	"Indeed it would be all over with us every moment, unless God equipped us for the battle with his armour, and strengthened us by his hand." (A 291)	"By ourselves we are too weak to hold our own even for a moment." (A 127)

As we saw with the exposition of the Ten Commandments, some of the commonalities here between Luther's Small Catechism, the GC, and the HC might be explained by the influence of Luther's catechism on both of the later documents, either independently or on the HC by way of the

GC. And the HC's commentary on the Lord's Prayer may at times reflect even broader patterns of interpretation that by this time had developed across the Protestant world. But there are also distinctive strands of text here from Melanchthon's *EO*, Luther's Small Catechism, and Calvin's GC which the HC almost certainly employed. As in the previous subsection on gratitude and the law, these are woven into this subsection on prayer in a way that reflects both the Lutheran and Reformed catechetical traditions without being partial to either. In these last fourteen questions, therefore, the catechism ends in much the same way as it began back in HC 1: with a synthesis of thematic and textual material that helped to create a doctrinal platform on which all theological parties in the Palatinate could comfortably stand.

9

ECUMENICAL REFLECTIONS ON THE HEIDELBERG CATECHISM

In the foregoing chapters, we found throughout the text of the HC a synthesis of Lutheran and Reformed sources and themes that followed the pattern of the Palatinate reformation as a whole and the religious development of two of its most important leaders, Frederick III and Zacharias Ursinus. To round out this interpretation of the HC, however, we should reflect on how ecumenical this theological synthesis really was and whether it has any significance for Christian churches and individuals involved in ecumenical efforts today. In this last chapter, therefore, we will briefly examine first the limitations of the HC's ecumenism, then the ecumenical spirit it exhibits despite those limitations, and finally its ecumenical potential for our own day and age.

THE HEIDELBERG CATECHISM'S ECUMENICAL LIMITATIONS

However irenic, sweet-spirited, and consensus-minded the HC might be, one must acknowledge that it does have its limits. This is borne out, in the first place, by the various polemical statements in the text.[1] The most frequent target of these polemics is the Roman Catholic Church, which is explicitly named only in HC 80:

> Q. **How does the Lord's Supper differ from the Roman Catholic [literally: papal or papist] Mass?**
>
> A. The Lord's Supper declares to us that all our sins are completely forgiven through the one sacrifice of Jesus Christ, which he himself accomplished on the cross once for all. It also declares to us that the Holy Spirit grafts us into Christ, who with his true body is now in heaven at the right hand of the Father where he wants us to worship him.
>
> But the Mass teaches that the living and the dead do not have their sins forgiven through the suffering of Christ unless Christ is still offered for them daily by the priests. It also teaches that Christ is bodily present under the form of bread and wine where Christ is therefore to be worshiped. Thus the Mass is basically nothing but a denial of the one sacrifice and suffering of Jesus Christ and a condemnable idolatry.

There is no doubt, however, that the HC also has Roman Catholicism in view when it rejects all reliance on self or saints (HC 29–30, 94, 102), any contribution of good works to justification (HC 62–64), baptismal regeneration (HC 72), transubstantiation (HC 78), good works based on human tradition (HC 91), and the worship of images (HC 97–98). Furthermore, many of the HC's positive statements of Protestant doctrine function as implicit anti-Catholic barbs: Christ has *fully* paid for sin with his blood (HC 1); we are totally unable to do any good apart from the regenerating work of the Holy Spirit (HC 8); neither we ourselves nor any other creature can make satisfaction for sin (HC 13–14); Jesus Christ completely delivers us and makes us right with God (HC 18); Christ has delivered us by the *one* sacrifice of his body (HC 31[2]); it is not with gold and silver but with Christ's blood that we are redeemed (HC 34); only Christ's death can pay for sins (HC 40); at death our souls go *immediately* to Christ (HC 57); it is through faith alone that we are righteous (HC 60–61); Christ instituted only two sacraments (HC 68); and the keys of the kingdom are preaching and church discipline (HC 83–85).

In addition, as we saw earlier, the HC's doctrine of Christ's ascension (HC 46–49), and perhaps its treatment of the two natures of Christ the Mediator (HC 15–18), were directed at the ubiquitarian view of Christ's human nature held by some Gnesio-Lutherans and codified in the Stuttgart Confession of 1559. These ubiquitarian Lutherans may also have been the object, along with the Catholics, of the invective in HC 78 and 80 against any bodily presence of Christ at the Lord's table.[3] Finally, the catechism repudiates Anabaptist teachings on baptism (HC 74), the swearing of oaths (HC 101), and civil government (HC 101, 104, 105), and probably the anti-trinitarianism of the day as well (HC 24–25), even though, once again, no names are mentioned and the polemical tone here is not as sharp as it is against the Catholics.[4]

A second reason why we should probably not think of the HC as ecumenical in the modern sense of the term has to do with the motivation behind its ecumenism. Even when the catechism is at its most ecumenical in constructing doctrinal bridges among the Protestant factions in the Palatinate, the motives for such bridge-building may have been as much political as religious. The catechism was composed in an age of what historians of early modern Europe are now calling "confessionalization," that is, a process by which Protestant and Catholic rulers solidified their power by using the state churches and religious confessions of their territories as instruments of social and political control.[5] In such a context it is difficult to sort out religious and political motives for seeking doctrinal unity, even for someone as pious as Frederick III, because religion and politics were so closely intertwined and religious unity usually had a political payoff. The composition of the HC could be interpreted, therefore, as an important phase in the confessionalization of the Palatinate, one facet of a strategy by Frederick III to enhance his political strength by overcoming the theological divisions in his territory.[6]

That the HC was intended to play such a political role might be hinted at in its own explanation of the commandment to honor our fathers and mothers:

> **104 Q. What is God's will for you in the fifth commandment?**
>
> A. That I honor, love, and be loyal to my father and mother and all those in authority over me; that I submit myself with proper obedience to all their good teaching and discipline; and also that I be patient with their failings—for through them God chooses to rule us.

According to this answer, honor, love, and loyalty are owed not only by children to their parents but also by subjects to their magistrates, one of the primary authorities through whom God chooses to rule us (Romans 13:1 is cited as one of HC 104's source texts). As with all those in authority over us, our posture toward civil rulers should be one of submission and obedience, including submission and obedience to the teaching and moral discipline that they provide their citizens. The catechism speaks only in generalities in this answer, but close to the surface is the implication that God's will in the fifth commandment for a citizen of the Palatinate is that he or she be loyal to Frederick III and obediently submit to the doctrinal and moral standards he has established, including and especially those in the HC.

The foundation and goal of such obedience is made clear by Frederick himself in his preface to the HC. There he remarks that it is the duty of a civil ruler not only to promote "quiet and peaceable living" among his subjects, but also "constantly to admonish and lead them to devout knowledge and fear of the Almighty and His holy word of salvation, as the only *foundation of all virtue and obedience*." His predecessors had instituted various measures "for the furtherance of the glory of God *and the upholding of civil discipline and order*," but they had been largely unsuccessful. Since, therefore, "*government and family discipline* cannot otherwise be maintained—and in order that *discipline and obedience to authority* and all other virtues may increase and be multiplied among subjects," it is imperative that both youth and lay adults be instructed in the true knowledge of God, which is "the pure and consistent doctrine of the holy gospel." This will require "a fixed form and model" of instruction, namely the catechism that has just been prepared. Only then will it "please Almighty God also to grant reformation of public and private morals, and temporal and eternal welfare."[7] Clearly, for Frederick the stability of the social and political order rested in large part on the religious foundation of a common interpretation of Scripture.

A final reason why we should not be too quick to label the HC as "ecumenical" is what one scholar has called "the paradoxical relationship between the intention and effect of the HC" as a consensus builder.[8] However much the catechism was intended to bridge the gap between the Reformed and Lutheran traditions, the fact remains that outside of the Palatinate, at least, it had quite the opposite effect. As we have seen, there are a number of elements of the HC that are rooted in Lutheran texts: the theme and structure of the catechism; the wedding of law and gospel to parts 1 and 2; the subthemes in the trinitarian division of part 2; and the definitions of such major topics as faith, providence, and sacraments. Moreover, there is substantial agreement between the HC and Melanchthon's AC on the doctrines of sin, reconciliation, justification, preaching, the relationship between Word and Spirit, and much, if not all, of the doctrine of the Lord's Supper.[9] Nevertheless, within four months of the HC's publication in January 1563, three neighboring Gnesio-Lutheran princes denounced it in the sharpest terms, particularly its doctrine of the Lord's Supper:

> We know by the grace of God that Zwinglianism and Calvinism in the article on the Lord's Supper are a seductive and a damned error, directly contradicting the holy divine Scriptures, the true Apostolic Church, the Christian sense of the Augsburg Confession, and the generally accepted and defended Peace of Augsburg.[10]

Why such a discrepancy between intent and response? After all, the HC stood in a line of confessions from this region of southern Germany, going back to the Tetrapolitan Confession of 1530 and the Wittenberg Concord of 1536, which sought common ground between Lutheran and Reformed expressions of Protestantism. The catechism could even be regarded as the fulfillment of what Bucer and the upper-German disciples of Zwingli had once strived so hard to achieve.[11] By the time the HC came into being in the 1560s, however, both Luther and Melanchthon had passed from the scene, and their followers were engaged in a bitter struggle for recognition as the rightful heirs of Luther's true legacy. As the catechism of a territory that was still legally bound to the AC, the HC could not avoid getting caught in the crossfire of this intra-Lutheran battle, especially when it came to the doctrine of the Lord's Supper. In their formulation of eucharistic teaching, the producers of the HC were not intending to rebel against the AC but rather to interpret it in a way that did not contradict the original text[12]—not even, as we have seen, the unaltered version of that text from 1530. Nevertheless, by sounding less than fully Gnesio-Lutheran in its eucharistic language, the HC was perceived by the stricter Lutherans to have cast its lot with the Philippists, Zwinglians, and Calvinists, and it did not take long for the rhetorical attacks against it to begin. When the

Gnesio-Lutherans ultimately prevailed over the Philippists in the Formula of Concord (1577), all chance of the HC serving as an ecumenical bridge to Lutheranism disappeared, and in the centuries that followed, the catechism became identified almost exclusively with Reformed Protestantism. However much it represented a Lutheran-Reformed theological synthesis and intended to build consensus on the basis of that synthesis, its impact in some of the Lutheran regions of the German empire was anything but ecumenical.

THE HEIDELBERG CATECHISM'S ECUMENICAL SPIRIT

Despite these limitations on its ecumenical character—a tone that is sometimes polemical, a consensus that was in part politically motivated, and an impact that in the short term created as much division as it did unity—there are still a number of ways that the HC models an ecumenical spirit. First of all, as we saw in the preceding chapters, the HC displays an ecumenical spirit by attempting to build a doctrinal synthesis between the Lutheran and Reformed traditions. In chapter 2 we noted a Lutheran, especially Melanchthonian-Lutheran, parentage to the theme and structure of the HC but with strands of Lutheran and Reformed texts woven into the pivotal first question and answer. Chapter 3 demonstrated how the Lutheran contrast between law and gospel, which is wedded to the first two divisions of the HC, is fleshed out with Reformed textual and thematic material that blunts the sharpness of the distinction and helps to create middle ground. The same is true, as we saw in chapter 4, of the explanation of providence in HC 26–28, which under Luther's heading "God the Father and our creation" draws largely on Reformed sources and language but with a soteriological slant that reflects the influence of Luther's Small Catechism. Moreover, the near silence on predestination in the questions leading up to HC 26–28 follows the pattern of the AC exactly: not a single question in either confession is devoted specifically to election, but the AC's portrayal of faith as the work of the Holy Spirit in those in whom God pleases to effect it creates space for an implicit doctrine of election and perseverance throughout the HC.

In chapter 5 we observed that the HC's exposition of the creedal article on the Son (HC 29–52) once again fleshes out a Lutheran skeletal structure with source material from the Reformed tradition, and the HC's treatment of the Holy Spirit (HC 53–58) actually blends language from both traditions into a formulation that points toward common ground. In its doctrine of the sacraments (HC 65–85), we learned in chapter 6, the HC begins by drawing from Melanchthonian sources and following Melanchthon's advice, but it then incorporates language and emphases from the Reformed tradition that are neither found in Melanchthon's AC nor directly contradict it. The HC also sought to respect the Lutheran tradition in general and the boundaries of the AC in particular with a heavily muted doctrine of the covenant (see chapter 7). Finally, chapter 8 made the case that the HC's treatment of gratitude in relation to the Ten Commandments and the Lord's Prayer (HC 86–129) weaves together strands of text from both the Lutheran and Reformed catechetical traditions without being partial to either.

Throughout the course of this emerging doctrinal synthesis, the HC employed multiple ecumenical strategies: using source texts from all parties in the discussion, focusing largely on fundamental doctrines of the Christian faith,[13] emphasizing views held in common, staking out middle positions, stating doctrines positively without explicitly rejecting alternatives, avoiding or only lightly touching on disputed topics, and sometimes simply combining elements of both traditions into a single formulation. In these respects the HC can be considered a model ecumenical confession, at least within the limits of the Melanchthonian-Reformed synthesis it sought to achieve. It may not have been a consensus document in the formal sense, like, for example, the *Consensus Tigurinus* ("Zurich Consensus") of 1549, but in tone and strategy it certainly bears many of the earmarks of one.

The ecumenical spirit of the HC, however, is manifest in other ways as well. For one thing, the catechism does not simply use various strategies to build bridges; it consciously presents itself as more than a partisan statement of doctrine. This is suggested already on the title page, where the document is identified not with the familiar moniker "Heidelberg Catechism" but rather "Catechism or *Christian* Instruction as This Is Carried on in Churches and Schools of the Electoral Palatinate."[14] In the preface, too, Frederick III avoids all references to Luther, Melanchthon, Calvin, Beza, or Bullinger, and to the theological traditions they inspired. Instead he laments the lack of "*Christian* doctrine" and "*Christian* instruction" among the youth in the Palatinate and emphasizes the need for training in "the pure and consistent doctrine of the holy Gospel." The HC, therefore, is "a summary course of instruction or catechism of our *Christian* Religion, according to the Word of God" so that "the youth in churches and schools may be piously instructed in such *Christian* doctrine."[15]

This broader view of Christianity and the church in the preface is reinforced in the body of the HC.[16] In its lead-in to the exposition of the Apostles' Creed, HC 22 reads as follows:

> **Q. What then must a Christian believe?**
>
> A. All that is promised us in the gospel, a summary of which is taught us in the articles of our universal and undisputed Christian faith.

It is worth noting here that already in the question it is the *Christian* believer and belief that is in view. The answer then identifies the core of such Christian belief as the promises of the gospel summarized in the articles of the *universal* Christian faith. This anticipates the more detailed description of the worldwide church in HC 54:

> **Q. What do you believe concerning "the holy catholic church"?**
>
> A. I believe that the Son of God through his Spirit and Word, out of the entire human race, from the beginning of the world to its end, gathers, protects, and preserves for himself a community chosen for eternal life and united in true faith. And of this community I am and always will be a living member.

It is out of the *entire* human race that the Son of God in all times and places has been gathering *one* community, a community "*united* in true faith." Underlying the unity of "believers one and all" is that "as members of this community, [they] share in Christ and in all his treasures and gifts" (HC 55). And such unity in Christ and true faith comes to concrete expression when "each member . . . use[s] these gifts readily and joyfully for the service and enrichment of the other members" (HC 55). We should remember that this expansive view of the unity of the church is articulated in the HC's exposition of two topics in the Apostles' Creed—the one, holy, catholic church and the communion of saints—both of which, HC 22 has already informed us, are among the promises that lie at the heart of the gospel. For the HC, church unity—both spiritual and visible—is not something that threatens the truth of the gospel; it is part of that truth.

Finally, the HC manifests an ecumenical spirit in the way it relates its doctrinal teaching to the shared religious experience of Christian believers. Like all catechisms for hundreds of years before and after it, the HC is essentially an exposition of the basic elements of the Christian faith: the Apostles' Creed, the Ten Commandments, the Lord's Prayer, and the sacraments. Unlike other catechisms (except Ursinus's SC), however, the HC weaves its explanations of these elements into a threefold structure that we discussed in detail in chapters 2 and 3: human misery (HC 3–11), human deliverance (HC 12–85), and gratitude (HC 86–129). These three subtopics, in turn, elaborate on the overarching theme of the catechism introduced in HC 1: the comfort of the believer. This theme and threefold structure are striking because they set a tone for the HC that is not first of all theological but pastoral and devotional. By choosing as the very first question, "What is your only *comfort* in life and in death?," the authors of the catechism seem to have sensed a profound "discomfort" in the religious lives and experience of their audience, and all the doctrinal material to follow is intended to address that spiritual anxiety. The HC explains not just the meaning of a doctrine, but its meaning for *us*, its relation to the life and experience of the believer. How does it help us (HC 28)? How does it benefit us (HC 36, 43, 45, 49, 51)? How does it comfort us (HC 52, 57, 58)? What good is it to us (HC 59)? How does it remind and assure us (HC 69, 75)? Like Calvin's first edition of the *Institutes* (1536), the HC is more of a handbook on piety than a manual of doctrine.

In this pastoral approach to the gospel as a message of comfort, the HC is operating on a plane of Christian experience that transcends differences on the finer points of doctrine. The essential story line of the catechism is that we are in misery, that is, alienated and estranged from God; that through faith we belong to Christ, who has delivered us from such estrangement and brought us back into fellowship with God; and that our thankfulness to God for that work of reconciliation comes to expression in lives of good works. This is not a narrow or theologically partisan description of the Christian life; it is the grand narrative of "lostness" and "foundness" that lies at the heart of Scripture itself and that Christians across the theological spectrum can identify with. This way of connecting doctrine to the shared experience of the Christian life gives the HC a broad ecumenical scope—even broader than the Lutheran-Reformed theological synthesis that shapes so much of the text.

THE HEIDELBERG CATECHISM'S ECUMENICAL POTENTIAL

There is still the question, however, of whether a 450-year-old confessional document like the HC can play a role in the contemporary ecumenical movement beyond inspiring us with an ecumenical spirit that was restricted to some extent by its own context. We will suggest four ways that this can be done by using some recent examples from North American ecumenism that have involved or could have involved the HC. First, even some of the sharpest polemical language in the HC can lead to fruitful ecumenical dialogue. In 1998, the synod of the Christian Reformed Church in North America (CRC), received an overture (a formal request for action) to remove question and answer 80 from the HC, one of the three Reformation-era confessions to which members of the CRC subscribe. HC 80, which is quoted in full near the beginning of this chapter, attacks the Roman Catholic Mass "as basically nothing but a denial of the one sacrifice and suffering of Jesus Christ and a condemnable [or accursed] idolatry." The overture argued, among other things, "that Christian love, unity, and understanding among Christians demand" the removal of such harsh language from the CRC's body of confessions.[17]

In response to this overture, the synod instructed the CRC's Ecumenical and Interfaith Relations Committee (EIRC) to engage the Roman Catholic Church in a dialogue to clarify the RCC's official doctrine of the Mass. This led to two face-to-face meetings between representatives of the CRC and of both the United States and Canadian Conferences of Catholic Bishops (since the CRC is a binational denomination). These discussions made clear that, when measured against official Roman Catholic teaching, much of HC 80's portrayal and evaluation of the doctrine of the Mass was inaccurate. The EIRC wrote up its findings in a report to the synod of 2002, a report that was later reviewed also by the United States and Canadian conferences of bishops and by the Pontifical Council for Promoting Christian Unity in the Vatican. All three Catholic bodies concluded that the CRC summary clearly and accurately represented the Roman Catholic doctrine of the Mass, and the Pontifical Council praised the whole process as "a welcome addition to the efforts at healing memories between separated Christians."

The questions that had been raised in this dialogue about the accuracy of HC 80 led the CRC synod of 2004 to declare that "Q. and A. 80 can no longer be held in its current form as part of our confession." The 2006 synod then brought the matter to a final resolution by directing that HC 80 remain in the text of the confession but that brackets be placed around the paragraphs describing and condemning the Mass to indicate that they did not accurately reflect the official teaching and practice of the RCC and were no longer confessionally binding on members of the CRC.

HC 80, therefore, was central to a process that produced several ecumenical advances. It led to a conversation between a Reformed denomination that subscribed to the HC and the very part of the Christian church that HC 80 had targeted four and a half centuries before. More importantly, perhaps, it led the CRC, a relative newcomer to the ecumenical movement, to wrestle with what it means to be a denomination that takes both its confessional and ecumenical commitments seriously. In other words, how could a church maintain its confessional identity with any integrity if one of its own confessional documents bore false witness against a neighbor? The only way it could do this was to bring its confessional witness into line with its ecumenical perspective. Finally, as a result of its work on HC 80, the CRC was invited to join the next round of the United States Catholic-Reformed dialogue, in which representatives of the Roman Catholic Church and four Reformed denominations spent seven years (2003–10) studying the sacraments of baptism and the Lord's Supper/Eucharist. It is no small irony, therefore, that the most divisive statement in the whole HC helped, in one case at least, to put churches on both sides of the Reformation divide on a path toward greater unity.[18]

Second, the HC can serve as a resource in some of the ecumenical discussions today that focus on social and economic issues. For example, in 2004 the theme of the General Council of the World Alliance (now Communion) of Reformed Churches (WARC) that met in Accra, Ghana, was "That All May Have Life in Fullness," an adaptation of Jesus' words in John 10:10. In a study paper I wrote for the Theology Committee of the Caribbean and North American Area Council in preparation for the Accra conference,[19] I noted that the concept of life that Jesus is talking about in John 10 is spiritual or eternal life, which throughout the Johannine writings and the rest of the New Testament is described as something distinct (though not entirely separate) from physical life and is more than just everlasting existence; it is a new quality or state of existence, a renewal in holiness and fellowship with God through the supernatural work of the Holy Spirit. The promotional materials for the general council, however, were reading Jesus' words in John 10 only in reference to such "life issues" as diversity, inclusiveness, gender justice, and peace, and to such threats and challenges to life in our day as environmental destruction, the AIDS pandemic, and worldwide economic injustice.

I suggested that the HC, in its own interpretation of the major themes of Scripture, might help to bridge the gap between these two views of life by linking the concept of eternal life given us by the Holy Spirit to an individual and communal response of thankfulness that should touch the lives of all our neighbors. In its famous concluding section on gratitude, the HC begins by stating that the Holy Spirit is restoring us into the image of God (HC 86), a lifelong process of conversion or repentance that involves "the dying-away of the old self and the rising-to-life of the new" (HC 88). This resurrection of the new self is a "wholehearted joy in God through Christ" (HC 90), which the catechism defined earlier as "life everlasting" (HC 58), as well as a delight "to live" according to the will of God as expressed in God's law (HC 90, 91). In this way we may show our thanks to God for all he has done for us, praise God, and even win our neighbors over to Christ (HC 86). Thus the experience of eternal life already now has implications for the way that we conduct ourselves in this world.

Such conduct includes a comprehensive social morality, a concern for the quality of life of all our neighbors. Already in its treatment of the third commandment, for example, the HC calls us to use the name of God in such a way that God is praised not only in all we say but in everything that we do (HC 99). This includes the swearing of oaths in God's name when the government demands it as part of its promotion of trustworthiness and truth for the sake of God's glory and our neighbor's good (HC 101). The implication, of course, is that institutions of government are enlisted in the cause of truth, trustworthiness, and neighborly good and that if they betray that cause, they are complicit in the blasphemy of God's name.

Citizens have both a right to expect integrity and justice from the government and a responsibility to work toward those goals. The very honor and praise of God's name is at stake (HC 122).

The fourth commandment, too, has social implications, according to the HC. The references to observing a day of rest and regularly gathering as Christian communities in part "to bring Christian offerings for the poor" (HC 103) echo the social legislation of the Old Testament, where Sabbath days, sabbatical years, years of Jubilee, and other provisions were made for the rest and well-being of those who toiled the hardest and earned the least.

Likewise, the sixth commandment for the HC is more than just about the prohibition of murder. It is about human relationships on a broad scale. We are certainly not to *kill* our neighbors, but also not to belittle, hate, or insult them, nor be a party to this in others, nor harm or willfully endanger ourselves (HC 105). Rather, we are to put away all desire for revenge (HC 105), "to love our neighbors as ourselves, to be patient, peace-loving, gentle, merciful, and friendly toward them, to protect them from harm as much as we can, and to do good even to our enemies" (HC 107). This concern for neighbor and respect for human life has a bearing on a number of social "life issues" today: certainly war, capital punishment, abortion, and euthanasia, but also gender discrimination, homophobia, AIDS, environmental damage, and economic injustice. Regardless of where one stands on such controversial issues, "a church that confesses the [Heidelberg] catechism may and must have these social issues, and the meaning of political responsibility with respect to them, on its agenda as a community of moral discourse and discernment."[20]

Finally, the HC interprets the eighth commandment as forbidding not only "outright theft and robbery" but also "all scheming and swindling in order to get our neighbor's goods for ourselves, whether by force or means that appear legitimate, such as inaccurate measurements of weight, size, or volume; fraudulent merchandising; counterfeit money; excessive interest." It also prohibits "all greed and pointless squandering of [God's] gifts" (HC 110). What God requires instead is "that I do whatever I can for my neighbor's good, that I treat others as I would like them to treat me, and that I work faithfully so that I may share with those in need" (HC 111).

These are but a few examples of where the HC moves from doctrine to practice, that is, from the doctrine of eternal life to its practical outworking in the actions of those born of the Spirit. That is the connection between the "life" that Jesus was talking about in John 10 and the "life issues" on WARC's agenda in 2004. The eradication of violence, pollution, and disease or the experience of greater economic, racial, and gender justice are not by themselves the new life that Jesus meant, but they should be priorities in the community of those who claim to have received this new spiritual life. On that point the HC can speak as eloquently into ecumenical discussions of social issues today as it did to its own social context in the sixteenth century.

A third way the HC can function ecumenically today is as a common voice for the Reformed tradition when more than one Reformed denomination is at an ecumenical table. In the recent U.S. Catholic-Reformed dialogue on the sacraments, for example, the Reformed side was represented by four denominations: the Presbyterian Church (U.S.A), the Reformed Church in America, the United Church of Christ, and the Christian Reformed Church in North America. When it came to identifying the authoritative sources that they would be appealing to in the discussions with the Catholics, the four Reformed delegations found themselves in something of a quandary, since the Reformed and Presbyterian tradition as a whole has never had a confession or body of confessions to which all its denominations subscribe. Indeed, one partial collection of such confessions, E. F. K. Müller's *Die Bekenntnisschriften der reformierten Kirche*, is no fewer than 976 pages long! Even when the list was reduced to those confessions recognized by at least one of the four Reformed churches at the table, the number still stood at ten, and of those ten eight were used by only a single denomination. The only confessional statement that all four Reformed denominations had in common was the HC. As such the HC played a rather significant role in the dialogue as a text that helped to unify and speak for the Reformed churches in this conversation with the Roman Catholics.

Finally, all of the examples cited so far have been of the ecumenical potential of the HC for *Reformed* churches involved in the ecumenical movement. As we have seen throughout this study, however, the HC created a synthesis of theological language and themes from both Reformed and Lutheran sources. It was only for reasons peculiar to its sixteenth-century context that the catechism soon became identified with the Reformed tradition. Even in the attempts in early nineteenth-century Germany to organize territorial union churches of Lutheran and Reformed congregations, the HC remained a representative Reformed catechism alongside of or amalgamated with key confessions from the Lutheran tradition.[21] Is there any possibility, therefore, that the HC could again become a bridge between those two traditions today?

It is certainly difficult to overcome historical inertia, but there is at least one recent ecumenical development in North America in which the HC might have been able to play this role. In 1997, four denominations of Reformation heritage, one Lutheran and the other three Reformed, adopted "A Formula of Agreement" to enter into full communion with one another. The four denominations were the Evangelical Lutheran Church in

America, the Presbyterian Church (U.S.A.), the Reformed Church in America, and the United Church of Christ. Their full communion meant, among other things, that they would:

- recognize each other as churches in which the gospel is rightly preached and the sacraments rightly administered according to the Word of God;
- withdraw any historic condemnation by one side or the other as inappropriate for the life and faith of our churches today;
- continue to recognize each other's baptism and authorize and encourage the sharing of the Lord's Supper among their members;
- recognize each other's various ministries and make provision for the orderly exchange of ordained ministers of Word and Sacrament.[22]

In a subsection titled "A Fundamental Doctrinal Consensus," the Formula locates a basis for the essential conditions of full communion in art. 7 of the AC: "For the true unity of the church it is enough to agree (*satis est consentire*) concerning the teaching of the Gospel and the administration of the sacraments." Surprisingly, however, that is the only reference to a Reformation-era confession in the entire document. Given that this was an agreement between Lutheran and Reformed churches and that the HC had made a serious attempt to find common ground between these same two traditions 450 years earlier, it would have been appropriate to make some mention of the HC in this modern consensus—if for no other reason than to show how contemporary efforts at bridging the Lutheran-Reformed divide have deep historical roots.

This is particularly true for some of the doctrinal issues discussed in the agreement. The Formula's identification of the wholeness of the gospel as both forgiveness of sins and renewal of life resonates perfectly with one of the major threads running through the HC (see chapter 7). The Formula's description of baptism as a reception into fellowship with Christ and a call to daily repentance echoes HC 70–74 and 88–90, respectively. The joint affirmation of the full presence of Christ in the Lord's Supper without explaining precisely *how* he is present and received there reflects what we identified in chapter 6 as one of key silences in the HC, namely the precise relationship between the signs of the Lord's Supper and that which they signify. While the Formula seeks a way around "the differing 'accents' of Calvin and Luther on the relation of . . . law and gospel . . . [and] the role of God's law in the Christian life," the HC had demonstrated already centuries ago a way to balance these accents in its own handling of the law (see chapter 8) and the relation between law and gospel (see chapter 3). Finally, although the Formula has to reckon with the fact that "the doctrine of predestination has been one of the issues separating the two traditions," we found already in the HC not only a reluctance to address the issue but also, where there are hints of it, a formulation that is careful to follow the lead of the AC.

In all of these instances, the Formula displays theological and ecumenical instincts that are remarkably similar to those of its famous predecessor in Palatine Germany. The Formula, like the Leuenberg Agreement in Europe in 1973, is another important plank in the bridge between Lutheran and Reformed Protestantism for which the HC helped to lay the groundwork more than 400 years before. It may be too much to expect, as Eugene Carson Blake proposed in 1960, "that such a Reformation confession as the Heidelburg [sic] Catechism, partly because of its Lutheran elements, might be lifted up in some acceptable formula as having a proper place in the confession of the whole Church."[23] But the HC can still serve today as an inspiration and foundation for efforts to unite at least the two major branches of the church, Lutheran and Reformed, that are represented in the catechism's theological synthesis.

APPENDIX

The Heidelberg Catechism

INTRODUCTION

The Heidelberg Catechism (1563) was composed in the city of Heidelberg, Germany, at the request of Elector Frederick III, who ruled the province of the Palatinate from 1559 to 1576. The new catechism was intended as a tool for teaching young people, a guide for preaching in the provincial churches, and a form of confessional unity among the several Protestant factions in the Palatinate. An old tradition credits Zacharias Ursinus and Caspar Olevianus with being the coauthors of the catechism, but the project was actually the work of a team of ministers and university theologians under the watchful eye of Frederick himself. Ursinus probably served as the primary writer on the team, and Olevianus had a lesser role. The catechism was approved by a synod in Heidelberg in January 1563. A second and third German edition, each with small additions, as well as a Latin translation were published the same year in Heidelberg. The third edition was included in the Palatinate Church Order of November 15, 1563, at which time the catechism was divided into fifty-two sections or Lord's Days, so that one Lord's Day could be explained in an afternoon worship service each Sunday of the year.

The Synod of Dort approved the Heidelberg Catechism in 1619, and it soon became the most ecumenical of the Reformed catechisms and confessions. It has been translated into many European, Asian, and African languages and is still the most widely used and warmly praised catechism of the Reformation period.

Most of the footnoted biblical references in this translation of the catechism were included in the early German and Latin editions, but the precise selection was approved by Synod 1975 of the Christian Reformed Church.

LORD'S DAY 1

1 **Q. What is your only comfort
in life and in death?**

A. That I am not my own,[1]
but belong—
body and soul,
in life and in death—[2]
to my faithful Savior, Jesus Christ.[3]

He has fully paid for all my sins with his precious blood,[4]
and has set me free from the tyranny of the devil.[5]
He also watches over me in such a way[6]
that not a hair can fall from my head
without the will of my Father in heaven;[7]
in fact, all things must work together for my salvation.[8]

Because I belong to him,
Christ, by his Holy Spirit,
assures me of eternal life[9]
and makes me wholeheartedly willing and ready
from now on to live for him.[10]

[1] 1 Cor. 6:19–20
[2] Rom. 14:7–9
[3] 1 Cor. 3:23; Titus 2:14
[4] 1 Pet. 1:18–19; 1 John 1:7–9; 2:2
[5] John 8:34–36; Heb. 2:14–15; 1 John 3:1–11
[6] John 6:39–40; 10:27–30; 2 Thess. 3:3; 1 Pet. 1:5
[7] Matt. 10:29–31; Luke 21:16–18
[8] Rom. 8:28
[9] Rom. 8:15–16; 2 Cor. 1:21–22; 5:5; Eph. 1:13–14
[10] Rom. 8:1–17

2 **Q. What must you know to
live and die in the joy of this comfort?**

A. Three things:
first, how great my sin and misery are;[1]
second, how I am set free from all my sins and misery;[2]
third, how I am to thank God for such deliverance.[3]

[1] Rom. 3:9–10; 1 John 1:10
[2] John 17:3; Acts 4:12; 10:43
[3] Matt. 5:16; Rom. 6:13; Eph. 5:8–10; 2 Tim. 2:15; 1 Pet. 2:9–10

Part I: Misery

LORD'S DAY 2

3 **Q. How do you come to know your misery?**
A. The law of God tells me.[1]

[1] Rom. 3:20; 7:7–25

4 **Q. What does God's law require of us?**
A. Christ teaches us this in summary in Matthew 22:37–40:

"'You shall love the Lord your God
with all your heart,
and with all your soul,
and with all your mind.'[1]
This is the greatest and first commandment.

"And a second is like it:
'You shall love your neighbor as yourself.'[2]

"On these two commandments hang
all the law and the prophets."

[1] Deut. 6:5
[2] Lev. 19:18

5 **Q. Can you live up to all this perfectly?**
A. No.[1]
I have a natural tendency
to hate God and my neighbor.[2]

[1] Rom. 3:9–20, 23; 1 John 1:8, 10
[2] Gen. 6:5; Jer. 17:9; Rom. 7:23–24; 8:7; Eph. 2:1–3; Titus 3:3

LORD'S DAY 3

6 **Q. Did God create people
so wicked and perverse?**

A. No.
God created them good[1] and in his own image,[2]
that is, in true righteousness and holiness,[3]
so that they might
truly know God their creator,[4]
love him with all their heart,
and live with God in eternal happiness,
to praise and glorify him.[5]

[1] Gen. 1:31
[2] Gen. 1:26–27
[3] Eph. 4:24
[4] Col. 3:10
[5] Ps. 8

7 **Q. Then where does this corrupt human nature come from?**

A. The fall and disobedience of our first parents,
Adam and Eve, in Paradise.[1]
This fall has so poisoned our nature[2]
that we are all conceived and born
in a sinful condition.[3]

[1] Gen. 3
[2] Rom. 5:12, 18–19
[3] Ps. 51:5

8 **Q. But are we so corrupt
that we are totally unable to do any good
and inclined toward all evil?**

A. Yes,[1] unless we are born again
by the Spirit of God.[2]

[1] Gen. 6:5; 8:21; Job 14:4; Isa. 53:6
[2] John 3:3–5

LORD'S DAY 4

9 **Q. But doesn't God do us an injustice
by requiring in his law
what we are unable to do?**

A. No, God created human beings with the ability to keep the law.[1]
They, however, provoked by the devil,[2]
in willful disobedience,[3]
robbed themselves and all their descendants of these gifts.[4]

[1] Gen. 1:31; Eph. 4:24
[2] Gen. 3:13; John 8:44
[3] Gen. 3:6
[4] Rom. 5:12, 18, 19

10 **Q. Does God permit
such disobedience and rebellion
to go unpunished?**

A. Certainly not.
God is terribly angry
with the sin we are born with
as well as the sins we personally commit.

As a just judge,
God will punish them both now and in eternity,[1]
having declared:
"Cursed is everyone who does not observe and obey
all the things written in the book of the law."[2]

[1] Ex. 34:7; Ps. 5:4–6; Nah. 1:2; Rom. 1:18; Eph. 5:6; Heb. 9:27
[2] Gal. 3:10; Deut. 27:26

11 **Q. But isn't God also merciful?**

A. God is certainly merciful,[1]
but also just.[2]
God's justice demands
that sin, committed against his supreme majesty,
be punished with the supreme penalty—
eternal punishment of body and soul.[3]

[1] Ex. 34:6–7; Ps. 103:8–9
[2] Ex. 34:7; Deut. 7:9–11; Ps. 5:4–6; Heb. 10:30–31
[3] Matt. 25:35–46

Part II: Deliverance

LORD'S DAY 5

12 **Q. According to God's righteous judgment**
we deserve punishment
both now and in eternity:
how then can we escape this punishment
and return to God's favor?

A. God requires that his justice be satisfied.[1]
Therefore the claims of this justice
must be paid in full,
either by ourselves or by another.[2]

[1] Ex. 23:7; Rom. 2:1–11
[2] Isa. 53:11; Rom. 8:3–4

13 **Q. Can we make this payment ourselves?**

A. Certainly not.
Actually, we increase our debt every day.[1]

[1] Matt. 6:12; Rom. 2:4–5

14 **Q. Can another creature—any at all—**
pay this debt for us?

A. No.
To begin with,
God will not punish any other creature
for what a human is guilty of.[1]
Furthermore,
no mere creature can bear the weight
of God's eternal wrath against sin
and deliver others from it.[2]

[1] Ezek. 18:4, 20; Heb. 2:14–18
[2] Ps. 49:7–9; 130:3

15 **Q. What kind of mediator and deliverer**
should we look for then?

A. One who is a true[1] and righteous[2] human,
yet more powerful than all creatures,
that is, one who is also true God.[3]

[1] Rom. 1:3; 1 Cor. 15:21; Heb. 2:17
[2] Isa. 53:9; 2 Cor. 5:21; Heb. 7:26
[3] Isa. 7:14; 9:6; Jer. 23:6; John 1:1

LORD'S DAY 6

16 Q. Why must the mediator be a true and righteous human?

A. God's justice demands
that human nature, which has sinned,
must pay for sin;[1]
but a sinful human could never pay for others.[2]

[1] Rom. 5:12, 15; 1 Cor. 15:21; Heb. 2:14–16
[2] Heb. 7:26–27; 1 Pet. 3:18

17 Q. Why must the mediator also be true God?

A. So that the mediator,
by the power of his divinity,
might bear the weight of God's wrath in his humanity
and earn for us
and restore to us
righteousness and life.[1]

[1] Isa. 53; John 3:16; 2 Cor. 5:21

**18 Q. Then who is this mediator—
true God and at the same time
a true and righteous human?**

A. Our Lord Jesus Christ,[1]
who was given to us
to completely deliver us
and make us right with God.[2]

[1] Matt. 1:21–23; Luke 2:11; 1 Tim. 2:5
[2] 1 Cor. 1:30

19 Q. How do you come to know this?

A. The holy gospel tells me.

God began to reveal the gospel already in Paradise;[1]
later God proclaimed it
by the holy patriarchs[2] and prophets[3]
and foreshadowed it
by the sacrifices and other ceremonies of the law;[4]
and finally God fulfilled it
through his own beloved Son.[5]

[1] Gen. 3:15
[2] Gen. 22:18; 49:10
[3] Isa. 53; Jer. 23:5–6; Mic. 7:18–20; Acts 10:43; Heb. 1:1–2
[4] Lev. 1–7; John 5:46; Heb. 10:1–10
[5] Rom. 10:4; Gal. 4:4–5; Col. 2:17

LORD'S DAY 7

20 **Q. Are all people then saved through Christ just as they were lost through Adam?**

A. No.
Only those are saved
who through true faith
are grafted into Christ
and accept all his benefits.[1]

[1] Matt. 7:14; John 3:16, 18, 36; Rom. 11:16–21

21 **Q. What is true faith?**

A. True faith is
not only a sure knowledge by which I hold as true
all that God has revealed to us in Scripture;[1]
it is also a wholehearted trust,[2]
which the Holy Spirit creates in me[3] by the gospel,[4]
that God has freely granted,
not only to others but to me also,[5]
forgiveness of sins,
eternal righteousness,
and salvation.[6]
These are gifts of sheer grace,
granted solely by Christ's merit.[7]

[1] John 17:3, 17; Heb. 11:1–3; James 2:19
[2] Rom. 4:18–21; 5:1; 10:10; Heb. 4:14–16
[3] Matt. 16:15–17; John 3:5; Acts 16:14
[4] Rom. 1:16; 10:17; 1 Cor. 1:21
[5] Gal. 2:20
[6] Rom. 1:17; Heb. 10:10
[7] Rom. 3:21–26; Gal. 2:16; Eph. 2:8–10

22 **Q. What then must a Christian believe?**
A. All that is promised us in the gospel,[1]
a summary of which is taught us
in the articles of our universal
and undisputed Christian faith.

[1] Matt. 28:18–20; John 20:30–31

23 **Q. What are these articles?**
A. I believe in God, the Father almighty,
creator of heaven and earth.

I believe in Jesus Christ, his only begotten Son, our Lord,
who was conceived by the Holy Spirit
and born of the virgin Mary.
He suffered under Pontius Pilate,
was crucified, died, and was buried;
he descended to hell.
The third day he rose again from the dead.
He ascended to heaven
and is seated at the right hand of God the Father almighty.
From there he will come to judge the living and the dead.

I believe in the Holy Spirit,
the holy catholic church,
the communion of saints,
the forgiveness of sins,
the resurrection of the body,
and the life everlasting. Amen.

LORD'S DAY 8

24 **Q. How are these articles divided?**
A. Into three parts:
God the Father and our creation;
God the Son and our deliverance;
and God the Holy Spirit and our sanctification.

25 **Q. Since there is only one divine being,[1]**
why do you speak of three:
Father, Son, and Holy Spirit?
A. Because that is how
God has revealed himself in his Word:[2]
these three distinct persons
are one, true, eternal God.

[1] Deut. 6:4; 1 Cor. 8:4, 6
[2] Matt. 3:16–17; 28:18–19; Luke 4:18 (Isa. 61:1); John 14:26; 15:26; 2 Cor. 13:14; Gal. 4:6; Tit. 3:5–6

God the Father

LORD'S DAY 9

26 **Q. What do you believe when you say,**
"I believe in God, the Father almighty,
creator of heaven and earth"?

A. That the eternal Father of our Lord Jesus Christ,
who out of nothing created heaven and earth
and everything in them,[1]
who still upholds and rules them
by his eternal counsel and providence,[2]
is my God and Father
because of Christ the Son.[3]

I trust God so much that I do not doubt
he will provide
whatever I need
for body and soul,[4]
and will turn to my good
whatever adversity he sends upon me
in this sad world.[5]

God is able to do this because he is almighty God[6]
and desires to do this because he is a faithful Father.[7]

[1] Gen. 1–2; Ex. 20:11; Ps. 33:6; Isa. 44:24; Acts 4:24; 14:15
[2] Ps. 104; Matt. 6:30; 10:29; Eph. 1:11
[3] John 1:12–13; Rom. 8:15–16; Gal. 4:4–7; Eph. 1:5
[4] Ps. 55:22; Matt. 6:25–26; Luke 12:22–31
[5] Rom. 8:28
[6] Gen. 18:14; Rom. 8:31–39
[7] Matt. 7:9–11

LORD'S DAY 10

27 **Q. What do you understand**
by the providence of God?

A. The almighty and ever present power of God[1]
by which God upholds, as with his hand,
heaven
and earth
and all creatures,[2]
and so rules them that
leaf and blade,
rain and drought,
fruitful and lean years,
food and drink,
health and sickness,
prosperity and poverty—[3]
all things, in fact,
come to us
not by chance[4]
but by his fatherly hand.[5]

[1] Jer. 23:23–24; Acts 17:24–28
[2] Heb. 1:3
[3] Jer. 5:24; Acts 14:15–17; John 9:3; Prov. 22:2
[4] Prov. 16:33
[5] Matt. 10:29

28 **Q. How does the knowledge**
of God's creation and providence help us?

A. We can be patient when things go against us,[1]
thankful when things go well,[2]
and for the future we can have
good confidence in our faithful God and Father
that nothing in creation will separate us from his love.[3]
For all creatures are so completely in God's hand
that without his will
they can neither move nor be moved.[4]

[1] Job 1:21–22; James 1:3
[2] Deut. 8:10; 1 Thess. 5:18
[3] Ps. 55:22; Rom. 5:3–5; 8:38–39
[4] Job 1:12; 2:6; Prov. 21:1; Acts 17:24–28

God the Son

LORD'S DAY 11

29 Q. **Why is the Son of God called "Jesus," meaning "savior"?**

A. Because he saves us from our sins,[1]
and because salvation should not be sought
and cannot be found in anyone else.[2]

[1] Matt. 1:21; Heb. 7:25
[2] Isa. 43:11; John 15:5; Acts 4:11–12; 1 Tim. 2:5

30 Q. **Do those who look for their salvation in saints, in themselves, or elsewhere really believe in the only savior Jesus?**

A. No.
Although they boast of being his,
by their actions they deny
the only savior, Jesus.[1]

Either Jesus is not a perfect savior,
or those who in true faith accept this savior
have in him all they need for their salvation.[2]

[1] 1 Cor. 1:12–13; Gal. 5:4
[2] Col. 1:19–20; 2:10; 1 John 1:7

LORD'S DAY 12

31 Q. Why is he called "Christ," meaning "anointed"?

A. Because he has been ordained by God the Father
and has been anointed with the Holy Spirit[1]
to be
our chief prophet and teacher[2]
who fully reveals to us
the secret counsel and will of God concerning our deliverance;[3]
our only high priest[4]
who has delivered us by the one sacrifice of his body,[5]
and who continually pleads our cause with the Father;[6]
and our eternal king[7]
who governs us by his Word and Spirit,
and who guards us and keeps us
in the freedom he has won for us.[8]

[1] Luke 3:21–22; 4:14–19 (Isa. 61:1); Heb. 1:9 (Ps. 45:7)
[2] Acts 3:22 (Deut. 18:15)
[3] John 1:18; 15:15
[4] Heb. 7:17 (Ps. 110:4)
[5] Heb. 9:12; 10:11–14
[6] Rom. 8:34; Heb. 9:24
[7] Matt. 21:5 (Zech. 9:9)
[8] Matt. 28:18–20; John 10:28; Rev. 12:10–11

32 Q. But why are you called a Christian?

A. Because by faith I am a member of Christ[1]
and so I share in his anointing.[2]
I am anointed
to confess his name,[3]
to present myself to him as a living sacrifice of thanks,[4]
to strive with a free conscience against sin and the devil in this life,[5]
and afterward to reign with Christ
over all creation
for eternity.[6]

[1] 1 Cor. 12:12–27
[2] Acts 2:17 (Joel 2:28); 1 John 2:27
[3] Matt. 10:32; Rom. 10:9–10; Heb. 13:15
[4] Rom. 12:1; 1 Pet. 2:5, 9
[5] Gal. 5:16–17; Eph. 6:11; 1 Tim. 1:18–19
[6] Matt. 25:34; 2 Tim. 2:12

LORD'S DAY 13

33 Q. Why is he called God's "only begotten Son" when we also are God's children?

A. Because Christ alone is the eternal, natural Son of God.[1]
We, however, are adopted children of God—
adopted by grace through Christ.[2]

[1] John 1:1–3, 14, 18; Heb. 1
[2] John 1:12; Rom. 8:14–17; Eph. 1:5–6

34 Q. Why do you call him "our Lord"?

A. Because—
not with gold or silver,
but with his precious blood—[1]
he has set us free
from sin and from the tyranny of the devil,[2]
and has bought us,
body and soul,
to be his very own.[3]

[1] 1 Pet. 1:18–19
[2] Col. 1:13–14; Heb. 2:14–15
[3] 1 Cor. 6:20; 1 Tim. 2:5–6

LORD'S DAY 14

35 Q. What does it mean that he "was conceived by the Holy Spirit and born of the virgin Mary"?

A. That the eternal Son of God,
who is and remains
true and eternal God,[1]
took to himself,
through the working of the Holy Spirit,[2]
from the flesh and blood of the virgin Mary,[3]
a truly human nature
so that he might also become David's true descendant,[4]
like his brothers and sisters in every way[5]
except for sin.[6]

[1] John 1:1; 10:30–36; Acts 13:33 (Ps. 2:7); Col. 1:15–17; 1 John 5:20
[2] Luke 1:35
[3] Matt. 1:18–23; John 1:14; Gal. 4:4; Heb. 2:14
[4] 2 Sam. 7:12–16; Ps. 132:11; Matt. 1:1; Rom. 1:3
[5] Phil. 2:7; Heb. 2:17
[6] Heb. 4:15; 7:26–27

36 Q. How does the holy conception and birth of Christ benefit you?

A. He is our mediator[1]
and, in God's sight,
he covers with his innocence and perfect holiness
my sinfulness in which I was conceived.[2]

[1] 1 Tim. 2:5–6; Heb. 9:13–15
[2] Rom. 8:3–4; 2 Cor. 5:21; Gal. 4:4–5; 1 Pet. 1:18–19

LORD'S DAY 15

37 **Q. What do you understand by the word "suffered"?**

A. That during his whole life on earth,
but especially at the end,
Christ sustained
in body and soul
the wrath of God against the sin of the whole human race.[1]

This he did in order that,
by his suffering as the only atoning sacrifice,[2]
he might deliver us, body and soul,
from eternal condemnation,[3]
and gain for us
God's grace,
righteousness,
and eternal life.[4]

[1] Isa. 53; 1 Pet. 2:24; 3:18
[2] Rom. 3:25; Heb. 10:14; 1 John 2:2; 4:10
[3] Rom. 8:1–4; Gal. 3:13
[4] John 3:16; Rom. 3:24–26

38 **Q. Why did he suffer "under Pontius Pilate" as judge?**

A. So that he,
though innocent,
might be condemned by an earthly judge,[1]
and so free us from the severe judgment of God
that was to fall on us.[2]

[1] Luke 23:13–24; John 19:4, 12–16
[2] Isa. 53:4–5; 2 Cor. 5:21; Gal. 3:13

39 **Q. Is it significant that he was "crucified" instead of dying some other way?**

A. Yes.
By this I am convinced
that he shouldered the curse
which lay on me,
since death by crucifixion was cursed by God.[1]

[1] Gal. 3:10–13 (Deut. 21:23)

LORD'S DAY 16

40 Q. Why did Christ have to suffer death?

A. Because God's justice and truth require it: [1]
nothing else could pay for our sins
except the death of the Son of God.[2]

[1] Gen. 2:17
[2] Rom. 8:3–4; Phil. 2:8; Heb. 2:9

41 Q. Why was he "buried"?

A. His burial testifies
that he really died.[1]

[1] Isa. 53:9; John 19:38–42; Acts 13:29; 1 Cor. 15:3–4

**42 Q. Since Christ has died for us,
why do we still have to die?**

A. Our death does not pay the debt of our sins.[1]
Rather, it puts an end to our sinning
and is our entrance into eternal life.[2]

[1] Ps. 49:7
[2] John 5:24; Phil. 1:21–23; 1 Thess. 5:9–10

**43 Q. What further benefit do we receive
from Christ's sacrifice and death on the cross?**

A. By Christ's power
our old selves are crucified, put to death, and buried with him,[1]
so that the evil desires of the flesh
may no longer rule us,[2]
but that instead we may offer ourselves
as a sacrifice of gratitude to him.[3]

[1] Rom. 6:5–11; Col. 2:11–12
[2] Rom. 6:12–14
[3] Rom. 12:1; Eph. 5:1–2

44 **Q. Why does the creed add,**
"He descended to hell"?

A. To assure me during attacks of deepest dread and temptation
that Christ my Lord,
by suffering unspeakable anguish, pain, and terror of soul,
on the cross but also earlier,
has delivered me from hellish anguish and torment.[1]

[1] Isa. 53; Matt. 26:36–46; 27:45–46; Luke 22:44; Heb. 5:7–10

LORD'S DAY 17

45 Q. How does Christ's resurrection benefit us?

A. First, by his resurrection he has overcome death,
so that he might make us share in the righteousness
he obtained for us by his death.[1]

Second, by his power we too
are already raised to a new life.[2]

Third, Christ's resurrection
is a sure pledge to us of our blessed resurrection.[3]

[1] Rom. 4:25; 1 Cor. 15:16–20; 1 Pet. 1:3–5
[2] Rom. 6:5–11; Eph. 2:4–6; Col. 3:1–4
[3] Rom. 8:11; 1 Cor. 15:12–23; Phil. 3:20–21

LORD'S DAY 18

46 Q. What do you mean by saying, "He ascended to heaven"?

A. That Christ,
while his disciples watched,
was taken up from the earth into heaven[1]
and remains there on our behalf[2]
until he comes again
to judge the living and the dead.[3]

[1] Luke 24:50–51; Acts 1:9–11
[2] Rom. 8:34; Eph. 4:8–10; Heb. 7:23–25; 9:24
[3] Acts 1:11

47 Q. But isn't Christ with us until the end of the world as he promised us?[1]

A. Christ is true human and true God.
In his human nature Christ is not now on earth;[2]
but in his divinity, majesty, grace, and Spirit
he is never absent from us.[3]

[1] Matt. 28:20
[2] Acts 1:9–11; 3:19–21
[3] Matt. 28:18–20; John 14:16–19

48 Q. If his humanity is not present wherever his divinity is, then aren't the two natures of Christ separated from each other?

A. Certainly not.
Since divinity
is not limited
and is present everywhere,[1]
it is evident that
Christ's divinity is surely beyond the bounds of the humanity that has been taken on,
but at the same time his divinity is in
and remains personally united to
his humanity.[2]

[1] Jer. 23:23–24; Acts 7:48–49 (Isa. 66:1)
[2] John 1:14; 3:13; Col. 2:9

49 **Q. How does Christ's ascension to heaven benefit us?**

A. First, he is our advocate
in heaven
in the presence of his Father.[1]

Second, we have our own flesh in heaven
as a sure pledge that Christ our head
will also take us, his members,
up to himself.[2]

Third, he sends his Spirit to us on earth
as a corresponding pledge.[3]
By the Spirit's power
we seek not earthly things
but the things above, where Christ is,
sitting at God's right hand.[4]

[1] Rom. 8:34; 1 John 2:1
[2] John 14:2; 17:24; Eph. 2:4–6
[3] John 14:16; 2 Cor. 1:21–22; 5:5
[4] Col. 3:1–4

LORD'S DAY 19

50 Q. Why the next words:
"and is seated at the right hand of God"?

A. Because Christ ascended to heaven
to show there that he is head of his church,[1]
the one through whom the Father rules all things.[2]

[1] Eph. 1:20–23; Col. 1:18
[2] Matt. 28:18; John 5:22–23

51 Q. How does this glory of Christ our head benefit us?

A. First, through his Holy Spirit
he pours out gifts from heaven
upon us his members.[1]

Second, by his power
he defends us and keeps us safe
from all enemies.[2]

[1] Acts 2:33; Eph. 4:7–12
[2] Ps. 110:1–2; John 10:27–30; Rev. 19:11–16

52 Q. How does Christ's return
"to judge the living and the dead"
comfort you?

A. In all distress and persecution,
with uplifted head,
I confidently await the very judge
who has already offered himself to the judgment of God
in my place and removed the whole curse from me.[1]
Christ will cast all his enemies and mine
into everlasting condemnation,
but will take me and all his chosen ones
to himself
into the joy and glory of heaven.[2]

[1] Luke 21:28; Rom. 8:22–25; Phil. 3:20–21; Tit. 2:13–14
[2] Matt. 25:31–46; 2 Thess. 1:6–10

God the Holy Spirit

LORD'S DAY 20

53 Q. What do you believe
concerning "the Holy Spirit"?

A. First, that the Spirit, with the Father and the Son,
is eternal God.[1]

Second, that the Spirit is given also to me,[2]
so that, through true faith,
he makes me share in Christ and all his benefits,[3]
comforts me,[4]
and will remain with me forever.[5]

[1] Gen. 1:1–2; Matt. 28:19; Acts 5:3–4
[2] 1 Cor. 6:19; 2 Cor. 1:21–22; Gal. 4:6
[3] Gal. 3:14
[4] John 15:26; Acts 9:31
[5] John 14:16–17; 1 Pet. 4:14

LORD'S DAY 21

54 Q. What do you believe concerning "the holy catholic church"?

A. I believe that the Son of God
through his Spirit and Word,[1]
out of the entire human race,[2]
from the beginning of the world to its end,[3]
gathers, protects, and preserves for himself
a community chosen for eternal life[4]
and united in true faith.[5]
And of this community I am[6] and always will be[7]
a living member.

[1] John 10:14–16; Acts 20:28; Rom. 10:14–17; Col. 1:18
[2] Gen. 26:3b–4; Rev. 5:9
[3] Isa. 59:21; 1 Cor. 11:26
[4] Matt. 16:18; John 10:28–30; Rom. 8:28–30; Eph. 1:3–14
[5] Acts 2:42–47; Eph. 4:1–6
[6] 1 John 3:14, 19–21
[7] John 10:27–28; 1 Cor. 1:4–9; 1 Pet. 1:3–5

55 Q. What do you understand by "the communion of saints"?

A. First, that believers one and all,
as members of this community,
share in Christ
and in all his treasures and gifts.[1]

Second, that each member
should consider it a duty
to use these gifts
readily and joyfully
for the service and enrichment
of the other members.[2]

[1] Rom. 8:32; 1 Cor. 6:17; 12:4–7, 12–13; 1 John 1:3
[2] Rom. 12:4–8; 1 Cor. 12:20–27; 13:1–7; Phil. 2:4–8

56 Q. What do you believe
concerning "the forgiveness of sins"?

A. I believe that God,
because of Christ's satisfaction,
will no longer remember
any of my sins[1]
or my sinful nature
which I need to struggle against all my life.[2]

Rather, by grace
God grants me the righteousness of Christ
to free me forever from judgment.[3]

[1] Ps. 103:3–4, 10, 12; Mic. 7:18–19; 2 Cor. 5:18–21; 1 John 1:7; 2:2
[2] Rom. 7:21–25
[3] John 3:17–18; Rom. 8:1–2

LORD'S DAY 22

57 Q. How does "the resurrection of the body" comfort you?

A. Not only will my soul
be taken immediately after this life
to Christ its head,[1]
but also my very flesh will be
raised by the power of Christ,
reunited with my soul,
and made like Christ's glorious body.[2]

[1] Luke 23:43; Phil. 1:21–23
[2] 1 Cor. 15:20, 42–46, 54; Phil. 3:21; 1 John 3:2

58 Q. How does the article concerning "life everlasting" comfort you?

A. Even as I already now
experience in my heart
the beginning of eternal joy,[1]
so after this life I will have
perfect blessedness such as
no eye has seen,
no ear has heard,
no human heart has ever imagined:
a blessedness in which to praise God forever.[2]

[1] Rom. 14:17
[2] John 17:3; 1 Cor. 2:9

LORD'S DAY 23

59 Q. What good does it do you, however, to believe all this?

A. In Christ I am righteous before God
and heir to life everlasting.[1]

[1] John 3:36; Rom. 1:17 (Hab. 2:4); Rom. 5:1–2

60 Q. How are you righteous before God?

A. Only by true faith in Jesus Christ.[1]

Even though my conscience accuses me
of having grievously sinned against all God's commandments,
of never having kept any of them,[2]
and of still being inclined toward all evil,[3]
nevertheless,
without any merit of my own,[4]
out of sheer grace,[5]
God grants and credits to me
the perfect satisfaction, righteousness, and holiness of Christ,[6]
as if I had never sinned nor been a sinner,
and as if I had been as perfectly obedient
as Christ was obedient for me.[7]

All I need to do
is accept this gift with a believing heart.[8]

[1] Rom. 3:21–28; Gal. 2:16; Eph. 2:8–9; Phil 3:8–11
[2] Rom. 3:9–10
[3] Rom. 7:23
[4] Tit. 3:4–5
[5] Rom. 3:24; Eph. 2:8
[6] Rom. 4:3–5 (Gen. 15:6); 2 Cor. 5:17–19; 1 John 2:1–2
[7] Rom. 4:24–25; 2 Cor. 5:21
[8] John 3:18; Acts 16:30–31

61 **Q. Why do you say that**
through faith alone
you are righteous?

A. Not because I please God
by the worthiness of my faith.
It is because only Christ's satisfaction, righteousness, and holiness
make me righteous before God,[1]
and because I can accept this righteousness and make it mine
in no other way
than through faith.[2]

[1] 1 Cor. 1:30–31
[2] Rom. 10:10; 1 John 5:10–12

LORD'S DAY 24

62 Q. **Why can't our good works
be our righteousness before God,
or at least a part of our righteousness?**

A. Because the righteousness
which can pass God's judgment
must be entirely perfect
and must in every way measure up to the divine law.[1]
But even our best works in this life
are imperfect
and stained with sin.[2]

[1] Rom. 3:20; Gal. 3:10 (Deut. 27:26)
[2] Isa. 64:6

63 Q. **How can our good works
be said to merit nothing
when God promises to reward them
in this life and the next?[1]**

A. This reward is not earned;
it is a gift of grace.[2]

[1] Matt. 5:12; Heb. 11:6
[2] Luke 17:10; 2 Tim. 4:7–8

64 Q. **But doesn't this teaching
make people indifferent and wicked?**

A. No.
It is impossible
for those grafted into Christ through true faith
not to produce fruits of gratitude.[1]

[1] Luke 6:43–45; John 15:5

The Holy Sacraments

LORD'S DAY 25

65 **Q. It is through faith alone**
that we share in Christ and all his benefits:
where then does that faith come from?

A. The Holy Spirit produces it in our hearts[1]
by the preaching of the holy gospel,[2]
and confirms it
by the use of the holy sacraments.[3]

[1] John 3:5; 1 Cor. 2:10–14; Eph. 2:8
[2] Rom. 10:17; 1 Pet. 1:23–25
[3] Matt. 28:19–20; 1 Cor. 10:16

66 **Q. What are sacraments?**

A. Sacraments are visible, holy signs and seals.
They were instituted by God so that
by our use of them
he might make us understand more clearly
the promise of the gospel,
and seal that promise.[1]

And this is God's gospel promise:
to grant us forgiveness of sins and eternal life
by grace
because of Christ's one sacrifice
accomplished on the cross.[2]

[1] Gen. 17:11; Deut. 30:6; Rom. 4:11
[2] Matt. 26:27–28; Acts 2:38; Heb. 10:10

67 **Q. Are both the word and the sacraments then**
intended to focus our faith
on the sacrifice of Jesus Christ on the cross
as the only ground of our salvation?

A. Yes!
In the gospel the Holy Spirit teaches us
and by the holy sacraments confirms
that our entire salvation
rests on Christ's one sacrifice for us on the cross.[1]

[1] Rom. 6:3; 1 Cor. 11:26; Gal. 3:27

68 **Q. How many sacraments**
did Christ institute in the New Testament?

A. Two: holy baptism and the holy supper.[1]

[1] Matt. 28:19–20; 1 Cor. 11:23–26

Holy Baptism

LORD'S DAY 26

69 **Q. How does holy baptism**
remind and assure you
that Christ's one sacrifice on the cross
benefits you personally?

A. In this way:
Christ instituted this outward washing[1]
and with it promised that,
as surely as water washes away the dirt from the body,
so certainly his blood and his Spirit
wash away my soul's impurity,
that is, all my sins.[2]

[1] Acts 2:38
[2] Matt. 3:11; Rom. 6:3–10; 1 Pet. 3:21

70 **Q. What does it mean**
to be washed with Christ's blood and Spirit?

A. To be washed with Christ's blood means
that God, by grace, has forgiven our sins
because of Christ's blood
poured out for us in his sacrifice on the cross.[1]

To be washed with Christ's Spirit means
that the Holy Spirit has renewed
and sanctified us to be members of Christ,
so that more and more
we become dead to sin
and live holy and blameless lives.[2]

[1] Zech. 13:1; Eph. 1:7–8; Heb. 12:24; 1 Pet. 1:2; Rev. 1:5
[2] Ezek. 36:25–27; John 3:5–8; Rom. 6:4; 1 Cor. 6:11; Col. 2:11–12

71 **Q. Where does Christ promise**
that we are washed with his blood and Spirit
as surely as we are washed
with the water of baptism?

A. In the institution of baptism, where he says:

"Go therefore and make disciples of all nations,
baptizing them in the name of the Father
and of the Son
and of the Holy Spirit."[1]

"The one who believes and is baptized will be saved;
but the one who does not believe will be condemned."[2]

This promise is repeated when Scripture calls baptism
"the water of rebirth"[3] and
the washing away of sins.[4]

[1] Matt. 28:19
[2] Mark 16:16
[3] Tit. 3:5
[4] Acts 22:16

LORD'S DAY 27

72 Q. Does this outward washing with water itself wash away sins?

A. No, only Jesus Christ's blood and the Holy Spirit cleanse us from all sins.[1]

[1] Matt. 3:11; 1 Pet. 3:21; 1 John 1:7

73 Q. Why then does the Holy Spirit call baptism the water of rebirth and the washing away of sins?

A. God has good reason for these words.
To begin with, God wants to teach us that
the blood and Spirit of Christ take away our sins
just as water removes dirt from the body.[1]

But more important,
God wants to assure us, by this divine pledge and sign,
that we are as truly washed of our sins spiritually
as our bodies are washed with water physically.[2]

[1] 1 Cor. 6:11; Rev. 1:5; 7:14
[2] Acts 2:38; Rom. 6:3–4; Gal. 3:27

74 Q. Should infants also be baptized?

A. Yes.
Infants as well as adults
are included in God's covenant and people,[1]
and they, no less than adults, are promised
deliverance from sin through Christ's blood
and the Holy Spirit who produces faith.[2]

Therefore, by baptism, the sign of the covenant,
they too should be incorporated into the Christian church
and distinguished from the children
of unbelievers.[3]
This was done in the Old Testament by circumcision,[4]
which was replaced in the New Testament by baptism.[5]

[1] Gen. 17:7; Matt. 19:14
[2] Isa. 44:1–3; Acts 2:38–39; 16:31
[3] Acts 10:47; 1 Cor. 7:14
[4] Gen. 17:9–14
[5] Col. 2:11–13

The Holy Supper of Jesus Christ

LORD'S DAY 28

75 **Q. How does the holy supper**
remind and assure you
that you share in
Christ's one sacrifice on the cross
and in all his benefits?

A. In this way:
Christ has commanded me and all believers
to eat this broken bread and to drink this cup
in remembrance of him.
With this command come these promises:[1]

First,
as surely as I see with my eyes
the bread of the Lord broken for me
and the cup shared with me,
so surely
his body was offered and broken for me
and his blood poured out for me
on the cross.

Second,
as surely as
I receive from the hand of the one who serves,
and taste with my mouth
the bread and cup of the Lord,
given me as sure signs of Christ's body and blood,
so surely
he nourishes and refreshes my soul for eternal life
with his crucified body and poured-out blood.

[1] Matt. 26:26–28; Mark 14:22–24; Luke 22:19–20; 1 Cor. 11:23–25

76 Q. What does it mean
to eat the crucified body of Christ
and to drink his poured-out blood?

A. It means
to accept with a believing heart
the entire suffering and death of Christ
and thereby
to receive forgiveness of sins and eternal life.[1]

But it means more.
Through the Holy Spirit, who lives both in Christ and in us,
we are united more and more to Christ's blessed body.[2]
And so, although he is in heaven[3] and we are on earth,
we are flesh of his flesh and bone of his bone.[4]
And we forever live on and are governed by one Spirit,
as the members of our body are by one soul.[5]

[1] John 6:35, 40, 50–54
[2] John 6:55–56; 1 Cor. 12:13
[3] Acts 1:9–11; 1 Cor. 11:26; Col. 3:1
[4] 1 Cor. 6:15–17; Eph. 5:29–30; 1 John 4:13
[5] John 6:56–58; 15:1–6; Eph. 4:15–16; 1 John 3:24

77 **Q. Where does Christ promise**
to nourish and refresh believers
with his body and blood
as surely as
they eat this broken bread
and drink this cup?

A. In the institution of the Lord's Supper:

"The Lord Jesus on the night when he was betrayed
took a loaf of bread, and when he had given thanks,
he broke it and said,
'This is my body that is [broken]* for you.
Do this in remembrance of me.'
In the same way he took the cup also, after supper, saying,
'This cup is the new covenant in my blood.
Do this, as often as you drink it,
in remembrance of me.'
For as often as you eat this bread and drink the cup,
you proclaim the Lord's death
until he comes."[1]

This promise is repeated by Paul in these words:

"The cup of blessing that we bless,
is it not a sharing in the blood of Christ?
The bread that we break,
is it not a sharing in the body of Christ?
Because there is one bread, we who are many are one body,
for we all partake of the one bread."[2]

[1] 1 Cor. 11:23–26
[2] 1 Cor. 10:16–17
*The word "broken" does not appear in the NRSV text, but it was present in the original German of the Heidelberg Catechism.

LORD'S DAY 29

78 Q. Do the bread and wine become the real body and blood of Christ?

A. No.
Just as the water of baptism
is not changed into Christ's blood
and does not itself wash away sins
but is simply a divine sign and assurance[1] of these things,
so too the holy bread of the Lord's Supper
does not become the actual body of Christ,[2]
even though it is called the body of Christ[3]
in keeping with the nature and language of sacraments.[4]

[1] Eph. 5:26; Tit. 3:5
[2] Matt. 26:26–29
[3] 1 Cor. 10:16–17; 11:26–28
[4] Gen. 17:10–11; Ex. 12:11, 13; 1 Cor. 10:1–4

79 Q. Why then does Christ call the bread his body and the cup his blood, or the new covenant in his blood, and Paul use the words, a sharing in Christ's body and blood?

A. Christ has good reason for these words.
He wants to teach us that
just as bread and wine nourish the temporal life,
so too his crucified body and poured-out blood
are the true food and drink of our souls for eternal life.[1]

But more important,
he wants to assure us, by this visible sign and pledge,
that we, through the Holy Spirit's work,
share in his true body and blood
as surely as our mouths
receive these holy signs in his remembrance,[2]
and that all of his suffering and obedience
are as definitely ours
as if we personally
had suffered and made satisfaction for our sins.[3]

[1] John 6:51, 55
[2] 1 Cor. 10:16–17; 11:26
[3] Rom. 6:5–11

LORD'S DAY 30

80* Q. How does the Lord's Supper differ from the Roman Catholic Mass?

A. The Lord's Supper declares to us
that all our sins are completely forgiven
through the one sacrifice of Jesus Christ,
which he himself accomplished on the cross once for all.[1]
It also declares to us
that the Holy Spirit grafts us into Christ,[2]
who with his true body
is now in heaven at the right hand of the Father[3]
where he wants us to worship him.[4]

[But the Mass teaches
that the living and the dead
do not have their sins forgiven
through the suffering of Christ
unless Christ is still offered for them daily by the priests.
It also teaches
that Christ is bodily present
under the form of bread and wine
where Christ is therefore to be worshiped.
Thus the Mass is basically
nothing but a denial
of the one sacrifice and suffering of Jesus Christ
and a condemnable idolatry.]**

[1] John 19:30; Heb. 7:27; 9:12, 25–26; 10:10–18
[2] 1 Cor. 6:17; 10:16–17
[3] Acts 7:55–56; Heb. 1:3; 8:1
[4] Matt. 6:20–21; John 4:21–24; Phil. 3:20; Col. 3:1–3

*Q&A 80 was altogether absent from the first edition of the catechism but was present in a shorter form in the second edition. The translation here given is of the expanded text of the third edition.

**In response to a mandate from Synod 1998, the Christian Reformed Church's Interchurch Relations Committee conducted a study of Q&A 80 and the Roman Catholic Mass. Based on this study, Synod 2004 declared that "Q&A 80 can no longer be held in its current form as part of our confession." Synod 2006 directed that Q&A 80 remain in the CRC's text of the Heidelberg Catechism but that the last three paragraphs be placed in brackets to indicate that they do not accurately reflect the official teaching and practice of today's Roman Catholic Church and are no longer confessionally binding on members of the CRC.

The Reformed Church in America retains the original full text, choosing to recognize that the catechism was written within a historical context which may not accurately describe the Roman Catholic Church's current stance.

81 **Q. Who should come**
to the Lord's table?

A. Those who are displeased with themselves
because of their sins,
but who nevertheless trust
that their sins are pardoned
and that their remaining weakness is covered
by the suffering and death of Christ,
and who also desire more and more
to strengthen their faith
and to lead a better life.

Hypocrites and those who are unrepentant, however,
eat and drink judgment on themselves.[1]

[1] 1 Cor. 10:19–22; 11:26–32

82 **Q. Should those be admitted**
to the Lord's Supper
who show by what they profess and how they live
that they are unbelieving and ungodly?

A. No, that would dishonor God's covenant
and bring down God's wrath upon the entire congregation.[1]
Therefore, according to the instruction of Christ
and his apostles,
the Christian church is duty-bound to exclude such people,
by the official use of the keys of the kingdom,
until they reform their lives.

[1] 1 Cor. 11:17–32; Ps. 50:14–16; Isa. 1:11–17

LORD'S DAY 31

83 **Q. What are the keys of the kingdom?**
A. The preaching of the holy gospel
and Christian discipline toward repentance.
Both of them
open the kingdom of heaven to believers
and close it to unbelievers.[1]

[1] Matt. 16:19; John 20:22–23

84 **Q. How does preaching the holy gospel open and close the kingdom of heaven?**
A. According to the command of Christ:

The kingdom of heaven is opened
by proclaiming and publicly declaring
to all believers, each and every one, that,
as often as they accept the gospel promise in true faith,
God, because of Christ's merit,
truly forgives all their sins.

The kingdom of heaven is closed, however,
by proclaiming and publicly declaring
to unbelievers and hypocrites that,
as long as they do not repent,
the wrath of God and eternal condemnation
rest on them.

God's judgment, both in this life and in the life to come,
is based on this gospel testimony.[1]

[1] Matt. 16:19; John 3:31–36; 20:21–23

85 **Q. How is the kingdom of heaven closed and opened by Christian discipline?**

A. According to the command of Christ:

Those who, though called Christians,
profess unchristian teachings or live unchristian lives,
and who after repeated personal and loving admonitions,
refuse to abandon their errors and evil ways,
and who after being reported to the church, that is,
to those ordained by the church for that purpose,
fail to respond also to the church's admonitions—
such persons the church excludes
from the Christian community
by withholding the sacraments from them,
and God also excludes them from the kingdom of Christ.[1]

Such persons,
when promising and demonstrating genuine reform,
are received again
as members of Christ
and of his church.[2]

[1] Matt. 18:15–20; 1 Cor. 5:3–5, 11–13; 2 Thess. 3:14–15
[2] Luke 15:20–24; 2 Cor. 2:6–11

Part III: Gratitude

LORD'S DAY 32

86 **Q. Since we have been delivered**
from our misery
by grace through Christ
without any merit of our own,
why then should we do good works?

A. Because Christ, having redeemed us by his blood,
is also restoring us by his Spirit into his image,
so that with our whole lives
we may show that we are thankful to God
for his benefits,[1]
so that he may be praised through us,[2]
so that we may be assured of our faith by its fruits,[3]
and so that by our godly living
our neighbors may be won over to Christ.[4]

[1] Rom. 6:13; 12:1–2; 1 Pet. 2:5–10
[2] Matt. 5:16; 1 Cor. 6:19–20
[3] Matt. 7:17–18; Gal. 5:22–24; 2 Pet. 1:10–11
[4] Matt. 5:14–16; Rom. 14:17–19; 1 Pet. 2:12; 3:1–2

87 **Q. Can those be saved**
who do not turn to God
from their ungrateful
and unrepentant ways?

A. By no means.
Scripture tells us that
no unchaste person,
no idolater, adulterer, thief,
no covetous person,
no drunkard, slanderer, robber,
or the like
will inherit the kingdom of God.[1]

[1] 1 Cor. 6:9–10; Gal. 5:19–21; Eph. 5:1–20; 1 John 3:14

LORD'S DAY 33

88 Q. What is involved in genuine repentance or conversion?

A. Two things:
the dying-away of the old self,
and the rising-to-life of the new.[1]

[1] Rom. 6:1–11; 2 Cor. 5:17; Eph. 4:22–24; Col. 3:5–10

89 Q. What is the dying-away of the old self?

A. To be genuinely sorry for sin
and more and more to hate
and run away from it.[1]

[1] Ps. 51:3–4, 17; Joel 2:12–13; Rom. 8:12–13; 2 Cor. 7:10

90 Q. What is the rising-to-life of the new self?

A. Wholehearted joy in God through Christ[1]
and a love and delight to live
according to the will of God
by doing every kind of good work.[2]

[1] Ps. 51:8, 12; Isa. 57:15; Rom. 5:1; 14:17
[2] Rom. 6:10–11; Gal. 2:20

91 Q. What are good works?

A. Only those which
are done out of true faith,[1]
conform to God's law,[2]
and are done for God's glory;[3]
and not those based
on our own opinion
or human tradition.[4]

[1] John 15:5; Heb. 11:6
[2] Lev. 18:4; 1 Sam. 15:22; Eph. 2:10
[3] 1 Cor. 10:31
[4] Deut. 12:32; Isa. 29:13; Ezek. 20:18–19; Matt. 15:7–9

The Ten Commandments

LORD'S DAY 34

92 **Q. What is God's law?**
A. God spoke all these words:

THE FIRST COMMANDMENT
"I am the LORD your God,
who brought you out of the land of Egypt,
out of the house of slavery;
you shall have no other gods before me."

THE SECOND COMMANDMENT
"You shall not make for yourself an idol,
whether in the form of anything that is in heaven above,
or that is on the earth beneath,
or that is in the water under the earth.
You shall not bow down to them or worship them;
for I the LORD your God am a jealous God,
punishing children for the iniquity of parents,
to the third and the fourth generation
of those who reject me,
but showing love to the thousandth generation of those
who love me and keep my commandments."

THE THIRD COMMANDMENT
"You shall not make wrongful use of the name of the LORD
your God,
for the LORD will not acquit anyone
who misuses his name."

THE FOURTH COMMANDMENT

"Remember the sabbath day, and keep it holy.
Six days you shall labor and do all your work.
But the seventh day is a sabbath to the LORD your God;
you shall not do any work—
you, your son or your daughter,
your male or female slave,
your livestock,
or the alien resident in your towns.
For in six days the LORD made
heaven and earth, the sea,
and all that is in them,
but rested the seventh day;
therefore the LORD blessed the sabbath day
and consecrated it."

THE FIFTH COMMANDMENT

"Honor your father and your mother,
so that your days may be long
in the land that the LORD your God is giving to you."

THE SIXTH COMMANDMENT

"You shall not murder."

THE SEVENTH COMMANDMENT

"You shall not commit adultery."

THE EIGHTH COMMANDMENT

"You shall not steal."

THE NINTH COMMANDMENT

"You shall not bear false witness
against your neighbor."

THE TENTH COMMANDMENT

"You shall not covet your neighbor's house;
you shall not covet your neighbor's wife,
or male or female slave,
or ox, or donkey,
or anything that belongs to your neighbor."[1]

[1] Ex. 20:1–17; Deut. 5:6–21

93 **Q. How are these commandments divided?**
A. Into two tables.
The first has four commandments,
teaching us how we ought to live in relation to God.
The second has six commandments,
teaching us what we owe our neighbor.[1]

[1] Matt. 22:37–39

94 **Q. What does the Lord require in the first commandment?**
A. That I, not wanting to endanger my own salvation,
avoid and shun
all idolatry,[1] sorcery, superstitious rites,[2]
and prayer to saints or to other creatures.[3]

That I rightly know the only true God,[4]
trust him alone,[5]
and look to God for every good thing[6]
humbly[7] and patiently,[8]
and love,[9] fear,[10] and honor[11] God
with all my heart.
In short,
that I give up anything
rather than go against God's will in any way.[12]

[1] 1 Cor. 6:9–10; 10:5–14; 1 John 5:21
[2] Lev. 19:31; Deut. 18:9–12
[3] Matt. 4:10; Rev. 19:10; 22:8–9
[4] John 17:3
[5] Jer. 17:5, 7
[6] Ps. 104:27–28; James 1:17
[7] 1 Pet. 5:5–6
[8] Col. 1:11; Heb. 10:36
[9] Matt. 22:37 (Deut. 6:5)
[10] Prov. 9:10; 1 Pet. 1:17
[11] Matt. 4:10 (Deut. 6:13)
[12] Matt. 5:29–30; 10:37–39

95 **Q. What is idolatry?**
A. Idolatry is
having or inventing something in which one trusts
in place of or alongside of the only true God,
who has revealed himself in the Word.[1]

[1] 1 Chron. 16:26; Gal. 4:8–9; Eph. 5:5; Phil. 3:19

LORD'S DAY 35

96 **Q. What is God's will for us**
in the second commandment?

A. That we in no way make any image of God[1]
nor worship him in any other way
than has been commanded in God's Word.[2]

[1] Deut. 4:15–19; Isa. 40:18–25; Acts 17:29; Rom. 1:22–23
[2] Lev. 10:1–7; 1 Sam. 15:22–23; John 4:23–24

97 **Q. May we then not make**
any image at all?

A. God can not and may not
be visibly portrayed in any way.

Although creatures may be portrayed,
yet God forbids making or having such images
if one's intention is to worship them
or to serve God through them.[1]

[1] Ex. 34:13–14, 17; 2 Kings 18:4–5

98 **Q. But may not images be permitted in churches**
in place of books for the unlearned?

A. No, we should not try to be wiser than God.
God wants the Christian community instructed
by the living preaching of his Word—[1]
not by idols that cannot even talk.[2]

[1] Rom. 10:14–15, 17; 2 Tim. 3:16–17; 2 Pet. 1:19
[2] Jer. 10:8; Hab. 2:18–20

LORD'S DAY 36

99 Q. What is the aim of the third commandment?

A. That we neither blaspheme nor misuse the name of God
by cursing,[1] perjury,[2] or unnecessary oaths,[3]
nor share in such horrible sins
by being silent bystanders.[4]

In summary,
we should use the holy name of God
only with reverence and awe,[5]
so that we may properly
confess God,[6]
pray to God,[7]
and glorify God in all our words and works.[8]

[1] Lev. 24:10–17
[2] Lev. 19:12
[3] Matt. 5:37; James 5:12
[4] Lev. 5:1; Prov. 29:24
[5] Ps. 99:1–5; Jer. 4:2
[6] Matt. 10:32–33; Rom. 10:9–10
[7] Ps. 50:14–15; 1 Tim. 2:8
[8] Col. 3:17

100 Q. Is blasphemy of God's name by swearing and cursing really such serious sin that God is angry also with those who do not do all they can to help prevent and forbid it?

A. Yes, indeed.[1]
No sin is greater
or provokes God's wrath more
than blaspheming his name.
That is why God commanded it to be punished with death.[2]

[1] Lev. 5:1
[2] Lev. 24:10–17

LORD'S DAY 37

101 Q. But may we swear an oath in God's name if we do it reverently?

A. Yes, when the government demands it,
or when necessity requires it,
in order to maintain and promote truth and trustworthiness
for God's glory and our neighbor's good.

Such oaths are grounded in God's Word[1]
and were rightly used by the people of God
in the Old and New Testaments.[2]

[1] Deut. 6:13; 10:20; Jer. 4:1–2; Heb. 6:16
[2] Gen. 21:24; Josh. 9:15; 1 Kings 1:29–30; Rom. 1:9; 2 Cor. 1:23

102 Q. May we also swear by saints or other creatures?

A. No.
A legitimate oath means calling upon God
as the only one who knows my heart
to witness to my truthfulness
and to punish me if I swear falsely.[1]
No creature is worthy of such honor.[2]

[1] Rom. 9:1; 2 Cor. 1:23
[2] Matt. 5:34–37; 23:16–22; James 5:12

LORD'S DAY 38

103 Q. What is God's will for you in the fourth commandment?

A. First,

that the gospel ministry and education for it be maintained,[1]
and that, especially on the festive day of rest,
I diligently attend the assembly of God's people[2]
to learn what God's Word teaches,[3]
to participate in the sacraments,[4]
to pray to God publicly,[5]
and to bring Christian offerings for the poor.[6]

Second,

that every day of my life
I rest from my evil ways,
let the Lord work in me through his Spirit,
and so begin in this life
the eternal Sabbath.[7]

[1] Deut. 6:4–9, 20–25; 1 Cor. 9:13–14; 2 Tim. 2:2; 3:13–17; Tit. 1:5
[2] Deut. 12:5–12; Ps. 40:9–10; 68:26; Acts 2:42–47; Heb. 10:23–25
[3] Rom. 10:14–17; 1 Cor. 14:31–32; 1 Tim. 4:13
[4] 1 Cor. 11:23–25
[5] Col. 3:16; 1 Tim. 2:1
[6] Ps. 50:14; 1 Cor. 16:2; 2 Cor. 8 & 9
[7] Isa. 66:23; Heb. 4:9–11

LORD'S DAY 39

104 Q. What is God's will for you in the fifth commandment?

A. That I honor, love, and be loyal
to my father and mother
and all those in authority over me;
that I submit myself with proper obedience
to all their good teaching and discipline;[1]
and also that I be patient with their failings—[2]
for through them God chooses to rule us.[3]

[1] Ex. 21:17; Prov. 1:8; 4:1; Rom. 13:1–2; Eph. 5:21–22; 6:1–9; Col. 3:18– 4:1
[2] Prov. 20:20; 23:22; 1 Pet. 2:18
[3] Matt. 22:21; Rom. 13:1–8; Eph. 6:1–9; Col. 3:18–21

LORD'S DAY 40

105 Q. What is God's will for you in the sixth commandment?

A. I am not to belittle, hate, insult, or kill my neighbor—
not by my thoughts, my words, my look or gesture,
and certainly not by actual deeds—
and I am not to be party to this in others;[1]
rather, I am to put away all desire for revenge.[2]

I am not to harm or recklessly endanger myself either.[3]
Prevention of murder is also why
government is armed with the sword.[4]

[1] Gen. 9:6; Lev. 19:17–18; Matt. 5:21–22; 26:52
[2] Prov. 25:21–22; Matt. 18:35; Rom. 12:19; Eph. 4:26
[3] Matt. 4:7; 26:52; Rom. 13:11–14
[4] Gen. 9:6; Ex. 21:14; Rom. 13:4

106 Q. Does this commandment refer only to murder?

A. By forbidding murder God teaches us
that he hates the root of murder:
envy, hatred, anger, vindictiveness.[1]

In God's sight all such are disguised forms of murder.[2]

[1] Prov. 14:30; Rom. 1:29; 12:19; Gal. 5:19–21; 1 John 2:9–11
[2] 1 John 3:15

107 Q. Is it enough then that we do not murder our neighbor in any such way?

A. No.
By condemning envy, hatred, and anger
God wants us
to love our neighbors as ourselves,[1]
to be patient, peace-loving, gentle,
merciful, and friendly toward them,[2]
to protect them from harm as much as we can,
and to do good even to our enemies.[3]

[1] Matt. 7:12; 22:39; Rom. 12:10
[2] Matt. 5:3–12; Luke 6:36; Rom. 12:10, 18; Gal. 6:1–2; Eph. 4:2; Col. 3:12; 1 Pet. 3:8
[3] Ex. 23:4–5; Matt. 5:44–45; Rom. 12:20–21 (Prov. 25:21–22)

LORD'S DAY 41

108 Q. What does the seventh commandment teach us?

A. That God condemns all unchastity,[1]
and that therefore we should thoroughly detest it[2]
and live decent and chaste lives,[3]
within or outside of the holy state of marriage.

[1] Lev. 18:30; Eph. 5:3–5
[2] Jude 22–23
[3] 1 Cor. 7:1–9; 1 Thess. 4:3–8; Heb. 13:4

109 Q. Does God, in this commandment, forbid only such scandalous sins as adultery?

A. We are temples of the Holy Spirit, body and soul,
and God wants both to be kept clean and holy.
That is why God forbids
all unchaste actions, looks, talk, thoughts, or desires,[1]
and whatever may incite someone to them.[2]

[1] Matt. 5:27–29; 1 Cor. 6:18–20; Eph. 5:3–4
[2] 1 Cor. 15:33; Eph. 5:18

LORD'S DAY 42

110 Q. What does God forbid in the eighth commandment?

A. God forbids not only outright theft and robbery,
punishable by law.[1]

But in God's sight theft also includes
all scheming and swindling
in order to get our neighbor's goods for ourselves,
whether by force or means that appear legitimate,[2]
such as
inaccurate measurements of weight, size, or volume;
fraudulent merchandising;
counterfeit money;
excessive interest;
or any other means forbidden by God.[3]

In addition God forbids all greed[4]
and pointless squandering of his gifts.[5]

[1] Ex. 22:1; 1 Cor. 5:9–10; 6:9–10
[2] Mic. 6:9–11; Luke 3:14; James 5:1–6
[3] Deut. 25:13–16; Ps. 15:5; Prov. 11:1; 12:22; Ezek. 45:9–12; Luke 6:35
[4] Luke 12:15; Eph. 5:5
[5] Prov. 21:20; 23:20–21; Luke 16:10–13

111 Q. What does God require of you in this commandment?

A. That I do whatever I can
for my neighbor's good,
that I treat others
as I would like them to treat me,
and that I work faithfully
so that I may share with those in need.[1]

[1] Isa. 58:5–10; Matt. 7:12; Gal. 6:9–10; Eph. 4:28

LORD'S DAY 43

112 Q. What is the aim of the ninth commandment?

A. That I
never give false testimony against anyone,
twist no one's words,
not gossip or slander,
nor join in condemning anyone
rashly or without a hearing.[1]

Rather, in court and everywhere else,
I should avoid lying and deceit of every kind;
these are the very devices the devil uses,
and they would call down on me God's intense wrath.[2]
I should love the truth,
speak it candidly,
and openly acknowledge it.[3]
And I should do what I can
to guard and advance my neighbor's good name.[4]

[1] Ps. 15; Prov. 19:5; Matt. 7:1; Luke 6:37; Rom. 1:28–32
[2] Lev. 19:11–12; Prov. 12:22; 13:5; John 8:44; Rev. 21:8
[3] 1 Cor. 13:6; Eph. 4:25
[4] 1 Pet. 3:8–9; 4:8

LORD'S DAY 44

113 Q. What is the aim of the tenth commandment?

A. That not even the slightest desire or thought
contrary to any one of God's commandments
should ever arise in our hearts.

Rather, with all our hearts
we should always hate sin
and take pleasure in whatever is right.[1]

[1] Ps. 19:7–14; 139:23–24; Rom. 7:7–8

**114 Q. But can those converted to God
obey these commandments perfectly?**

A. No.
In this life even the holiest
have only a small beginning of this obedience.[1]

Nevertheless, with all seriousness of purpose,
they do begin to live
according to all, not only some,
of God's commandments.[2]

[1] Eccles. 7:20; Rom. 7:14–15; 1 Cor. 13:9; 1 John 1:8–10
[2] Ps. 1:1–2; Rom. 7:22–25; Phil. 3:12–16

115 Q. Since no one in this life
can obey the Ten Commandments perfectly,
why does God want them
preached so pointedly?

A. First, so that the longer we live
the more we may come to know our sinfulness
and the more eagerly look to Christ
for forgiveness of sins and righteousness.[1]

Second, so that
we may never stop striving,
and never stop praying to God for the grace of the Holy Spirit,
to be renewed more and more after God's image,
until after this life we reach our goal:
perfection.[2]

[1] Ps. 32:5; Rom. 3:19–26; 7:7, 24–25; 1 John 1:9
[2] 1 Cor. 9:24; Phil. 3:12–14; 1 John 3:1–3

The Lord's Prayer

LORD'S DAY 45

116 Q. Why do Christians need to pray?
A. Because prayer is the most important part
of the thankfulness God requires of us.[1]
And also because God gives his grace and Holy Spirit
only to those who pray continually and groan inwardly,
asking God for these gifts
and thanking God for them.[2]

[1] Ps. 50:14–15; 116:12–19; 1 Thess. 5:16–18
[2] Matt. 7:7–8; Luke 11:9–13

117 Q. What is the kind of prayer that pleases God and that he listens to?
A. First, we must pray from the heart
to no other than the one true God,
revealed to us in his Word,
asking for everything God has commanded us to ask for.[1]

Second, we must fully recognize our need and misery,
so that we humble ourselves in God's majestic presence.[2]

Third, we must rest on this unshakable foundation:
even though we do not deserve it,
God will surely listen to our prayer
because of Christ our Lord.
That is what God promised us in his Word.[3]

[1] Ps. 145:18–20; John 4:22–24; Rom. 8:26–27; James 1:5; 1 John 5:14–15
[2] 2 Chron. 7:14; Ps. 2:11; 34:18; 62:8; Isa. 66:2; Rev. 4
[3] Dan. 9:17–19; Matt. 7:8; John 14:13–14; 16:23; Rom. 10:13; James 1:6

118 **Q. What did God command us to pray for?**
A. Everything we need, spiritually and physically,[1]
as embraced in the prayer
Christ our Lord himself taught us.

[1] James 1:17; Matt. 6:33

119 **Q. What is this prayer?**
A. Our Father in heaven,
hallowed be your name.
Your kingdom come.
Your will be done,
on earth as it is in heaven.
Give us this day our daily bread.
And forgive us our debts,
as we also have forgiven our debtors.
And do not bring us to the time of trial,
but rescue us from the evil one.*
For the kingdom
and the power
and the glory are yours forever.
Amen.[1]**

[1] Matt. 6:9–13; Luke 11:2–4
*This text of the Lord's Prayer is from the New Revised Standard Version in keeping with the use of the NRSV throughout this edition of the catechism. Most biblical scholars agree that it is an accurate translation of the Greek text and carries virtually the same meaning as the more traditional text of the Lord's Prayer.
**Earlier and better manuscripts of Matthew 6 omit the words "For the kingdom and . . . Amen."

LORD'S DAY 46

120 Q. Why did Christ command us to call God "our Father"?

A. To awaken in us
at the very beginning of our prayer
what should be basic to our prayer—
a childlike reverence and trust
that through Christ God has become our Father,
and that just as our parents do not refuse us
the things of this life,
even less will God our Father refuse to give us
what we ask in faith.[1]

[1] Matt. 7:9–11; Luke 11:11–13

121 Q. Why the words "in heaven"?

A. These words teach us
not to think of God's heavenly majesty
as something earthly,[1]
and to expect everything
needed for body and soul
from God's almighty power.[2]

[1] Jer. 23:23–24; Acts 17:24–25
[2] Matt. 6:25–34; Rom. 8:31–32

LORD'S DAY 47

122 Q. What does the first petition mean?
A. "Hallowed be your name" means:

Help us to truly know you,[1]
to honor, glorify, and praise you
for all your works
and for all that shines forth from them:
your almighty power, wisdom, kindness,
justice, mercy, and truth.[2]

And it means,

Help us to direct all our living—
what we think, say, and do—
so that your name will never be blasphemed because of us
but always honored and praised.[3]

[1] Jer. 9:23–24; 31:33–34; Matt. 16:17; John 17:3
[2] Ex. 34:5–8; Ps. 145; Jer. 32:16–20; Luke 1:46–55, 68–75; Rom. 11:33–36
[3] Ps. 115:1; Matt. 5:16

LORD'S DAY 48

123 Q. What does the second petition mean?

A. "Your kingdom come" means:
Rule us by your Word and Spirit in such a way
that more and more we submit to you.[1]

Preserve your church and make it grow.[2]

Destroy the devil's work;
destroy every force which revolts against you
and every conspiracy against your holy Word.[3]
Do this until your kingdom fully comes,
when you will be
all in all.[4]

[1] Ps. 119:5, 105; 143:10; Matt. 6:33
[2] Ps. 122:6–9; Matt. 16:18; Acts 2:42–47
[3] Rom. 16:20; 1 John 3:8
[4] Rom. 8:22–23; 1 Cor. 15:28; Rev. 22:17, 20

LORD'S DAY 49

124 Q. What does the third petition mean?
A. "Your will be done, on earth as it is in heaven" means:

Help us and all people
to reject our own wills
and to obey your will without any back talk.
Your will alone is good.[1]

Help us one and all to carry out the work we are called to,[2]
as willingly and faithfully as the angels in heaven.[3]

[1] Matt. 7:21; 16:24–26; Luke 22:42; Rom. 12:1–2; Tit. 2:11–12
[2] 1 Cor. 7:17–24; Eph. 6:5–9
[3] Ps. 103:20–21

LORD'S DAY 50

125 Q. What does the fourth petition mean?
A. "Give us this day our daily bread" means:

Do take care of all our physical needs[1]
so that we come to know
that you are the only source of everything good,[2]
and that neither our work and worry
nor your gifts
can do us any good without your blessing.[3]

And so help us to give up our trust in creatures
and trust in you alone.[4]

[1] Ps. 104:27–30; 145:15–16; Matt. 6:25–34
[2] Acts 14:17; 17:25; James 1:17
[3] Deut. 8:3; Ps. 37:16; 127:1–2; 1 Cor. 15:58
[4] Ps. 55:22; 62; 146; Jer. 17:5–8; Heb. 13:5–6

LORD'S DAY 51

126 Q. What does the fifth petition mean?

A. "Forgive us our debts,
as we also have forgiven our debtors" means:

Because of Christ's blood,
do not hold against us, poor sinners that we are,
any of the sins we do
or the evil that constantly clings to us.[1]

Forgive us just as we are fully determined,
as evidence of your grace in us,
to forgive our neighbors.[2]

[1] Ps. 51:1–7; 143:2; Rom. 8:1; 1 John 2:1–2
[2] Matt. 6:14–15; 18:21–35

LORD'S DAY 52

127 Q. What does the sixth petition mean?

A. "And do not bring us to the time of trial,
but rescue us from the evil one" means:

By ourselves we are too weak
to hold our own even for a moment.[1]
And our sworn enemies—
  the devil,[2] the world,[3] and our own flesh—[4]
never stop attacking us.

And so, Lord,
uphold us and make us strong
  with the strength of your Holy Spirit,
so that we may not go down to defeat
  in this spiritual struggle,[5]
but may firmly resist our enemies
  until we finally win the complete victory.[6]

[1] Ps. 103:14–16; John 15:1–5
[2] 2 Cor. 11:14; Eph. 6:10–13; 1 Pet. 5:8
[3] John 15:18–21
[4] Rom. 7:23; Gal. 5:17
[5] Matt. 10:19–20; 26:41; Mark 13:33; Rom. 5:3–5
[6] 1 Cor. 10:13; 1 Thess. 3:13; 5:23

128 Q. What does your conclusion to this prayer mean?

A. "For the kingdom
and the power
and the glory are yours forever" means:

We have made all these petitions of you
because, as our all-powerful king,
  you are both willing and able
  to give us all that is good;[1]
and because your holy name,
  and not we ourselves,
should receive all the praise, forever.[2]

[1] Rom. 10:11–13; 2 Pet. 2:9
[2] Ps. 115:1; John 14:13

129 **Q. What does that little word "Amen" express?**
A. "Amen" means:

This shall truly and surely be!

It is even more sure
that God listens to my prayer
than that I really desire
what I pray for.[1]

[1] Isa. 65:24; 2 Cor. 1:20; 2 Tim. 2:13

NOTES

1. INTRODUCTION

1. "More Than a Memorial," *The Christian Century* 80, no. 7 (February 13, 1963): 198.

2. James I. McCord, "The Heidelberg Catechism: An Ecumenical Confession," *The Princeton Seminary Bulletin* 56, no. 2 (February 1963): 13–14.

3. Shirley C. Guthrie Jr., translator's preface to *Learning Jesus Christ through the Heidelberg Catechism*, by Karl Barth (Grand Rapids: Wm. B. Eerdmans, 1964), 12.

4. Arie F. N. Lekkerkerker, *Gespreken over de Heidelberger* (Wageningen: Zomer & Keunings, 1964), 26.

5. Howard Hageman, "The Lasting Significance of Ursinus," in *Controversy and Conciliation: The Reformation and the Palatinate 1559–1583*, ed. Derk Visser (Allison Park, PA: Pickwick, 1986), 228–30.

6. Barth, *Learning Jesus Christ*, 24–25.

7. Karin Y. Maag, "Early Editions and Translations of the Heidelberg Catechism," in *An Introduction to the Heidelberg Catechism: Sources, History, and Theology*, by Lyle D. Bierma et al., Texts and Studies in Reformation and Post-Reformation Thought, ed. Richard A. Muller (Grand Rapids: Baker Academic, 2005), 103–17, esp. p. 107: "The range of languages into which the Catechism was translated, the speed at which this translation process was done, and the large number of reprints all point to the popularity of the Heidelberg Catechism as a key document in the creation and upholding of Reformed identity."

8. Nicolaas H. Gootjes, *The Belgic Confession: Its History and Sources*, Texts and Studies in Reformation and Post-Reformation Thought, ed. Richard A. Muller (Grand Rapids: Baker Academic, 2007), 148.

9. John W. Nevin, *History and Genius of the Heidelberg Catechism* (Chambersburg, PA.: Publication Office of the German Reformed Church, 1847), 126. Cf. also Friedrich Winter, *Confessio Augustana und Heidelberger Katechismus in vergleichender Betrachtung* (Berlin: Evangelische Verlagsanstalt, 1954), 69; August Lang, *Der Heidelberger Katechismus: Zum 350 jährigen Gedächtnis seiner Entstehung*, Schriften des Vereins für Refomationsgeschichte, no. 113 (Leipzig: Verein für Refomationsgeschichte, 1913), 47: "Durch den Heidelberger Katechismus hat der gesamte refomierte Protestantismus eine Art ökumenisches Symbol erhalten."

10. Recent attempts at classifying the labels that have been applied to the HC's theology can be found in Thorsten Latzel, *Theologische Grundzüge des Heidelberger Katechismus: Eine fundamentaltheologische Untersuchung seines Ansatzes zur Glaubenskommunikation*, vol. 83, Marburger Theologische Studien, ed. Wilfired Härle and Dieter Lührmann, (Marburg: Elwert, 2004), 7n40; and Lyle D. Bierma, "The Sources and Theological Orientation of the Heidelberg Catechism," in Bierma et al., *Introduction to the Heidelberg Catechism*, 76–77.

11. "Wie in der Sakramentslehre, so stimmt der Katechismus auch in allem Uebrigen mit der Gemeinlehre der auswärtigen Reformierten überein und steht mit deren Bekenntnissen in vollem Einklang." Karl Sudhoff, *C. Olevianus und Z. Ursinus: Leben und ausgewählte Schriften*, Leben und ausgewählte Schriften der Väter und Begründer der reformierten Kirche, vol. 8 (Elberfeld: Friderichs, 1857), 118. On perseverance and predestination, see pp. 119–24.

12. A. E. Dahlmann, "The Theology of the Heidelberg Catechism," *The Reformed Church Review*, 4th ser., 17 (April 1913): 176.

13. August Lang, "The Religious and Theological Character of the Heidelberg Catechism," *The Reformed Church Review*, 4th ser., 18 (October 1914): 462.

14. Winter, *Confessio Augustana*, 81.

15. Gustav A. Benrath, "Die Eigenart der pfälzischen Reformation und die Vorgeschichte des Heidelberger Katechismus," *Heidelberger Jahrbuch* 7 (1963): 25.

16. Fred H. Klooster, "The Heidelberg Catechism—An Ecumenical Creed?" *Bulletin of the Evangelical Theological Society* 8, no. 1 (Winter 1965): 30.

17. Fred H. Klooster, *Our Only Comfort: A Comprehensive Commentary on the Heidelberg Catechism*, 2 vols. (Grand Rapids: Faith Alive, 2001), 1:46. See also idem, *A Mighty Comfort: The Christian Faith according to the Heidelberg Catechism* (Grand Rapids: CRC Publications, 1990), 35–37.

18. Maurits Gooszen, *De Heidelbergsche Catechismus: textus receptus met toelichtenden teksten* ("Inleiding") (Leiden: Brill, 1890), x, 149–50, 155–56; idem, *De Heidelbergsche Catechismus en het boekje van de breking des broods, in het jaar 1563–1564 bestreden en verdedigd* (Leiden: Brill, 1892), 276, 331–32, 401, 406, 408–9, 411.

19. G. P. Hartvelt, *Alles in Hem*, vol. 1 of *Nieuwe Commentaar Heidelbergse Catechismus* (Aalten: Graafschap, 1966), 17–18.

20. Joachim Staedtke, "Entstehung und Bedeutung des Heidelberger Katechismus," in *Warum Wirst Du Ein Christ Genannt?*, ed. Walter Herrenbrück and Udo Smidt (Neukirchen Vluyn: Neukirchener Verlag des Erziehungsvereins, 1965), 15–18; Walter Hollweg, *Heinrich Bullingers Hausbuch: Eine Untersuchung über die Anfänge der reformierten Predigtliteratur*, Beiträge zur Geschichte und Lehre der Reformierten Kirche, vol. 8 (Neukirchen: Verlag der Buchhandlung des Erziehungsvereins, 1956), 238–41.

21. Johannes H. A. Ebrard, *Das Dogma vom heiligen Abendmahl und seine Geschichte*, 2 vols. (Frankfurt: Zimmer, 1846), 2:596–606.

22. Nevin, *History and Genius*, 143.

23. John W. Nevin, introduction to *The Commentary of Dr. Zacharias Ursinus on the Heidelberg Catechism*, trans. G. W. Williard (Grand Rapids: Wm. B. Eerdmans, 1954), xvi.

24. Philip Schaff, "Geschichte, Geist und Bedeutung des Heidelberger Katechismus: Ein Beitrag zur dreihundertjährigen Jubilfeier," *Zeitschrift für die historische Theologie* 3 (1864): 328, quoted in Bard Thompson et al., *Essays on the Heidelberg Catechism* (Philadelphia: United Church Press, 1963), 91–92.

25. Bard Thompson, "Reformed Liturgies: An Historical and Doctrinal Interpretation of the Palatinate Liturgy of 1563, Mercersburg Provisional Liturgy of 1858, Evangelical and Reformed Order of 1944, and Their Sources" (B.D. thesis, Union Theological Seminary [New York], 1949), 7–8. See also p. 1n2.

26. J. F. Gerhard Goeters, "Christologie und Rechtfertigung nach dem Heidelberger Katechismus," in *Das Kreuz Jesu Christi als Grund des Heils*, ed. Ernst Bizer (Gütersloh: Mohn, 1967), 34. See also Benno Gassmann, *Ecclesia Reformata: Die*

Kirche in den reformierten Bekenntnisschriften (Freiburg: Herder, 1968), 239: "Wenn auch der direkte, quellenmässig aufweisbare Einfluss Melanchthons auf die Formulierungen des Katechismus minimum ist, ist doch die Theologie von seiner, ja von deutsch-lutherischen Stimmung allgemein, getragen. Sie is daher nicht mit dem Calvinismus identisch."

27. Eberhard Busch, *Drawn to Freedom: Christian Faith Today in Conversation with the Heidelberg Catechism*, trans. William H. Rader (Grand Rapids: Wm. B. Eerdmans, 2010), 14.

28. "[The HC] hat lutherische Innigkeit, melanchthonische Klarheit, zwinglische Einfachheit, und calvinsches Feuer in Eins verschmolzen." *Realencyclopädie für protestantische Theologie und Kirche*, 2nd ed., s.v. "Katechismus, Heidelberger oder Pfälzer," quoted in Wilhelm Neuser, "Die Väter des Heidelberger Katechismus," *Theologische Zeitschrift* 35 (1979): 180.

29. Staedtke, "Entstehung und Bedeutung," 15.

30. Neuser, "Väter des Heidelberger Katechismus,"181–87.

31. Jan Rohls, *Reformed Confessions: Theology from Zurich to Barmen*, trans. John Hoffmeyer, Columbia Series in Reformed Theology (Louisville, KY: Westminster John Knox Press, 1997), 20.

32. Ulrich Hutter, "Zacharias Ursinus und der Heidelberger Katechismus," in *Martin Luther und die Reformation in Ostdeutschland und Sudosteuropa: Wirkungen und Wechselwirkungen*, ed. Ulrich Hutter and Hans-Günther Parplies, Beihefte zum Jahrbuch für Schlesische Kirchengeschichte 8 (Sigmaringen: Jan Thorbecke, 1991), 96–98. Hutter claims, for example, that "der Heidelberger Katechismus ist eine Verbindung melanchthonischer Lehrformeln mit der calvinischen Lehrweise," 97.

33. Willem Verboom, *De Theologie van de Heidelbergse Catechismus* (Zoetermeer: Boekencentrum, 1996), 24–25.

34. August Lang, ed., *Der Heidelberger Katechismus und vier verwandte Katechismen* (Leipzig: Deichert, 1907), CIII. See also idem., *Heidelberger Katechismus: Zum 350 jährigen Gedächtnis*, 46–47.

35. Winter, *Confessio Augustana*, 70, 81.

36. Benrath, "Eigenart der pfälzischen Reformation," 25.

37. For a concise overview of the history of the Palatinate before and during the Protestant Reformation, see Charles D. Gunnoe Jr., "The Reformation of the Palatinate and the Origins of the Heidelberg Catechism, 1500–1562," in Bierma et al., *Introduction to the Heidelberg Catechism*, 15–47.

38. Ibid., 20.

39. For the details of Melanchthon's life, see Clyde L. Manschreck, *Melanchthon: The Quiet Reformer* (New York: Abingdon Press, 1958), and Robert Stupperich, *Melanchthon*, trans. Robert H. Fischer (London: Lutterworth, 1965).

40. Gunnoe, "Reformation of the Palatinate," 34–35.

41. Fred H. Klooster, "The Heidelberg Catechism: Origin and History" (photocopied manuscript, Calvin Theological Seminary, 1982), 60–61.

42. Benrath, "Eigenart der pfälzischen Reformation," 16. See also Gunnoe, "Reformation of the Palatinate," 36–37, and Christa Boerke, "The People behind the Heidelberg Catechism," in *The Church's Book of Comfort*, ed. Willem van 't Spijker, trans. Gerrit Bilkes (Grand Rapids: Reformation Heritage Books, 2009), 74–88.

43. For the first hypothesis, see Ruth Wesel-Roth, *Thomas Erastus* (Lahr: Schauenberg, 1954), 17. For the second, see Derk Visser, *Zacharias Ursinus, the Reluctant Reformer: His Life and Times* (New York: United Church Press, 1983), 103–4.

44. Gunnoe, "Reformation of the Palatinate," 36.

45. For Boquinus as a Calvinist, see Boerke, "People behind the Heidelberg Catechism," 74; for Boquinus as a Bullingerian, see Hartvelt, *Alles in Hem*, 17–18.

46. Gunnoe, "Reformation of the Palatinate," 37. See also James I. Good, *The Origin of the Reformed Church in Germany* (Reading, PA: Daniel Miller, 1887), 128, 134; idem, *The Heidelberg Catechism in Its Newest Light* (Philadelphia: Publication and Sunday School Board of the Reformed Church in the United States, 1914), 133; Klooster, "Heidelberg Catechism: Origin and History," 83, 104; Walter Henss, *Der Heidelberger Katechismus im konfessionspolitischen Kräftespiel seiner Frühzeit* (Zurich: Theologischer Verlag, 1983), 8–11; Visser, *Zacharias Ursinus*, 1; and Christopher J. Burchill, "On the Consolation of a Christian Scholar: Zacharias Ursinus (1534–83) and the Reformation in Heidelberg," *Journal of Ecclesiastical History* 37, no. 4 (1986): 569.

47. For an overview of the Heshusius-Klebitz controversy, see Klooster, "Heidelberg Catechism: Origin and History," 84–92, and Gunnoe, "Reformation of the Palatinate," 37–40.

48. Bard Thompson, "Historical Background of the Catechism," in *Essays on the Heidelberg Catechism*, by Bard Thompson et al. (Philadelphia: United Church Press, 1963), 29–30.

49. Gunnoe, "Reformation of the Palatinate," 47.

50. Ibid., 40–44.

51. Ibid., 44–46; Boerke, "People behind the Heidelberg Catechism," 67–74, 76–78, 85–86.

52. Quoted in George W. Richards, *The Heidelberg Catechism: Historical and Doctrinal Studies* (Philadelphia: Publication and Sunday School Board of the Reformed Church in the United States, 1913), 193, 195. On pp. 182–99 Richards provides a facsimile of the German text of the preface and an English translation on the facing pages. The German text can also be found in Lang, *Heidelberger Katechismus und vier verwandte Katechismen*, 2–4.

53. Gerrit den Hartogh, *Voorzienigheid in donker licht: Herkomst en gebruik van het begrip 'Providentia Dei' in de reformatorische theologie, in het bijzonder bij Zacharias Ursinus* (Heerenveen: Groen, 1999), 31; Boerke, "People behind the Heidelberg Catechism," 78–83.

54. J. F. Gerhard Goeters, "Caspar Olevianus als Theologe," *Monatshefte für Evangelische Kirchengeschichte des Rheinlandes* 37–38 (1988—89): 303; Boerke, "People behind the Catechism," 83–88.

55. Lyle D. Bierma, "The Purpose and Authorship of the Heidelberg Catechism," in Bierma et al., *Introduction to the Heidelberg Catechism*, 71–74.

56. Detailed biographical information on Ursinus can be found in Sudhoff, *C. Olevianus und Z. Ursinus*; Good, *Heidelberg Catechism*; G. Bouwmeester, *Zacharias Ursinus en de Heidelbergse Catechismus* (The Hague: Willem de Zwijgerstichting, 1954); Erdmann Sturm, *Der junge Zacharias Ursinus: Sein Weg vom Philippismus zum Calvinismus* (Neukirchen-Vluyn: Neukirchener Verlag, 1972); and Visser, *Reluctant Reformer*.

57. Letter to Crato (January 10, 1557), quoted in translation in Good, *Heidelberg Catechism*, 246. The original text of the entire letter is in Wilhelm Becker, "Zacharias Ursins Briefe an Crato von Crafftheim," *Theologische Arbeiten aus dem rheinischen wissenschaftlichen Prediger-Verein* 12 (1892): 46–50. A month later, Ursinus wrote that "when Philip has spoken, I cannot and dare not think otherwise." Letter to Crato (February 27, 1557), in Becker, "Ursins Briefe," 58.

58. Zacharias Ursinus, "Theses complectentes breviter et perspicue summam verae Doctrinae de Sacramentis," in *Zachariae Ursini . . . volumen tractationum theologicarum*, 2 vols. (Neustadt: Harnisch, 1584), 1:339–82.

59. According to Sudhoff (*C. Olevianus und Z. Ursinus*, 5), Melanchthon's reaction was reported in a letter Ursinus received from his friend Ferinarius.

60. Richards, *Heidelberg Catechism*, 28, 133; Good, *Heidelberg Catechism*, 45; Sturm, *Zacharias Ursinus*, 1–3; Richard A. Muller, *Christ and the Decree: Christology and Predestination in Reformed Theology from Calvin to Perkins* (Durham, NC: Labyrinth, 1986), 124. Burchill goes so far as to say that Melanchthon "remained a dominant influence throughout [Ursinus's] career," "Consolation of a Christian Scholar," 580.

61. Heinrich Alting, *Historia ecclesiae Palatinae* (1644), in *Monumenta pietatis & literaria virorum in republica & literaria illustrium, selecta*, ed. Ludwig Christian Mieg and Daniel Nebel (Frankfurt: Maximillian, 1701), 130, quoted in Benrath, "Eigenart der pfälzischen Reformation," 14.

2. THEME AND STRUCTURE OF THE HEIDELBERG CATECHISM

1. All quotations from the Heidelberg Catechism are taken from the recently revised and adopted CRC-RCA-PC(USA) translation found in the appendix at the back of this book. To save space, in-text quotations have been changed from verse form to paragraph form.

2. Here I take a slightly different approach than I did in "What Hath Wittenberg to Do with Heidelberg? Philip Melanchthon and the Heidelberg Catechism," in *Melanchthon in Europe: His Work and Influence beyond Wittenberg*, ed. Karin Maag, Studies and Texts in Reformation and Post-Reformation Thought, ed. Richard A. Muller (Grand Rapids: Baker, 1999), 103–21. There my argument was that the actual sources that the authors of the HC drew from for the theme and structure of the catechism were not necessarily Melanchthonian; here it is that the theme and threefold structure have their earliest and broadest expression in the Lutheran tradition.

3. Italics added in all four quotations.

4. Klooster, *Our Only Comfort*, 1:34. On the meaning of the term *comfort* in the HC, see also Latzel, *Theologische Grundzüge*, 44–49.

5. See, e.g., Gooszen, *Heidelbergsche Catechismus* ("Catechismus"), 1–241; Lang, *Heidelberger Katechismus und vier verwandte Katechismen*, I–CIV; Bard Thompson, "The Palatinate Church Order of 1563," *Church History* 23, no. 4 (1954): 347.

6. For a detailed textual comparison of the HC with Ursinus's SC and LC, see Lang, *Heidelberger Katechismus und vier verwandte Katechismen*, LXXXVII–XCVI.

7. Zacharias Ursinus, "The Smaller Catechism," trans. Lyle D. Bierma, in Bierma et al., *Introduction to the Heidelberg Catechism*, 141. The Latin text on which this English translation is based, "Catechesis minor, perspicua brevitate christianam fidem complectens," is found in Lang, *Heidelberger Katechismus und vier verwandte Katechismen*, 200–218.

8. Zacharias Ursinus, "The Larger Catechism," trans. Lyle D. Bierma, in Bierma et al., *Introduction to the Heidelberg Catechism*, 163. The Latin text on which this English translation is based can be found in Lang, *Heidelberger Katechismus und vier verwandte Katechismen*, 152–99.

9. These counterparts are SC 38, 39, 43, and 44, respectively.

10. E.g., Goeters, "Christologie und Rechtfertigung," 34; Neuser, "Väter des Heidelberger Katechismus," 181–82.

11. Martin Luther, "The Small Catechism," in *The Book of Concord: The Confessions of the Evangelical Lutheran Church*, ed. Robert Kolb and Timothy J. Wengert, trans. Charles Arand et al. (Minneapolis: Fortress Press, 2000), 355. The German text is found in *Die Bekenntnisschriften der evangelisch-lutherischen Kirche*, 4th ed. (Göttingen: Vandenhoeck & Ruprecht, 1959), 511.

12. "Was ist dein Trost für [vor] aller Welt auff Erden?" Joachim Mörlin, "Der Katechismus des Joachim W[M]örlin von 1547 resp. 1566," in *Quellen zur Geschichte des kirchlichen Unterrichts in der evangelischen Kirche Deutschlands zwischen 1530 und 1600*, ed. Johann M. Reu, pt. 1, *Quellen zur Geschichte des Katechismusunterrichts*, vol. 3, *Ost-, Nord-, und Westdeutsche Katechismen*, sec. 2, bk. 2, *Texte* (1920; reprint, Hildesheim: Olms, 1976), 860. For references to the parallel between this question and HC Q 1, see Sturm, *Zacharias Ursinus*, 249, and Latzel, *Theologische Grundzüge*, 44n8.

13. For the actual opening question of the 1547 edition, see Mörlin, "Katechismus" 860n2.

14. Sturm, *Zacharias Ursinus*, 249; Latzel, *Theologische Grundzüge*, 24.

15. The Latin text of the AC uses the noun *consolatio* and verb *consolare*, which the 2000 English edition of the *Book of Concord* usually translates as "consolation" and "console," respectively. The German text of the AC uses the noun *Trost* and verb *trösten*, both of which the 2000 English edition of the *Book of Concord* translates as "comfort," and the adjective *tröstlich*, which is translated as "comforting." We will be quoting the translation of the German text. It is worth noting that the HC uses these very same terms for *comfort* in both its German and Latin versions.

16. Philip Melanchthon, "The Augsburg Confession [German text]," in *The Book of Concord: The Confessions of the Evangelical Lutheran Church*, ed. Robert Kolb and Timothy J. Wengert (Minneapolis: Fortress Press, 2000), 38 (italics added).

17. Ibid., 44 (italics added).

18. Ibid., 54 (italics added).

19. Ibid., 68 (italics added).

20. Ibid., 72 (italics added).

21. Ibid., 76 (italics added).

22. Arie de Reuver, "De Augsburgse Confessie en de Heidelbergse Catechismus—een kritische vergelijking," *Theologia Reformata* 49, no. 4 (2006): 349. Cf. also ibid., 361: "In de onvolprezen openingszin van Zondag 1 is niet alleen de spiritualiteit van Heidelberg vertolkt maar even zeer die van Augsburg."

23. Walter Hollweg, "Zur Quellenfrage des Heidelberger Katechismus," in *Neue Untersuchungen zur Geschichte und Lehre des Heidelberger Katechismus: Zweite Folge*, Beiträge zur Geschichte und Lehre der Reformierten Kirche, ed. Hannelore Erhart et al., vol. 28 (Neukirchen-Vluyn: Neukirchener Verlag, 1968), 43–47.

24. Sturm, *Zacharias Ursinus*, 249. In n16, Sturm mentions only "mehr als vierzig Stellen" where comfort is found. I found at least fifty-one.

25. Philip Melanchthon, "Examen ordinandorum 1552," in *Melanchthons Werke in Auswahl*, ed. Robert Stupperich, vol. 6, *Bekenntnisse und kleine Lehrschriften*, ed. Robert Stupperich (Gütersloh: Bertesmann, 1955), 185 (italics added).

26. Ibid., 192, 198, 217, 179 (italics added).

27. Ibid., 187 (italics added).

28. Ibid., 189 (italics added).

29. Ibid., 213 (italics added).

30. Ibid., 193 (italics added).

31. "In its central alignment on the soteriological question of the 'only comfort' [the HC] actually stood closer to Melanchthon than to the theologians in Zurich and Geneva." Busch, *Drawn to Freedom*, 14. See also Goeters, "Christologie und Rechtfertigung," 34.

32. See, e.g., Good, *Heidelberg Catechism*, 63–64.

33. Johannes à Lasco, *De catechismus, oft kinder leere, diemen te Londen, in de Duytsche ghemeynte, is ghebruyckende*, trans. [into Dutch] Jan Utenhove (London: Steven Myerdman, 1551), 45r-46v, http://eebo.chadwyck.com (italics added).

34. Marten Micronius, "Een corte undersouckinghe des gheloofs (1553) in der Fassung von 1555," ed. J. Marius J. Lange van Ravenswaay, in *Reformierte Bekenntnisschriften*, ed. Heiner Faulenbach, vol. 1/3, *1550–1558*, ed. Judith Becker et al. (Neukirchen-Vluyn: Neukirchener Verlag, 2007), 281.

35. Micronius, "Corte undersouckinghe," 288, 291.

36. Johannes à Lasco, "Der Kleine Emder Katechismus (1554) in der Fassung von 1579," ed. Alfred Rauhaus, in *Reformierte Bekenntnisschriften*, ed. Heiner Faulenbach, vol. 1/3, *1550–1558*, ed. Judith Becker et al. (Neukirchen-Vluyn: Neukirchener Verlag, 2007), 305. For the suggestion of this answer as a source for HC 1, see Sudhoff, *C. Olevianus und Z. Ursinus*, 89–90.

37. Lasco, "Kleine Emder Katechismus," 310.

38. Latzel, *Theologische Grundzüge*, 44n8.

39. Lang, *Heidelberger Katechismus und vier verwandte Katechismen*, LXXX.

40. Martin Luther, "Eine kurze Form der zehn Gebote, eine kurze Form des Glaubens, eine kurze Form des Vaterunsers. 1520," in *D. Martin Luthers Werke: Kritische Gesammtausgabe*, vol. 7 (1897; reprint, Graz: Akademische Druck- und Verlagsanstalt, 1966), 204–5. The material quoted here can also be found verbatim in Luther's "Betbüchlein. 1522," in *D. Martin Luthers Werke: Kritische Gesammtausgabe*, vol. 10, bk. 2 (1907; reprint, Graz: Akademische Druck- und Verlagsanstalt, 1966), 376–77. I have largely followed the English translation in "Personal Prayer Book, 1522," trans. Martin H. Bertram, in *Luther's Works*, ed. Helmut T. Lehmann, vol. 43, *Devotional Writings II*, ed. Gustav K. Wiencke (Philadelphia: Fortress Press, 1968), 15–16, but I have made some alterations based on the German text.

41. Lang, *Heidelberger Katechismus und vier verwandte Katechismen*, LXXX, CI.

42. Gooszen, *Heidelbergsche Catechismus* (Inleiding), 75.

43. Philip Melanchthon, "Loci Communes Theologici [1521]," trans. Lowell J. Satre, in *Melanchthon and Bucer*, ed. Wilhelm Pauck, Library of Christian Classics, vol. 19 (Philadelphia: Westminster, 1969), 18–152. The original text can be found in "Loci theologici [1521]," in *CR*, vols. 1–28, *Philippi Melanthonis opera quae supersunt omnia*, vol. 21, ed. C. G. Bretschneider and H. E. Bindseil (1854; reprint, New York: Johnson Reprint Corporation, 1963).

44. Timothy J. Wengert, "Philip Melanchthon's 1522 Annotations on Romans and the Lutheran Origins of Rhetorical Criticism," in *Biblical Interpretation in the Era of the Reformation: Essays Presented to David C. Steinmetz in Honor of His Sixtieth Birthday*, ed. Richard A. Muller and John L. Thompson (Grand Rapids: Wm. B. Eerdmans, 1996), 131.

45. "Ein Kurtze Ordenliche summa der rechten Waren Lehre unsers heyligen Christlichen Glaubens [1554 ed.]," in *Quellen zur Geschichte des kirchlichen Unterrichts in der evangelischen Kirche Deutschlands zwischen 1530 und 1600*, ed. Johann M. Reu, pt. 1, *Quellen zur Geschichte des Katechismus-Unterrichts*, vol. 1, *Süddeutsche Katechismen* (1904; reprint, Hildesheim: Olms, 1976), 720–34.

46. Johann M. Reu, ed., *Quellen zur Geschichte des kirchlichen Unterrichts in der evangelischen Kirche Deutschlands zwischen 1530 und 1600*, pt. 1, *Quellen zur Geschichte des Katechismus-Unterrichts*, vol. 1, *Süddeutsche Katechismen* (1904; reprint, Hildesheim: Olms, 1976), 198–99.

47. "Kurtze Ordenliche summa," 721, 724, 731.

48. Ibid., 724, 731.

49. Ibid., 734.

50. Reu, *Quellen*, 1/1:202–3.

51. Walter Hollweg, "Die Beiden Konfessionen Theodore von Bezas: Zwei bisher unbeachtete Quellen zum Heidelberger Katechismus," in *Neue Untersuchungen zur Geschichte und Lehre des Heidelberger Katechismus*, Beiträge zur Geschichte und Lehre der Reformierten Kirche, ed. Paul Jacobs et al., vol. 13 (Neukirchen: Neukirchener Verlag, 1961)," 86–123; idem, "Quellenfrage," 38–47.

52. Hollweg, "Beiden Konfessionen," 87–88.

53. Ibid., 88–94; Hollweg, "Quellenfrage," 39–41.

54. Hollweg, "Beide Konfessionen," 96–98. The text of the 1562 German translation of Beza's "Second Brief Confession" is appended to Hollweg's essay, 111–23 (arts. 17–21, pp. 116–18).

55. Hollweg, "Beiden Konfessionen," 98–105.

56. Mörlin, "Katechismus," 861–62.

57. One might make the same point about Calvin's first catechism (French, 1537; Latin, 1538), where Calvin moves in a general way from sin and the law, to the gospel and faith, to a life of obedience and prayer (see I. John Hesselink, *Calvin's First Catechism: A Commentary*, Columbia Series in Reformed Theology [Louisville, KY: Westminster John Knox Press, 1997], 8–33). But Calvin, too, never makes such a structure transparent and never connects it to gratitude.

58. Latzel, *Theologische Grundzüge*, 97.

59. "Kirchenordnung . . . [vom 15. November 1563]," in Emil Sehling, ed., *Die evangelischen Kirchenordnungen des XVI. Jahrhunderts*, vol. 14, *Kurpfalz* (Tübingen: Mohr, 1957), 337.

60. Ursinus, *The Commentary of Dr. Zacharias Ursinus on the Heidelberg Catechism*, trans. G. W. Williard (Grand Rapids: Wm. B. Eerdmans, 1954), 21.

61. Christoph Weismann, *Eine Kleine Biblia: Die Katechismen von Luther und Brenz* (Stuttgart: Calwer, 1985), 114.

62. Timothy J. Wengert, *Law and Gospel: Philip Melanchthon's Debate with John Agricola of Eisleben over Poenitentia*, Texts and Studies in Reformation and Post-Reformation Thought, ed. Richard A. Muller (Grand Rapids: Baker, 1997), 144–45.

63. Melanchthon, "Augsburg Confession [German text]," 44.

64. Melanchthon, "Die Augsburgische Konfession [German text]," in *BSLK*, 83.

65. Melanchthon, "Apology of the Augsburg Confession" in *The Book of Concord: The Confessions of the Evangelical Lutheran Church*, ed. Robert Kolb and Timothy J. Wengert, trans. Charles Arand et al. (Minneapolis: Fortress Press, 2000), 191–92. See also p. 194.

66. Christoph Weismann, *Die Katechismen des Johannes Brenz*, vol. 1, *Die Entstehungs-, Text-, und Wirkungsgeschichte*, Spätmittelalter und Reformation Texte und Untersuchungen, ed. Heiko A. Oberman, vol. 21 (Berlin: Walter de Gruyter, 1990), 596n98.

67. "Die Brandenburg-Nürnbergische Kirchenordnung (1533)" ed. Jürgen Lorz and Gottfried Seebass, in *Andreas Osiander d. Ä. Gesamtausgabe*, ed. Gerhard Müller, vol. 5, *Schriften und Briefe 1533 bis 1534*, ed. Gerhard Müller and Gottfried Seebass (Gütersloh: Mohn, 1983), 125.

68. Ibid., 127.

3. LAW AND GOSPEL

1. Verboom, *Theologie van de Heidelbergse Catechismus*, 251.

2. For a summary of Luther's view of law and gospel, see Philip S. Watson, *Let God be God! An Interpretation of the Theology of Martin Luther* (Philadelphia: Muhlenberg, 1950), 152–60, and Paul Althaus, *The Theology of Martin Luther*, trans. Robert C. Schultz (Philadelphia: Fortress Press, 1966), 251–73.

3. For a summary of Calvin's view of law and gospel, see Andrew J. Bandstra, "Law and Gospel in Calvin and Paul," in *Exploring the Heritage of John Calvin*, ed. David E. Holwerda (Grand Rapids: Baker, 1976), 11–39.

4. Note Hutter's comment that "die melanchthonische Reihenfolge von Gesetz und Evangelium wird mit calvinischem Inhalt gefüllt." "Ursinus und der Heidelberger Katechismus," 96.

5. Hollweg, "Beiden Konfessionen," 100–101.

6. My translation is based on the sixteenth-century German translation, Theodore Beza, "Kurtze Bekanntnuss des Christlichen glaubens" (Heidelberg: Ludwig Lück, 1562), in Hollweg, "Beiden Konfessionen," 111.

7. Ibid., 112.

8. Ibid., 111–12

9. Ibid., 112.

10. Ibid.

11. Ibid.

12. Ibid., 112–13.

13. Cornelis Graafland, *Van Calvijn tot Comrie: Oorsprong en ontwikkeling van de leer van het verbond in het Gereformeerd Protestantisme* (Zoetermeer: Boekcentrum, 1994), 2:19.

14. Ibid., 2:20.

15. "Kennzeichen des calvinischen Gesetzesverständnis ist, dass das Gesetz und das Evangelium die gnädige Gerechtigkeit Gottes aussagen—das Evangelium klarer als das Gesetz. Sündenerkenntnis kann auch am Evangelium entstehen." Neuser, "Väter des Heidelberger Katechismus," 189.

16. Note Klooster's comment that "Q&A's 12–14 are so closely linked to the catechism's discussion on misery that it's not immediately clear that the discussion on deliverance has begun." Klooster, *Our Only Comfort*, 1:143.

17. Goeters, "Christologie und Rechtfertigung," 38. Ursinus himself used similar terminology in his lectures on the HC: *Commentary of Dr. Zacharias Ursinus*, 77.

18. Goeters, "Christologie und Rechtfertigung," 38.

19. "Bemerkenswert ist dabei, dass ganz im Gegensatz zu dem namentlich in der lutherischen Theologie üblichen Reden von Gesetz und Evangelium im Sinne einer Scheidung zwischen Altem und Neuem Testament hier [in HC 19] das Evangelium, also die gute Botschaft Gottes, bereits als zentraler Gehalt des Alten Testaments, und zwar von der Paradiesszene an, betrachtet wird." Lothar Coenen, "Wort Gottes und Heiliger Geist," in *Handbuch zum Heidelberger Katechismus*, ed. Lothar Coenen (Neukirchen-Vluyn: Neukirchener Verlag, 1963), 86.

20. There is a passage in Melanchthon's "Examen" that sounds very much like HC 19, but Melanchthon does not identify Christ's preaching in the Old Testament as "gospel," nor does he make any mention of the foreshadowing of the gospel by the "law": "Die erste Predigt im Paradis, die der Son Gottes selb gethan hat, strafft erstlich die sünd in Adam und Heva seer schrecklich. Darnach gibt er jnen Trost und offenbart die wunderbarliche heimligkeit von der Erlösung der Menschen und vergebung der Sünden durch den künfftigen Samen, der der Schlangen den kopff zertretten würde . . . . Diese Predigt wird fur und fur in den Propheten erholet. Und wie der Son Gottes selbs im Paradis und ernach in den Propheten gepredigt, also spricht er auch da er sichtiglich im Ampt gewesen ist." "Examen ordinandorum 1552," 206–7.

21. Neuser, "Väter des Heidelberger Katechismus," 189–90. Neuser's claim that HC 4 suggests a Calvinistic approach to law and gospel had also been made earlier by Heinrich Graffmann, *Unterricht nach im Heidelberger Katechismus* (Neukirchen: Buchhandlung des Erziehungsvereins, 1951), 3:657. It should also be noted that Neuser regards the SC as a committee project and not the work of Ursinus alone ("Die Erwählungslehre im Heidelberger Katechismus," *Zeitschrift für Kirchengeschichte* 75 [1964]: 311).

22. Neuser, "Väter des Heidelberger Katechismus," 189.

23. Ursinus confirms this in his lectures on the HC: "The Decalogue belongs to the first part, in as far as it is the mirror through which we are brought to see ourselves, and thus led to a knowledge of our sins and misery, and to the third part in as far as it is the rule of true thankfulness and of a Christian life." *Commentary of Dr. Zacharias Ursinus*, 14.

24. Neuser, "Väter des Heidelberger Katechismus," 189.

25. Ludwig Couard, *Der Heidelberger Katechismus und sein Verhältnis zum kleinen lutherischen* (Gütersloh: Bertelsmann, 1904), 44. Goeters, too, argues that in the HC's doctrine of reconciliation through Christ the Mediator (HC 12–18) "hat der ehemalige Melanchthonschüler Ursinus offenkundig dem spätmelanchthonischen Synergismus zu entgehen versucht." "Christologie und Rechtfertigung," 47.

26. For a brief summary of the Lutheran synergistic controversy, see *Evangelical Dictionary of Theology*, 2nd. ed., s.v. "Synergism," by C. G. Fry (Grand Rapids: Baker, 1984).

27. ". . . bestimmten, aber doch schonenden und unanstösslichen Weise," Courard, *Heidelberger Katechismus*, 44.

28. De Reuver ("Augsburgse Confessie," 349–50) points out that HC 5–8 are doctrinally very consistent with AC art. 2 on original sin, except for the latter's reference to baptism. Art. 2 reads in part, "From birth [fallen human beings] are full of evil lust and inclination and cannot by nature possess true fear of God and true faith in God. Moreover, this same innate disease and original sin is truly sin and condemns to God's eternal wrath all who are not in turn born anew through

baptism and the Holy Spirit." Melanchthon, "The Augsburg Confession [German text]," 38.

29. Goeters, "Christologie und Rechtfertigung," 40–42. For more on Melanchthon's rejection of ubiquitarianism, see below, chapter 5, pp. 63–64.

30. Goeters (ibid., 37, 40) claims that we also find in the references to the sinlessness of Christ in HC 15 and 16 the old Reformed doctrine of the active obedience of Christ, which had its basis in the theses Ursinus had defended for his doctoral degree a year before. Goeters has in mind especially Ursinus's first thesis: "Postquam homo per peccatum a Deo avulsus erat, summa & perfectissima Dei iustitia, illum reconciliari cum Deo non sinebat, nisi aliquis verus homo, ex eo quod peccaverat, humano genere natus, ab omni tamen labe peccati immunis, poenam pro peccatis sufficientem luendo, integram divina legi obedientiam praestaret." Ursinus, "Theses de persona et officio unici mediatoris inter Deum et homines, domini nostri Iesu Christi," in *D. Zachariae Ursini . . . opera theologica*, ed. Quirinus Reuter (Heidelberg: Lancellot, 1612), 1:744. The last part of this thesis, however, can be translated as "by paying the penalty sufficient for sin, he [Christ] discharged full obedience to the divine law." It is not that Christ paid the penalty for sin (passive obedience) and also fully obeyed the law (active obedience) but that he obeyed the law through his payment. For more on the questions surrounding the doctrine of the active obedience of Christ in Ursinus and the HC, see Heber Carlos de Campos Júnior, "Johannes Piscator (1546–1625) and the Consequent Development of the Doctrine of the Imputation of Christ's Active Obedience" (Ph.D. diss., Calvin Theological Seminary, 2009), chap. 3.

31. Robert H. Culpepper, *Interpreting the Atonement* (Grand Rapids: Wm. B. Eerdmans, 1966), 93–95; Timothy George, "The Atonement in Luther's Theology," in *The Glory of the Atonement—Biblical, Historical & Practical Perspectives: Essays in Honor of Roger Nicole*, ed. Charles E. Hill and Frank A. James III (Downers Grove, IL: InterVarsity Press, 2004), 275.

32. Culpepper, *Interpreting the Atonement*, 102; Timothy George, *Theology of the Reformers* (Nashville: Broadman, 1988), 222; Henri Blocher, "The Atonement in John Calvin's Theology," in *The Glory of the Atonement*, ed. Charles E. Hill and Frank A. James III, 283–92.

33. "To the evil powers of sin, death, and the devil . . . Luther adds the law, and even the wrath of God. Over all of these personified evils Christ has won the decisive victory . . . . No creature, but only one who was truly and naturally God, could overcome sin, death, and the curse. Thus against these mighty forces it was necessary for God to set a mightier power—his own," Culpepper, *Interpreting the Atonement*, 93. See also Watson, *Let God be God!*, 116–17.

34. Ursinus, *Commentary of Dr. Zacharias Ursinus*, 78.

35. Ibid., (italics added).

4. PROVIDENCE AND PREDESTINATION

1. Melanchthon, "Examen Ordinandorum 1552," 190.

2. Melanchthon, "Examen Ordinandorum [1554]," in *CR*, vol. 23, *Philippi Melanthonis opera quae supersunt omnia*, ed. C. G. Bretschneider and H. E. Bindseil, (1855; reprint, New York: Johnson Reprint Corporation, 1963), 19. The similarity

between the first line of this definition and that of LC 38 is particularly striking. For parallels to the last line of this definition, see also Melanchthon, "Examen Ordinandorum 1552," 203, 208.

3. "Zum andern wirt yn gott geglaubt, das ist, wen ich nit alleyn glaub, das war sey, was von gott gesagt wirt, szondern setze meyn traw yn yhn." Luther, "Eine kurze Form," *WA* 7:215; *LW* 43:24.

4. The Latin translation of HC 21 uses the same terms for "knowledge" (*notitia*) and "trust" (*fiducia*) as the Latin text of the AC in its treatment of faith in art. 20. See *Catechesis Religionis Christianae, quae traditur in ecclesiis et scholis Palatinatus* (Heidelberg: Schirat et Mayer, 1563), 8; Melanchthon, "Augsburgische Konfession [Latin text]," in *BSLK*, 79–80.

5. For an overview of the definitions of faith in early Lutheran and Reformed theological literature, see Verboom, *Theologie van de Heidelbergse Catechismus*, 60–65.

6. Leo Jud, "Catechismus. Christliche klare und einfalte ynleitung in den Willenn unnd in die Gnad Gottes" (1534), in Gooszen, *Heidelbergsche Catechismus* ("Catechismus"), 33–34 (Q/A 21); John Calvin, *Institutes of the Christian Religion: 1536 edition*, trans. Ford Lewis Battles (Grand Rapids: Wm. B. Eerdmans, 1975), 42–43.

7. Marten Micronius, *Den kleynen cathechismus, oft kinder leere der Duytscher Ghemeynte van Londen* (1552) (London: Duvves, 1566), 11v, http://eebo.chadwyck.com/; Lasco, "Kleine Emder Katechismus," 311 (Q/A 27).

8. Neuser, "Väter des Heidelberger Katechismus," 182. By contrast, Calvin's GC ("The Catechism of the Church of Geneva" [1545], in *Calvin: Theological Treatises*, trans. and ed. J. K. S. Reid, The Library of Christian Classics, vol. 22 [Philadelphia: Westminster, 1960], 93 [Q/A 17–18]) divides the creed into four parts: Father, Son, Holy Spirit, and Church.

9. Luther, "Eine kurze Form," *WA* 7:214; *LW* 43:24.

10. See, for example, Micronius, *Kleynen cathechismus*, 12r–v: "Vraghe: Hoe wert dit Symbolum ghedeylt? Antwoorde: In drye sonderlicke stucken. D'eerste is van God den Vader, d'ander van den Sone, ende t'derde van den heylighen Gheest."

11. Bullinger's 1559 catechism also connects these works to the persons of the Trinity but in a scheme in which the creed is presented, as in the GC, in twelve articles divided into four parts, with the fourth part (the Church) illustrating the Spirit's work of sanctification introduced in the third part. "Catechesis pro adultoribus scripta, de his potissimum captibus" (Zurich: Froschauer, 1559), in Gooszen, *Heidelbergsche Catechismus* ("Catechismus"), 36 (Q/A 115).

12. Luther, "Small Catechism," 354, 355 (German text: *BSLK*, 510–11).

13. Ibid., (italics added).

14. Neuser, "Väter des Heidelberger Katechismus," 182.

15. Note the similarity to Q 19 of Calvin's GC (1545): "Since there is no God but one, why do you here mention three, Father, Son, and Holy Spirit?" "The Catechism of the Church of Geneva," 93. The HC's answer echoes both Leo Jud's (Large) Catechism of 1534 ("Gott stellt sich selbst uns in der Schrift auf dreyerley Wege vor, nähmlich mit diesen dreyen Namen" ["Catechismus," 40, Q/A 25]) and Melanchthon's 1552 *EO* ("Warum sol man drey Göttliche Personen erkennen . . . ? Denn Gottes wesen und willen sol man also erkennen, wie er sich selb geoffenbart hat. Und ist diese offenbarung offt in der Schrifft ausgedruckt," 178).

16. Sudhoff, *C. Olevianus und Z. Ursinus*, 93.

17. Paul Jacobs, *Theologie reformierter Bekenntnisschriften in Grundzügen* (Neukirchen Kreis Moers: Neukirchener Verlag, 1959), 26. Jacobs claims that "oft gewinnt der Genfer Katechismus eine unmittelbare, manchmal geradezu als Zitat erscheinende Einflussnahme auf den Heidelberger Katechismus" (ibid.).

18. Lang, *Heidelberger Katechismus und vier verwandte Katechismen*, XC.

19. Calvin, GC, 93.

20. Ibid.

21. Ibid., 94.

22. Calvin, GC, 93, 94. See also *Institutes* (1536), 49, and *Calvin: Institutes of the Christian Religion* (1559), edited by John T. McNeill, translated by Ford Lewis Battles, Library of Christian Classics, vols. 20–21 (Philadelphia: Westminster, 1960),1.17.6. Martin Bucer had used this image even earlier in his discussion of providence in his catechism of 1534. "Kurtze schrifftliche erklärung für die Kinder vnd angohnden," in *Quellen zur Geschichte*, ed. Johann M. Reu, pt. 1, 27, 28.

23. Calvin, *Institutes* (1536), 49; GC, 94 (Q/A 28, 29). See also *Institutes* (1559), 1.17.6.

24. Calvin, GC, 94. As den Hartogh notes, however, Calvin directs his answer more toward theodicy and Ursinus more toward providence in its totality, (*Voorzienigheid in donker licht*, 60–61.

25. Calvin, *Institutes* (1559) 1.17.7.

26. Bucer, "Kurtze schrifftliche erklärung," 27.

27. Bullinger, "Catechesis," 46, 47 (Q/A 117–19).

28. Micronius, *Kleynen cathechismus*, 12v.

29. Micronius, "Corte undersouckinghe," 285.

30. Lasco, "Kleine Emder Katechismus," 312.

31. Luther, "Small Catechism," 354 (German text: *BSLK*, 510). For a discussion of this point, see den Hartogh, *Voorzienigheid*, 59.

32. Luther, "Small Catechism," 354 (German text: *BSLK*, 510).

33. Melanchthon, "Examen Ordinandorum 1552," 181.

34. Emerich Gyenge, "Der Glaube, seine Gewissheit und Bewahrung," in *Handbuch zum Heidelberger Katechismus*, ed. Lothar Coenen (Neukirchen-Vluyn: Neukirchener Verlag, 1963), 120–21.

35. Latzel, *Theologische Grundzüge*, 74n225.

36. Verboom, *Theologie van de Heidelbergse Catechismus*, 85, 88.

37. Lasco, "Kleine Emder Katechismus," 312 (Q/A 30); Bullinger, "Catechesis," 46 (Q/A 118).

38. Luther, "Small Catechism," 354 (German text: *BSLK*, 510; italics added).

39. Bucer, "Kurtze schrifftliche erklärung," 27–28; Calvin, *Institutes* (1536), 49; Jud, "Catechismus," 45 (Q/A 24, 26); Bullinger, "Catechesis," 46–47 (Q/A 118–19); Micronius, *Kleynen cathechismus*, 12v (Q/A 48); idem., "Corte undersouckinghe," 285 (Q/A 12); Lasco, "Kleine Emder Katechismus," 312 (Q/A 30).

40. "Das christologisch formulierte Zentralkerygma von A 1 . . . findet seine schöpfungstheologische Entsprechung in der Kernaussage von A 26." Latzel, *Theologische Grundzüge*, 74. See also L. L. J. Visser, "Die Lehre von Gottes Vorsehung und Weltregiment," in *Handbuch zum Heidelberger Katechismus*, ed. Lothar Coenen, 107.

41. HC 50 ("Why the next words: 'and is seated at the right hand of God'?") also describes the ascended Christ as not only the head of the church but also "the

one through whom the Father rules all things." See Visser, "Gottes Vorsehung," 106–8.

42. Schaff, "Geschichte, Geist und Bedeutung," 126ff., cited in Couard, *Heidelberger Katechismus*, 46–47; Lang, *350 jährigen Gedächtnis*, 45–46.

43. Lothar Coenen, "Gottes Bund und Erwählung," in *Handbuch zum Heidelberger Katechismus*, ed. Lothar Coenen, 132–33; Klooster, *A Mighty Comfort*, 36.

44. Dahlmann, "Heidelberg Catechism," 176–77.

45. Neuser, "Erwählungslehre," 316.

46. "In een gebied als de Paltz, waar de verschillende confessionele stromingen op kwetsbare wijze de koers moesten volgen die de keurvorst Frederik III uitzette, was het belangrijk dat de leer van de predestinatie geen onnodige conflicten zou veroorzaken." Verboom, *Theologie van de Heidelbergse Catechismus*, 167. See also ibid., 142; and Neuser, "Väter des Heidelberger Katechismus," 191.

47. Timothy Wengert, "'We Will Feast Together in Heaven Forever': The Epistolary Friendship of John Calvin and Philip Melanchthon," in *Melanchthon in Europe: His Work and Influence beyond Wittenberg*, ed. Karin Maag, Studies and Texts in Reformation and Post-Reformation Thought, ed. Richard A. Muller (Grand Rapids: Baker, 1999), 27.

48. Calvin, *CO* 11:381, cited in Wengert, "Epistolary Friendship," 31.

49. Cornelis P. Venema, *Heinrich Bullinger and the Doctrine of Predestination: Author of 'the Other Reformed Tradition'?*, Texts & Studies in Reformation and Post-Reformation Thought, ed. Richard A. Muller (Grand Rapids: Baker, 2002), 119. See also pp. 105–7.

50. Winter suggests that this was because in 1530 predestination was not yet an important part of Protestant doctrinal discussions. *Confessio Augustana*, 81.

51. Melanchthon, "The Augsburg Confession [German text]," 40 (art. 5)`; "The Augsburg Confession [Latin text]," 41 (art. 5).

52. De Reuver, "Augsburgse Confessie," 352. Couard neglects to take this into account when he argues that HC 54's reference to the church as the elect is set over against the AC's portrayal of the church (art. 7) as the body of believers where the Word is preached and the sacraments administered. *Heidelberger Katechismus*, 43–44.

53. Goeters, "Christologie und Rechtfertigung," 46–47.

54. Sudhoff, *C. Olevianus und Z. Ursinus*, 119–20; Neuser, "Erwählungslehre," 315.

55. Visser, "Gottes Vorsehung," 106; den Hartogh, *Voorzienigheid*, 60.

56. Neuser, "Erwählungslehre," 315.

5. CHRIST AND THE HOLY SPIRIT

1. William E. Korn, "Die Lehre von Christi Person und Werk," in *Handbuch zum Heidelberger Katechismus*, ed. Lothar Coenen, 92.

2. See Lang, *Heidelberger Katechismus und vier verwandte Katechismen*, CIII.

3. Luther, "Small Catechism," 355; *BSLK*, 511.

4. De Reuver ("Augsburgse Confessie," 350) claims that there are parallels also between HC 1 and article 3 of the AC, but apart from the reference in the AC to the comfort that Christ provides the believer through the Holy Spirit, I do not find much similarity.

5. See above, pp. 16–17.
6. Luther, "Small Catechism," 355.
7. Neuser, "Väter des Heidelberger Katechismus," 181.
8. Luther, "Small Catechism," 355.
9. Latzel, *Theologische Grundzüge*, 31.
10. E.g., Jacobs, *Theologie reformierter Bekenntnisschriften*, 26–27; Neuser, "Väter des Heidelberger Katechismus," 184.
11. See Lang, *Heidelberger Katechismus und vier verwandte Katechismen*, XC–XCI.
12. Calvin, GC, 95.
13. Ibid.
14. Ibid., 96.
15. Ibid.
16. Ibid., 98.
17. Ibid.
18. Ibid., 99.
19. Ibid., 100.
20. Ibid., 99.
21. Ibid., 100.
22. Ibid.
23. Ibid., 100–101.
24. Others can be found in HC 31 and GC 37–39 (p. 95); HC 47 and GC 78–79 (p. 101); HC 50 and GC 80, 82 (p. 101); and HC 52 and GC 86–87 (p. 102).
25. Neuser, "Väter des Heidelberger Katechismus," 184.
26. See Lyle D. Bierma, "How Should Heidelberg Catechism Q/A 60 Be Translated?" *Calvin Theological Journal* 26 (April 1991): 129–32. I am indebted to Heber Carlos de Campos Júnior for pointing out how the threefold remedy is related to the other two triads. "Johannes Piscator," 89n108.
27. Theodore Beza, *Confessio christianae fidei, et eiusdem collation cum papisticis haeresibus* (London: Thomas Vautrollerius, 1575), 27–36, http://eebo.chadwyck.com. This only further confirms Hollweg's thesis that this confession served as one of the sources for the HC. Hollweg, "Beiden Konfessionen," 86–110.
28. Verboom, *Theologie van de Heidelbergse Catechismus*, 112–14.
29. See above, pp. 39–40.
30. As we pointed out earlier, the language in HC 34 of deliverance through Christ from the tyranny of the devil is found almost verbatim in Luther's Small Catechism (p. 355).
31. Melanchthon uses the same pair of verbs as HC 31 and 51 in talking about divine protection against the devil and his minions: "[God] *erhalte und schütze* [the Church] durch seinen Son Jhesum Christum *wider alle Teufel*." "Examen ordinandorum 1552," 224 (italics added). "Der Herr Christus selb uns aus der Helle zeucht und Trost und Leben in uns wircket und gibt uns seinen heiligen Geist, *schützt uns wider die Teufel und erhelt uns* wunderbarlich." Ibid., 231 (italics added).
32. We should not be surprised to find a concentration of this vocabulary also in the doctrine of justification at the end of the exposition of the creed (60–62) and in the treatment of the sacraments at the end of part 2 (HC 66, 67, 69, 75, 79, 80).
33. Klooster, *Our Only Comfort*, 1:525.
34. Couard, *Heidelberger Katechismus*, 34–35.
35. Winter, *Confessio Augustana*, 81.

36. "Formula of Concord [The Solid Declaration]," in *The Book of Concord: The Confessions of the Evangelical Lutheran Church*, ed. Robert Kolb and Timothy J. Wengert, trans. Charles Arand et al. (Minneapolis: Fortress Press, 2000), 634–35n305.

37. Althaus, *Theology of Martin Luther*, 207.

38. "Formula of Concord [The Solid Declaration]," 635.

39. Ibid., 634. See also "Formula of Concord [The Epitome]," 514.

40. It is worth noting that as with the threefold office of Christ in HC 31, the descent of Christ into hell in HC 44 is connected to the overall Lutheran theme of deliverance: "Christ my Lord . . . has *delivered* me from hellish anguish and torment" (italics added).

41. Couard, *Heidelberger Katechismus*, 35–36.

42. For a comprehensive treatment of the background to this doctrine and of the HC's treatment of it, see Klooster, *Our Only Comfort*, 1:592–623.

43. On the similarity here between Calvin and Melanchthon, see Richard A. Muller, "Calvin on Sacramental Presence, in the Shadow of Marburg and Zurich," *Lutheran Quarterly* 23 (2009): 152, and the primary sources cited there. For a contrary view of Melanchthon, see Good (*Heidelberg Catechism*, 173–83), who argued that Melanchthon held to a local presence of Christ's body in the Lord's Supper without resorting to a doctrine of ubiquity.

44. Winter, *Confessio Augustana*, 70–71. For the text of AC art. 3, see Melanchthon, "Augsburg Confession [German text]," 38.

45. Klooster, "Heidelberg Catechism: Origin and History," 97.

46. "Der Dritte Artikel. Von der Heiligung." Luther, "Dr. Martin Luther's Enchiridion: Der Kleine Katechismus," in Philip Schaff, ed., *The Creeds of Christendom: With a History and Critical Notes*, 6th ed., vol. 3, *The Evangelical Protestant Creeds with Translations* (1931; repr., Grand Rapids: Baker, 1990), 79.

47. Luther, "Small Catechism," 355–56 (italics added). Cf. also the similarity in language between HC 54 ("of this community I am and always will be a living member") and Luther's Large Catechism: "Of this community I also am a part and member." Luther, "The Large Catechism," in *The Book of Concord: The Confessions of the Evangelical Lutheran Church*, ed. Robert Kolb and Timothy J. Wengert, trans. Charles Arand et al. (Minneapolis: Fortress Press, 2000), 438.

48. Melanchthon, "Augsburg Confession [German text]," 38.

49. Melanchthon also talks about the comforting role of the Holy Spirit in his "Examen ordinandorum 1552," 178. It can also be found in the Reformed catechisms of Jud, "Der kürtzer Catechismus [1541]," in Lang, *Heidelberger Katechismus und vier verwandte Katechismen*, 90 (Q/A 141); Lasco, *Catechismus, oft kinder leere*, 62r; idem, "Kleine Emder Katechismus," 315 (Q/A 43); and Micronius, *Kleynen cathechismus*, 16r.

50. The giving of the Holy Spirit to us by Christ is also a fairly common expression in Melanchthon's "Examen ordinandorum 1552." See, pp. 193, 198, 208, and 236.

51. Daniel R. Hyde, "The Holy Spirit in the Heidelberg Catechism," *Mid-America Journal of Theology* 17 (2006): 215–19.

52. Luther, "Small Catechism," 355.

53. Calvin, GC, 102.

54. Ibid. See also GC, 103 (Q/A 100): "the company of those who, by secret election, [God] has adopted for salvation."

55. Ibid., 103.

56. Ibid.

57. Alfred Rauhaus, "Untersuchungen zu Entstehung, Gestaltung und Lehre des Kleinen Emder Katechismus von 1554" (Th.D. diss., University of Göttingen, 1977), 221–22, 224.

58. Lasco, "Kleine Emder Katechismus," 315.

59. Ibid.

60. The translators of the 2000 English edition of the Small Catechism prefer the latter rendering because "the English word 'sanctification' does not preserve the linguistic connection between the Holy [*heilig*] Spirit and the Holy Spirit's activity [*Heiligung*]." "Small Catechism," 355n56.

61. Luther, "Small Catechism," 355–56.

62. See GC, 102ff. (Q/A 92ff.). Neither Micronius's "Corte undersouckinghe" (pp. 287–89) nor Lasco's "Kleine Emder Katechismus" (pp. 315–16), two other sources for the HC, display such integration either.

63. GC, 102–3 (Q/A 95).

64. Verboom, *Theologie van de Heidelbergse Catechismus*, 141.

65. Furthermore, Melanchthon, too, uses the term "elect" in his description of the church, though also without further elaboration. See "Examen Ordinandorum 1552," 187, 212.

66. Latzel, *Theologische Grundzüge*, 145n30; see also Benrath, "Eigenart der pfälzischen Reformation," 26.

67. Verboom, *Theologie van de Heidelbergse Catechismus*, 138–39. Verboom concludes that "in de lutherse traditie komt een bespreking van de pneumatologie los van het Woord eenvoudigweg niet voor, terwijl in de gereformeerde geschriften over the pneumatologie, ook zonder he Woord wordt gesproken" (p. 138).

68. Latzel, *Theologische Grundzüge*, 52. For other allusions in the HC to union with Christ, see HC 1, 20, 64, 65, and 80.

69. Neuser, "Väter des Heidelberger Katechismus," 183; Latzel, *Theologische Grundzüge*, 53–54; Muller, "Calvin on Sacramental Presence," 153. See, for example, Melanchthon's "Loci Communes Theologici," in *LCC* 19:21, and "Examen ordinandorum 1552," 170.

70. Neuser ("Väter des Heidelberger Katechismus," 183) probably states it too strongly when he asserts that Melanchthon "keine Christusgemeinschaft im Glauben kennt." Cf., e.g., Melanchthon's statement on the Lord's Supper in his "Examen ordinandorum 1552": "[Christ] hat diese niessung eingesetzt, das er bezeuget, das er warhafftiglich und wesentlich bey uns und in uns sein wil und wil in den bekerten wonen" (p. 202).

71. Marcus Johnson, "Luther and Calvin on Union with Christ," *Fides et Historia* 39, no. 2 (2007): 59–77.

72. "Bedurfte der Mittler zu seinem Versöhnungswerk der potentia divinitatis, daβ er 'uns die Gerechtigkeit und das Leben erwerben und wiedergeben könnte' (Frage 17), so vollzieht er dies an uns als das erhöhte Haupt, indem er durch seinen Heiligen Geist in uns, seine Glieder, die himmlischen Gaben ausgieβt (Frage 51). . . . Der Katechismus führt hier nur konsequenterweise aus, was er bereits in seiner ersten Frage andeutet, in der Versöhnungslehre begründet und in seiner gesamten Erlösungslehre immer wieder unterstreicht—was also nicht eine belanglose, sondern eine höchst charakteristische und durchgängige Eigentümlichkeit reformierten Glaubens überhaupt ist—daβ Christus, der als der

Menschgewordene das Versöhnungswerk vollzogen hat, uns dies als der Erhöhte durch seinen Heiligen Geist zueignet." Goeters, "Christologie und Rechtfertigung," 41–42.

6. THE SACRAMENTS

1. Documentation for the first four views can be found in our discussion of the general theological orientation of the HC in chapter 1, pp. 2–5. For the fifth view, see Charles Hodge, *The Biblical Repertory and Princeton Review* 20 (1848): 241.

2. Neuser uses the terms "neuzwinglianisch"and "spätzwinglianisch,"respectively, in "Erwählungslehre," 311, and "Väter des Heidelberger Katechismus," 182. In addition, Rohls describes Bullinger's view as "modified Zwinglianism." *Reformed Confessions*, 16.

3. Lang acknowledged a distinctive Melanchthonian influence on Ursinus's LC (1562), one of the literary antecedents to the HC, but he found only traces of this influence in the HC itself, and none in the doctrine of the sacraments. *Heidelberger Katechismus undvier verwandte Katechismen*, CI. Neuser identified Melanchthon as one of four "fathers"of the HC, but, like Lang, did not extend this paternity to the doctrine of the sacraments. "Väter des Heidelberger Katechismus,"181ff. Visser claimed that "much of the *Heidelberg Catechism* can be found in the writings of Melanchthon," but he is not more specific. *Reluctant Reformer*, 142. Sturm argued that there was indeed a Philippist stamp on Ursinus's sacramental doctrine that was never completely overcome by Zwinglian and Calvinist influences, but he traced the development of Ursinus's thought only up to, not through, the HC. *Zacharias Ursinus*, 1.

4. E. F. Karl Müller, *Die Bekenntnisschriften der reformierten Kirche* (Leipzig: Deichert, 1903), LII; Jan Bavinck, *De Heidelbergsche Catechismus*, 2nd ed. (Kampen: Kok, 1913–14), 2:523–24; Hermann Hesse, "Zur Sakramentslehre des Heidelberger Katechismus nach den Fragen 65–68," in *Theologische Aufsätze: Karl Barth zum 50. Geburtstag*, ed. E. Wolf (Munich: Kaiser, 1936), 474ff.; Hendrikus Berkhof, "The Catechism in Its Historical Context," in Bard Thompson et al., *Essays on the Heidelberg Catechism* (Philadelphia: United Church Press, 1963), 88–89; idem, "The Catechism as an Expression of Our Faith," in Bard Thompson et al., *Essays*, 113; Klooster, *Mighty Comfort*, 37–38, 119.

5. Rohls, *Reformed Confessions*, 20, 210–11, 226–27.

6. Richards, *Heidelberg Catechism*, 90, 100. See also Couard, *Heidelberger Katechismus*, 42–43: "Die Abendmahlslehre des Heidelberger Katechismus ist eine geschickte Verschmelzung zwinglischer und calvinischer Anschauungen."

7. Good, *Heidelberg Catechism*, 54.

8. G. P. Hartvelt, *Verum Corpus: Een Studie over een Centraal Hoofdstuk uit de Avondmaalsleer van Calvijn* (Delft: Meinema, 1960), 200, 241; idem, "Petrus Boquinus,"*Gereformeerd Theologisch Tijdschrift* 62 (1962): 51, 76–77; idem, "De Avondmaalsleer van de Heidelbergse Catechismus en Haar Toepassing in de Prediking,"*Homiletica en Biblica* 23 (1964): 127–37; idem, *Tastbaar Evangelie*, vol. 3 of *Nieuwe Commentaar Heidelbergse Catechismus* (Aalten: Graafschap, 1966), 6.

9. Brian A. Gerrish, "Sign and Reality: The Lord's Supper in the Reformed Confessions," in *The Old Protestantism and the New: Essays on the Reformation Heritage* (Chicago: University of Chicago Press, 1982), 126.

10. Neuser, "Väter des Heidelberger Katechismus," 185–86; idem., "Erwählungslehre,"311.

11. Sudhoff, *C. Olevianus und Z. Ursinus*, 116; Gooszen, *Heidelbergsche Catechismus* ("Inleiding"), 153.

12. Gerrish, "Sign and Reality," 124, 126; Paul Rorem, "The *Consensus Tigurinus* (1549): Did Calvin Compromise?" in *Calvinus Sacrae Scripturae Professor: Calvin as Confessor of Holy Scripture*, ed. Wilhelm H. Neuser (Grand Rapids: Wm. B. Eerdmans, 1994), 90; Berkhof, "Catechism as an Expression of Our Faith,"113.

13. Gooszen, *Heidelbergsche Catechismus* ("Inleiding"), 153; Good, *Heidelberg Catechism*, 76. Neuser regards as late-Zwinglian (Bullingerian) the *absence* of any reference in the HC to the presence of Christ in the Lord's Supper! "Väter des Heidelberger Katechismus,"185.

14. Sudhoff, *C. Olevianus und Z. Ursinus*, 116; Rohls, *Reformed Confessions*, 210–11.

15. Verboom, *Theologie van de Heidelbergse Catechismus*, 215.

16. Gooszen, *Heidelbergsche Catechismus* ("Inleiding"), 65–66; Neuser, "Erwählungslehre ," 311.

17. "Sacramentum . . . ist ritus divinitus institutus, additus promissioni in Evangelio traditae, ut sit testimonium et pignus exhibitae et applicatae promissionis Gratiae." Melanchthon, "Examen Ordinandorum [1554]," *CR* 23:39.

18. Ursinus, "Theses complectentes," 344.

19. "Parum est quod admonent signa promissionum divinarum. Hoc vero magnum est, quod certum testimonium divinae voluntatis erga te sunt. . . . Quibus conscientia tua certa reddatur. . . ." Melanchthon, "Loci theologici [1521]," *CR* 21:209.

20. Melanchthon, "Loci theologici [1521]," *CR* 21:208–10; Ursinus, "Catechesis minor," 208, 209, 210; *Catechesis Religionis Christianae*, 26, 29.

21. Latzel, *Theologische Grundzüge*, 55.

22. Luther, "Small Catechism," 359, 362. It should be noted, however, that Melanchthon does talk about the sacrament of baptism as a washing that involves this double blessing: "[In baptism God] wescht dich mit dieser Tauff, zur bedeutung, das dir deine sünd mit seinem Blut abgewaschen sind und das er dich mit dem Heiligen Geist zu newer und ewiger gerechtigkeit und seligkeit heiligen wil." "Examen ordinandorum 1552," 201.

23. "Postremo admonet ritus de multis officiis: Primum de gratiarum actione praestanda Deo, postea de mutua benevolentia membrorum Ecclesiae." Melanchthon, "Loci Theologici [1543]," *CR* 21, 848. "First, we must consider what a sacrament is. It seems to me that a simple and proper definition would be that it is an outward sign by which the Lord seals on our consciences the promises of his good will toward us . . . and we in turn attest our piety toward him." Calvin, *Institutes* (1559), 4.14.1. "Postremo sacramenta instituta sunt, ut nos officii nostri admoneant, quo in unitate corporis Christi, in vera pietate & fraterno amore vitam peragamus." Heinrich Bullinger, *Compendium Christianae Religionis* (Zurich: Froschauer, 1569), 112v.

24. Gooszen, *Heidelbergsche Catechismus* ("Inleiding"), 105–7; Lang, *Heidelberger Katechismus und vier verwandte Katechismen*, XCIII; idem, *350 jährigen Gedächtnis*, 44; Hesse, "Sakramentslehre des Heidelberger Katechismus," 475–76; Walter Kreck, "Die Abendmahlslehre in den reformierten Bekenntnisschriften," in *Die Abendmahlslehre in den reformatorischen Bekenntnisschriften* (Munich: Kaiser, 1955), 43.

25. "Expone mihi quid intelliges per Sacramentum? . . . Sacramentum est symbolum sacrum vel ritus sanctus, aut actio sacra, a Deo . . . instituta, . . . quibus item

obsignat et repraesentat quid nobis praestat . . . ." Bullinger, "Catechesis," 131 (Q/A 246–47).

26. "figurat . . . ad obsignandas." Calvin, GC, 131 (Q/A 310; *OS* 2:130).

27. Bullinger, "Catechesis," 131 (Q/A 246–47).

28. Heinrich Bullinger, "Confessio Helvetica Posterior [The Second Helvetic Confession]" (1566), *CC*, 290 (20.3): "Deus . . . purgat nos a peccatis gratuito, per sanguine Filii sui . . . . Nam intus regeneramur, purificamur, et renovamur a Deo per Spiritum Sanctum." Calvin, GC, 133 (Q/A 324; *OS* 2:133). See also Sturm, *Zacharias Ursinus*, 150.

29. "sichtbare bildner." Jud, "Kürtzer Catechismus [1541]," 106 (Q/A 198).

30. "visibili signo." Calvin, GC, 131 (Q/A 311; *OS* 2:130).

31. Jud's Larger Catechism makes reference to "heiligen . . . Zeichen" and "heiligen Pflichtzeichen." "Catechismus," in Gooszen, *Heidelbergsche Catechismus*, 129 (Q/A 93). His Shorter Catechism refers to the "heilig Euangelium." "Kürtzer Catechismus [1541]," 92 (Q/A 152).

32. Bullinger, "Catechesis," 131 (Q/A 246–47).

33. Micronius (*Kleynen cathechismus*, 18r; "Corte undersouckinghe," 290) describes a sacrament as a "heylige oeffeninge." In Lasco's Small Emden Catechism, the adjective "holy" modifies a series of nouns related to the Word and sacraments: "hilligent Godlicken Wordes" (2x), "hilligen Sacramenten," "hilligen Euangelii" (3x), "hillige handelinge" (Q/A 51–54). "Kleine Emder Katechismus," 316–17 (Q/A 51–54).

34. Gerrish, "Sign and Reality," 128. For a summary of Calvin's view of the relationship between sign and signified, see also Ronald S. Wallace, *Calvin's Doctrine of the Word and Sacraments* (Edinburgh: Oliver and Boyd, 1953; Tyler, TX: Geneva Divinity School Press, 1982), 159ff.; Rohls, *Reformed Confessions*, 183–84, and Rorem, "*Consensus Tigurinus*," 73–75.

35. See, for example, Calvin's statement about baptism in the GC, 133 (Q/A 328; *OS* 2:134): "Sic figura sentio, ut simul annexa sit veritas. Neque enim, sua nobis dona pollicendo, nos Deus frustratur. Proinde et peccatorum veniam, et vitae novitatem offerri nobis in baptismo, et recipi a nobis certum est."

36. Gerrish, "Sign and Reality," 128; Rohls, *Reformed Confessions*, 182–83; Rorem, "*Consensus Tigurinus*," 75–78.

37. Rorem, "*Consensus Tigurinus*," 90.

38. "Die Sakramente sind Heilsmittel. Dem Einwand, 'bestätigen' bedeute, dem Glauben werde nur gegeben, was er schon besitze, tritt Frage 66 entgegen: Sakramente sind eingesetzt, damit Gott 'durch den Gebrauch derselben die Verheissung des Evangeliums desto besser zu verstehen gebe und versiegle.' Die Sakramente besitzen Gabecharakter." Neuser, "Väter des Heidelberger Katechismus," 185–86. This represents a change in Neuser's position from his earlier article, "Erwählungslehre," 311, where he characterizes HC 66, as "neuzwinglianisch."

39. Gerrish, "Sign and Reality," 126.

40. Rohls, *Reformed Confessions*, 211.

41. Ibid., 226–27.

42. Calvin, GC, 132–33 (Q/A 319, 320); *Institutes* (1559), 14.4.1.

43. Bullinger, "Confessio Helvetica Posterior," 285 (19.1): "Sunt autem sacramenta . . . quibus . . . fidem nostram, Spiritu Dei in cordibus nostris operante, roborat et auget."

44. See n35 above.

45. John Calvin, "Short Treatise on the Lord's Supper" (1541), in *Calvin: Theological Treatises*, trans. and ed. J. K. S. Reid, The Library of Christian Classics, vol. 22 (Philadelphia: Westminster, 1954), 147 (*OS* 1:508).

46. Rohls, *Reformed Confessions*, 227–28.

47. "Quemadmodum enim . . . aqua hominum corpora mundantur: ita similia in animis nostris Deus sanguine Christi per spiritum suum operatur." Bullinger, *Compendium*, 119r. See also idem, *The Decades of Henry Bullinger*, ed. Thomas Harding (1849–52; reprint, New York: Johnson Reprint, 1968), 4:328–29 (5.7), 364 (5.8).

48. Bullinger, *Decades*, 4:329 (5.7).

49. Calvin, GC, 133.

50. Calvin, GC, 135–36.

51. Gerrish, "Sign and Reality," 128.

52. Rohls, *Reformed Confessions*, 211.

53. See, e.g., Ulrich Zwingli, "Fidei Ratio" (1530), in Müller, *Die Bekenntnisschriften der reformierten Kirche*, 86: "Ex quibus hoc colligitur . . . sacramenta dari in Testimonium publicum eius gratiae, quae cuique privato prius adest."

54. According to Ernst Koch, "dass die Taufe in den Bund, die Familie und das Erbe der Kinder Gottes initiiert und aufnimmt, dass sie dem Täufling den Namen eines filius Dei beilegt, dass sie von den Sündenflecken reinigt und die Gnade Gottes zu einem neuen Leben verleiht [Second Helvetic Confession 20], heist, dass sie alle diese Tatbestände als bereits geschehen bezeichnet." *Die Theologie der Confessio Helvetica Posterior*, Beiträge zur Geschichte und Lehre der Reformierten Kirche, ed. H. Erhart et al., vol. 27 (Neukirchen-Vluyn: Neukirchener Verlag, 1968), 286. See also p. 288.

55. "Sacramentorum igitur proprium non est conferre gratiam & eius dona, sed collata nobis obsignare, id est, postquam res fide acceptae sunt vel accipiuntur, in sacramento accedit exhibitionis testimonium." Ursinus, "Theses complectentes," 350.

56. "In omni autem legitmo usu baptismi, id est, cum baptizatur conversus ritu et fine instituto, necesse est gratiam et donum per gratiam vel iam esse donatam vel certe simul donare. Non enim ideo efficimur filii Dei, quia baptizamur, sed ideo baptizandi sumus, quia sumus filii Dei et ut nos esse filios reddamur certiores." Ibid., 357.

57. Melanchthon, "Loci theologici [1521]," *CR* 21:213, 214, 215.

58. References are to the paragraph numbers. The Latin text of the *Consensus Tigurinus* can be found in *Calvini Opera* 7:733–48. An English translation by Ian Bunting was published in the *Journal of Presbyterian History* 44 (1966): 45–61.

59. See also Wallace, *Calvin's Doctrine*, 186.

60. "Fidei autem confirmandae et augendae baptismus adminiculum est, illi, tanquam inferiori medio, remissio peccatorum, quae fidei est effectus, annectitur." Calvin, *Calvini Opera* 20:53.

61. "Eos qui iam sunt recepti a Deo & renati, baptizari nihilo minus necesse est, & propter mandatum Dei, & quia nos de bonis acceptis baptismus confirmat: eius acceptionis apud alios testimonium est: & per eum ipsa in nobis dona augentur. . . . Etsi autem ad omnem legitimum baptismi usum concurrit rerum signatarum exhibitio: nulla tamen aquae & sanguinis vel Spiritus Christi mutatio aut coniunctio physica fingenda est." Ursinus, "Theses complectentes," 357.

62. "Cum autem res conferri per sacramenta dicuntur, simul eas, aut etiam abundantius communicari significatur." Ibid., 350.

63. Melanchthon, "Iudicium de Zwinglii doctrina" (1530), in *CR* 2:223: "Nos docemus, quod corpus Christ vere et realiter adsit cum pane, vel in pane." Ralph W. Quere notes than even though Melanchthon used the prepositions "with" and "in" up through his negotiations with Bucer in August 1530, the ongoing Reformed objection to the formula *in pane* led him to employ only *cum pane* in subsequent writings. "Christ's Efficacious Presence in the Lord's Supper: Directions in the Development of Melanchthon's Theology after Augsburg," *The Lutheran Quarterly* 29 (1977): 33–34.

64. "Dicuntur quandoque etiam per sacramenta conferri a Deo bona promissa: quod sit nequaquam vi aliqua sacramentis divinitatus infusa: sed primum ratione temporis, quia simul utraque accipiunt credentes. Et magis proprie dicitur, CUM vel IN sacramentis seu usu sacramentorum." Ursinus, "Theses complectes," 349.

65. Melanchthon, "Augsburg Confession [German text]," 44. German text: "Von dem Abendmahl des Herren wird also gelehrt, dass wahrer Leib und Blut Christi wahrhaftliglich unter der Gestalt des Brots und Weins im Abendmahl gegenwärtig sei und da ausgeteilt und genommen werde. . . ." *BSLK*, 64.

66. Melanchthon, "Augsburg Confession [Latin text]," 45. Latin text: "De coena Domini docent, quod corpus et sanguis Christi vere adsint et distribuantur vescentibus in coena Domini; . . ." *BSLK*, 64.

67. "De coena domini deocent, quod cum pane et vino vere exhibeantur corpus et sanguis Christi vescentibus in coena domini." *BSLK*, 65.

68. "Die Frage nach dem Verhältnis von Leib und Blut, Brot und Wein stand für sie [AC] nicht im Vordergrund." Winter, *Confessio Augustana*, 76. See also De Reuver, "Augsburgse Confessie," 356.

69. Good, *Heidelberg Catechism*, 246; Rohls, *Reformed Confessions*, 228.

70. Willem Verboom, "Waardering voor de Augsburgse Confessie," *Reformatorisch Dagblad*, June 11, 2003, http://www.refdag.nl/opinie/opinie/waardering_voor_de_augsburgse_confessie_1_415196 (accessed July 26, 2010).

71. Ursinus, *Gründtlicher Bericht vom heiligen Abendmal unsers Herren Jesu Christi* (Heidelberg: Mayer, 1564), 129r–130v. See also De Reuver, "Augsburgse Confessie," 360.

72. Good, *Heidelberg Catechism*, 143–45. Latin text: Melanchthon, "Responsio Philip. Melanth. ad quaestionem de controversia Heidelbergensi," *CR* 9:961–62.

73. See also SC 67 and LC 309.

74. Calvin, GC, 133.

75. Calvin, *Institutes* (1559), 4.17.5; see also Calvin, GC, 136 (Q/A 344).

76. Brian A. Gerrish, "Calvin Retrospect," *The Bulletin of the Institute for Reformed Theology* 8/3 (2009): 9.

77. Thomas Erastus, *Gründtlicher bericht, wie die wort Christi Das ist mein leib etc. zuuerstehen seien* (Heidelberg: Lück, 1562), 50.

78. Ibid., 49.

79. Ibid.

80. Ibid., 47.

81. Neuser, "Väter des Heidelberger Katechismus," 185.

82. Charles D. Gunnoe, Jr. "Thomas Erastus in Heidelberg: A Renaissance Physician during the Second Reformation, 1558–1580" (Ph.D. diss., University of Virginia, 1998), 141. However, I agree with Gunnoe's judgment that "the view of the Lord's Supper presented in this tract [Erastus's *Gründtlicher bericht*] represented something of a melding of the Philippist and late-Zwinglian positions, as would later be seen in the HC." Gunnoe, "Reformation of the Palatinate," 45.

83. Sturm, *Zacharias Ursinus*, 294.

84. Neuser, "Väter des Heidelberger Katechismus," 185; Rohls, *Reformed Confessions*, 226–27.

85. Calvin, GC, 133, 134 (Q/A 327, 330).

86. Ibid., 136–37.

87. Melanchthon, "Apology," 184 (*BSLK*, 247–48).

88. Calvin, GC, 137 (Q/A 353; *OS* 2: 140).

89. Ursinus, "Theses complectentes," 359.

90. Latin text: Lang, *Heidelberger Katechismus und vier verwandte Katechismen*, 195.

91. Neuser ("Erwählungslehre," 311n12), notes, e.g., that in 1557 Bullinger strongly rejected such terminology when Beza, with Calvin's approval, employed it in a proposed formula of unity. Neuser also points out that in the "Confessio Helvetica Posterior" (292; 21.4), Bullinger denies that we eat the body of Christ in the Lord's Supper *essentialiter*.

92. Gooszen, *Heidelbergsche Catechismus* ("Inleiding"), 87–88; Neuser, "Erwählungslehre," 311.

93. Ursinus, *Commentary*, 375. See also Bodo Nischan, "The 'Fractio Panis:' A Reformed Communion Practice in Late Reformation Germany," *Church History* 53 (1984): 17–29.

94. Sturm, *Zacharias Ursinus*, 300, 306.

95. Rohls, *Reformed Confessions*, 227.

96. Nischan, "'Fractio Panis,'" 20. See also Gooszen, *Heidelbergsche Catechismus en het boekje*.

97. Sturm, *Zacharias Ursinus*, 300. Sturm notes (ibid., 171) that Ursinus was well enough acquainted and impressed with Beza's larger confession to recommend it to friends.

98. On the linkage between Olevianus, Beza's Small Confession, and the HC, see Hollweg, "Quellenfrage," 39–41.

99. Sudhoff, *C. Olevianus und Z. Ursinus*, 116–17; Richards, *Heidelberg Catechism*, 90; Winter, *Confessio Augustana*, 76; Benrath, "Eigenart der pfälzischen Reformation," 25; Berkhof, "Catechism as an Expression of Our Faith," 113; Gerrish, "Sign and Reality," 125; Sturm, *Zacharias Ursinus*, 302, 304, 305.

100. For a summary of Calvin's view, see Muller, "Calvin on Sacramental Presence," 156–60. On Melanchthon, see Quere, "Christ's Efficacious Presence," 22–23, 25.

101. See also Bullinger, *Compendium*, 123v–124r: "Christi enim corpus in coelis est in gloria, non in his terris in corruptione. Spiritualiter autem corpus Christi comedendum, & sanguis eius bibendus est. Comeditur autem fide, sive per fidem. Nempe quod Dominus, qui verum habet corpus, & vere etiam passus est, Spiritu suo interne in cordibus hominum de coelo operatur, ac illis vitam & omnia quae suo sacro corpore seu passione sua adeptus est, confert."

102. Bullinger, "Confessio Helvetica Posterior," 294 (21.10).

103. Rohls, *Reformed Confessions*, 233. See also Bullinger, "Catechesis," 155 (Q/A 280): "Qui passus est pro nobis, et resurrexit a mortuis, et ascendit in coelum sedetque ad dextram Patris atque nos redemit, seipsum nobis cibum vivificum communicat per Spiritum suum sanctum: nos autem edimus et bibimus, id est recipimus ipsum per fidem, ut ipse in nobis vivat et nos vivamus in ipso."

104. Bullinger, "Confessio Helvetica Posterior," 292, 293 (21.5, 6). See also the statement by the Heidelberg Bullingerian Erastus: "Wer also in die gemainschafft

oder gesellschafft des leibs und blüts Christi auffgenommen, das ist, wer in seinem hertzen kräfftiglich vergwissert, überzeuget, und versichert ist, dass er im glauben und vertrauwen auff Christum, durch die unerforschliche wirckung des hailigen gaistes, ain lebendig glid Christi worden sei." *Gründtlicher bericht*, 48.

105. Verboom, *Theologie van de Heidelbergse Catechismus*, 215.

106. Latzel, *Theologische Grundzüge*, 193, esp. n55.

7. COVENANT

1. Heinrich Heppe, *Dogmatik des deutschen Protestantismus im sechzehnten Jahrhundert* (Gotha: Perthes, 1857), 1:139–44, 158, 160.

2. Lothar Coenen, "Gottes Bund und Erwählung," 128–32. Coenen's conclusion is "daß der Fortfall der Terminologie oder besonderer auf den Bundesgedanken bezugnehmender Fragen gerade nicht die Preisgabe des Bundesgedankens überhaupt zur Folge hatte, sondern vielmehr dessen Umgeißung und Integration in die Gesamtkonzeption des Katechismus." Ibid., 132n8. Verboom makes the same point about HC 27–28 (Lord's Day 10): "Hoewel de HC het woord verbond niet gebruikt, zou je ook kunnen zeggen dat de verbondsgedachte het cement van het bouwwerk in zondag 10 is." *Theologie van de Heidelbergse Catechismus*, 92.

3. Goeters, "Christologie und Rechtfertigung," 39. See also Goeters' conclusion (ibid.) concerning HC 19 that "auch wenn hier der Begriff des Gnadenbundes fehlt, so ist er der Sache nach hier augenfällig vorhanden."

4. Derk Visser, "The Covenant in Zacharias Ursinus," *The Sixteenth Century Journal* 18, no. 4 (1987): 532.

5. Ibid., 532–44.

6. See, e.g., Graafland, *Van Calvijn tot Comrie*, 2:13–15, 18–19, 27–28.

7. Gooszen, *Heidelbergsche Catechismus* ("Inleiding"), 74.

8. Lang, *Heidelberger Katechismus und vier verwandte Katechismen*, LXXVIII–LXXIX.

9. Sturm, *Zacharias Ursinus*, 239–41, 246. For a summary of Sturm's argument, see Bierma et al., *Introduction to the Heidelberg Catechism*, 138.

10. Sehling, ed., *Kirchenordnungen*, 337, 339–41, 385, 390.

11. Zacharias Ursinus, *Corpus doctrinae Christianae* (Hannover: Aubrius, 1634), 2–3, 96–100, 394–404, 418, 464 (English translation: Ursinus, *Commentary*, 2–3, 96–100, 366–76, 387–88, 430).

12. Sturm, *Zacharias Ursinus*, 238–41, 253; Graafland, *Van Calvijn tot Comrie*, 2:13–14.

13. Ursinus, *Corpus doctrinae*, 96–100 (ET: Commentary, 96–100).

14. Ibid., 367–468 passim (English Translation: *Commentary*, 340–440 passim).

15. Sturm, *Zacharias Ursinus*, 239.

16. Lang, *Heidelberger Katechismus und vier verwandte Katechismen*, LXIV.

17. Graafland, *Van Calvijn tot Comrie*, 2:13. Cf. also Sturm's assertion that covenant is the "tragende Gerüst" of the LC. *Zacharias Ursinus*, 254.

18. Sturm notes that "in einer solchen Summa [the LC] muβ er sich stärker als in Minor [the SC] der Loci-Methode bedienen." *Zacharias Ursinus*, 253.

19. Graafland is correct, however, in his conclusion that Ursinus retains the content of the creation covenant doctrine in the commentary even though he no longer uses the terminology. *Van Calvijn tot Comrie*, 2:28.

20. See Graafland's conclusion that "ook al komt het genadeverbond niet meer zo terug in de Heidelbergse Catechismus als in de Catechesis Maior [LC], het voor Ursinus' eigen geloofsconceptie toch een wezenlijke plaats is blijven innemen." *Van Calvijn tot Comrie*, 2:28.

21. Willem Verboom has suggested to me in personal correspondence (Nov. 23, 2006) that another factor we may need to consider here is the relationship in Ursinus's theology between covenant and election (see, e.g., LC 33). Minimal reference to covenant in the HC may follow from the minimal reference to election, to which theologically the concept of covenant was so closely tied.

22. See n1 above.

23. See n2 above.

24. Ursinus, *Corpus doctrinae*, 96 (English Translation: *Commentary*, 96).

25. See n3 above.

26. Ursinus, *Corpus doctrinae*, 101 (English Translation: *Commentary*, 101).

27. "Sol man die kleinen Kindlin auch teuffen?" "Examen ordinandorum 1552," 201. The German text of HC 74 reads as follows: "Sol man auch die jungen kinder tauffen?"

28. "Examen ordinandorum 1552," 201–2.

29. Ibid., 202.

30. Klooster, *Mighty Comfort*, 127.

31. See Verboom, *Theologie van de Heidelbergse Catechismus*, 141.

32. Klooster, *Mighty Comfort*, 127.

33. P. Ch. Marcel, "Die Lehre von der Kirche und den Sakramenten," in *Handbuch zum Heidelberger Katechismus*, ed. Lothar Coenen (Neukirchen-Vluyn: Neukirchener Verlag, 1963), 146.

34. The "he" in this question is the "mediator of the covenant" in the previous question. See also HC 18.

35. As we saw above, these are the same four blessings identified in Melanchthon's question on infant baptism in the "Examination of Ordinands." "Examen ordinandorum 1552," 202.

36. Italics added.

37. Italics added.

38. Salvation seems to be used as a synonym for eternal life or everlasting life here (see HC 58).

39. It should be noted that this is true also of Caspar Olevianus, who also served on the HC drafting committee but probably in a lesser role. In his *A Firm Foundation* (1567), a kind of catechetical commentary on the HC, Olevianus relates the covenant concept to the doctrines of the mediator (Q/A 6, 71, 73, 76–78), providence (Q/A 28, 29, 31, 43), the Son (Q/A 65, 66), the church (Q/A 132, 133), and the final resurrection (Q/A 151). *A Firm Foundation: An Aid to Interpreting the Heidelberg Catechism*, trans. and ed. Lyle D. Bierma, Texts and Studies in Reformation and Post-Reformation Thought, ed. Richard A. Muller (Grand Rapids: Baker, 1995). See also Caspar Olevianus, *An Exposition of the Apostles' Creed*, trans. Lyle D. Bierma, Classic Reformed Theology, ed. R. Scott Clark, vol. 2 (Grand Rapids: Reformation Heritage Books, 2009); Lyle D. Bierma, *The Covenant Theology of Caspar Olevianus*, rev. ed. (Grand Rapids: Reformation Heritage Books, 2005); and R. Scott Clark, *Caspar Olevian and the Substance of the Covenant: The Double Benefit of Christ*, Rutherford Series in Historical Theology (Edinburgh: Rutherford House, 2005).

8. GOOD WORKS AND GRATITUDE

1. Lang, *Heidelberger Katechismus und vier verwandte Katechismen*, CI–CII; Graffmann, *Unterricht im Heidelberger Katechismus*, 3:656; Hollweg, "Beiden Konfessionen," 98–105; *Evangelical Dictionary of Theology*, s. v. "Heidelberg Catechism"; Rohls, *Reformed Confessions*, 20; Klooster, *Mighty Comfort*, 37; *Encyclopedia of the Reformed Faith*, s. v. "Heidelberg Catechism"; and Berard, Marthaler, *The Catechism Today and Yesterday: The Evolution of a Genre* (Collegeville, MN: Liturgical Press, 1995), 30.

2. Jud, "Kürtzer Catechismus [1541]," 79 (Q/A 86); Lasco, *De catechismus, oft kinder leere*, 35r; Calvin, *Institutes* (1559), 2.16.2, 3.4.37. For the theme of gratitude in Calvin's theology as a whole, see Brian A. Gerrish, *Grace and Gratitude: The Eucharistic Theology of John Calvin* (Minneapolis: Fortress Press, 1993), esp. 86, 123, 156.

3. Jud, "Kürtzer Catechismus [1541]," 78–80 (Q/A 86). In his larger confession, Beza, too, includes the assurance of faith among the benefits of doing good works. *Confessio christianae fidei*, 56–57.

4. Neuser, "Väter des Heidelberger Katechismus,"186.

5. For the citations and their sources, see Bierma, "Sources and Theological Orientation," 86–87.

6. Weismann, *Eine Kleine Biblia*, 114.

7. Good, *Heidelberg Catechism*, 67.

8. Calvin, GC, 107 (Q/A 128).

9. Good, *Heidelberg Catechism*, 67.

10. Jud, "Kürtzer Catechismus [1541]," 78 (Q/A 85)

11. Hollweg, *Heinrich Bullingers Hausbuch*, 239.

12. Cited in Hollweg, *Heinrich Bullingers Hausbuch*, 240.

13. Melanchthon, "Examen ordinandorum 1552," 207–9.

14. Good, *Heidelberg Catechism*, 67; Neuser, "Väter des Heidelberger Katechismus,"184–85.

15. Rauhaus, "Untersuchungen," 224. His reference is to Lasco, *Catechismus, oft kinder leere*, 9v.

16. Hollweg (*Heinrich Bullingers Hausbuch*, 240–41) finds a similar linguistic parallel to this clause in Bullinger's *Hausbuch*.

17. Literally, the German reads "secret murder" (*heimlicher todtschlag*).

18. Rauhaus ("Untersuchungen," 225) notes correspondence also between Ursinus's SC 92 (on which HC 108–9 are based) and Lasco's *Catechismus, oft kinder leere* , 23r–24v.

19. Latzel, *Theologische Grundzüge*, 82n278, notes similarities between Luther's Small Catechism and HC 94, but as we shall see, the parallels extend well beyond the interpretation of the first commandment.

20. Luther, "Small Catechism," 351 ("Kleine Katechismus," 74).

21. Luther, "Small Catechism," 352 ("Kleine Katechismus," 74).

22. Luther, "Small Catechism," 352 ("Kleine Katechismus," 75).

23. Luther, "Small Catechism," 352 ("Kleine Katechismus," 75).

24. Luther, "Small Catechism," 353 ("Kleine Katechismus," 75).

25. Cf. HC 110–12 and Luther, "Small Catechism," 353 ("Kleine Katechismus," 76).

26. Luther, "Small Catechism," 351.

27. Calvin, GC, 108.

28. On this approach in Luther, see Albrecht Peters, *Kommentar zu Luthers Katechismen*, vol. 1, *Die Zehn Gebote; Luthers Vorreden*, ed. Gottfried Seebaß

(Göttingen: Vandenhoeck & Ruprecht, 1990), 95–96. For Calvin, see I. John Hesselink, *Calvin's Concept of the Law* (Allison Park, PA: Pickwick, 1992), 112–38. For the HC, see Klooster, *Mighty Comfort*, 100–101, and *Our Only Comfort*, 2:931–32.

29. "Diser angefangene gehorsam folget der Widergeburt. . . . Und ob gleich nach der Widergeburt dieser gehorsam angefangen wird, . . ." Melanchthon, "Examen ordinandorum 1552," 195. See also ibid., 209 ("angefangener Gehorsam"), 236 ("das der gehorsam angefangen werde").

30. Ibid., 236.

31. Ibid.

32. CR 21:719.

33. Calvin, GC, 118 (Q/A 229); *Institutes* (1559), 2.7.12.

34. Bierma, "Sources and Theological Orientation," 91.

35. Klooster, *Our Only Comfort*, 2:1111–12.

36. For additional examples, see Isomi Saito, "The Relation of the Law to Prayer in the Heidelberg Catechism" (Th.M. thesis, Calvin Theological Seminary, 2003), 89–93.

37. "Sed inter omnes fructus quos Fides universaliter in omnibus vere Christianis homnibus edit, principatum nostro iudicio facile tenent preces, id est, invocatio nominis Dei per Iesum Christum . . . sive quid ab eo postulemus, sive laudes eius canamus, sive gratias ei agamus pro acceptis beneficiis." Beza, *Confessio christianae fidei*, 42–43.

38. Hollweg, "Beiden Konfessionen," 103.

39. Latzel, *Theologische Grundzüge*, 58n125.

40. Luther, "Large Catechism," 440–41.

41. Ibid., 441. See also "Luther, "Small Catechism," 352.

42. Ibid., 394.

43. Ibid., 446.

44. HC Q 111 is the only other place where one of the commandments is introduced with the language of divine requiring. There, however, the verb is *gebieten*, not *erfordern*.

45. Melanchthon, "Examen ordinandorum 1552," 224.

46. Ibid., 227, 221–22.

47. Ibid., 224.

48. Ibid., 222.

49. Latzel, *Theologische Grundzüge*, 98n34. See GC, 123 (Q/A 257).

50. Good, *Heidelberg Catechism*, 66.

9. ECUMENICAL REFLECTIONS ON THE HEIDELBERG CATECHISM

1. For a fuller treatment of this point, see Latzel, *Theologische Grundzüge*, 195–98, and Bierma, "Sources and Theological Orientation," 78–80.

2. For references to the single sacrifice of Christ, cf. also HC 37, 66, 67, 69, 75, and 80.

3. Ulrich Asendorf certainly thinks so in "Luther's Small Catechism and the Heidelberg Catechism," in *Luther's Catechisms—450 Years: Essays Commemorating*

the Small and Large Catechisms of Dr. Martin Luther, ed. David P. Scaer and Robert D. Preus (Fort Wayne: Concordia Theological Seminary, 1979), 6.

4. Latzel, *Theologische Grundzüge*, 195–96.

5. See, for example, the ground-breaking essay by Heinz Schilling, "Confessionalization in the Empire: Religious and Societal Change in Germany between 1555 and 1620," in Schilling, *Religion, Political Culture and the Emergence of the Early Modern State: Essays in German and Dutch History*, Studies in Medieval and Reformation Thought, vol. 50 (Leiden: Brill, 1992), 205–45.

6. Cf. Busch's assertion that "the catechism that in 1562 he [Frederick III] commissioned his Heidelberg theologians to create, and that he helped to write, was unquestionably supposed to serve the cause of conciliatory living together by the various factions in his land. Therefore the catechism has features of a compromise document. Aside from a few points, it stays away from extreme statements of the various camps and at the same time takes up insights from the differing sides, in order to make possible their coexistence." *Drawn to Freedom*, 14.

7. German text and English translation in Richards, *Heidelberg Catechism*, 185–99 (italics added).

8. Latzel, *Theologische Grundzüge*, 193n57.

9. De Reuver, "Augsburgse Confessie," 349–61.

10. Cited in Richards, *Heidelberg Catechism*, 61. For a fuller discussion of the HC's reception, see pp. 60–69.

11. Lang, *350 jährigen Gedächtnis*, 47.

12. Nevin, *Heidelberg Catechism*, 142–43.

13. Cf. Latzel, *Theologische Grundzüge*, 195: "Zum einen ist der HK darum bemüht, sich auf die Grundbotschaft des christlichen Glaubens zu konzentrieren; er verzichtet auf die Entfaltung bestimmter Besonderheiten der eigene Lehre."

14. Cited in Richards, *Heidelberg Catechism*, 178–79 (italics added).

15. Cited in Richards, *Heidelberg Catechism*, 188–89, 192–93, 194–95 (italics added).

16. See Latzel, *Theologische Grundzüge*, 194–95.

17. For a detailed account of this entire matter, see Christian Reformed Church in North America, "The Lord's Supper and the Roman Catholic Mass: A Discussion on Question and Answer 80 of the Heidelberg Catechism," http://www.crcna.org/site_uploads/uploads/Lord%27sSupper&RCMass.pdf.

18. For a more detailed appraisal of the ecumenical significance of this project for the CRC, see Lyle D. Bierma, "Confessions and Ecumenicity: The Christian Reformed Church and Heidelberg Catechism 80," in *That the World May Believe: Essays on Mission & Unity in Honour of George Vandervelde*, ed. Michael W. Goheen and Margaret O'Gara (Lanham, MD: University Press of America, 2006), 149–53.

19. Lyle D. Bierma, "WARC, the Heidelberg Catechism, and the Concept of Life" (paper presented at the Theology Committee of the Caribbean and North American Area Council, Louisville, KY, February 2004). Much of this unpublished paper has been incorporated into the next several paragraphs.

20. Allen Verhey, *Living the Heidelberg: The Heidelberg Catechism and the Moral Life* (Grand Rapids: CRC Publications, 1986), 124.

21. Latzel, *Theologische Grundzüge*, 28n64.

22. "A Formula of Agreement," Presbyterian Church (U.S.A.), http://oga.pcusa.org/ecumenicalrelations/resources/formula.pdf.

23. Eugene Carson Blake, "A Proposal toward the Reunion of Christ's Church" (sermon preached at Grace Cathedral, San Francisco, CA, December 4, 1960), 10, http://keithwatkinshistorian.files.wordpress.com/2010/07/a-proposal-toward-the-reunion-of-christs-church.pdf.

BIBLIOGRAPHY

1. PRIMARY SOURCES

Becker, Wilhelm. "Zacharias Ursins Briefe an Crato von Crafftheim." *Theologische Arbeiten aus dem rheinischen wissenschaftlichen Prediger-Verein* 12 (1892): 41–107.

Die Bekenntnisschriften der evangelisch-lutherischen Kirche, 4th ed. Göttingen: Vandenhoeck & Ruprecht, 1959.

Beza, Theodore. *Confessio christianae fidei, et eiusdem collation cum papisticis haeresibus.* London: Thomas Vautrollerius, 1575. http://eebo.chadwyck.com.

———. "Kurtze Bekanntnuss des Christlichen glaubens." Heidelberg: Ludwig Lück, 1562. In Walter Hollweg, "Die Beiden Konfessionen Theodore von Bezas: Zwei bisher unbeachtete Quellen zum Heidelberger Katechismus," 111–23. *Neue Untersuchungen zur Geschichte und Lehre des Heidelberger Katechismus.* Beiträge zur Geschichte und Lehre der Reformierten Kirche, edited by Paul Jacobs et al., vol. 13. Neukirchen: Neukirchener Verlag, 1961.

"Die Brandenburg-Nürnbergische Kirchenordnung (1533)." Edited by Jürgen Lorz and Gottfried Seebass. In *Andreas Osiander d. Ä. Gesamtausgabe,* edited by Gerhard Müller. Vol. 5, *Schriften und Briefe 1533 bis 1534,* edited by Gerhard Müller and Gottfried Seebass. Gütersloh: Mohn, 1983.

Bucer, Martin. "Kurtze schrifftliche erklärung für die Kinder vnd angohnden." In *Quellen zur Geschichte des kirchlichen Unterrichts in der evangelischen Kirche Deutschlands zwischen 1530 und 1600,* edited by Johann M. Reu. Pt. 1, *Quellen zur Geschichte des Katechismus-Unterrichts.* Vol. 1, *Süddeutsche Katechismen.* 1904. Reprint, Hildesheim: Olms, 1976.

Bullinger, Heinrich. "Catechesis pro adultoribus scripta, de his potissimum captibus." Zurich: Froschauer, 1559. In Maurits Gooszen, *De Heidelbergsche Catechismus: textus receptus met toelichtenden teksten* ("Catechismus"). Leiden: Brill, 1890.

———. *Compendium Christianae Religionis.* Zurich: Froschauer, 1569.

———. "Confessio Helvetica Posterior [The Second Helvetic Confession]" (1566). In *The Creeds of Christendom: With a History and Critical Notes,* edited by Philip Schaff. 6th ed. Vol. 3, *The Evangelical Protestant Creeds with Translations.* 1931. Reprint, Grand Rapids: Baker, 1990.

———. *The Decades of Henry Bullinger.* Edited by Thomas Harding. 1849–52. Reprint, New York: Johnson Reprint, 1968.

Calvin, John. *Calvin: Institutes of the Christian Religion.* Edited by John T. McNeill. Translated by Ford Lewis Battles. The Library of Christian Classics, vols. 20–21. Philadelphia: Westminster, 1960.

———. "The Catechism of the Church of Geneva" (1545). In *Calvin: Theological Treatises,* translated and edited by J. K. S. Reid. The Library of Christian Classics, vol. 22. Philadelphia: Westminster, 1954.

———. *Institutes of the Christian Religion: 1536 Edition*. Translated by Ford Lewis Battles. Grand Rapids: Wm. B. Eerdmans, 1975.

———. *Ioannis Calvini opera quae supersunt omnia*. Edited by Guilielmus Baum, Eduardus Cunitz, and Eduardus Reuss. 59 vols. Brunswick: Schwetschke, 1863–1900.

———. "Short Treatise on the Lord's Supper " (1541). In *Calvin: Theological Treatises*, translated and edited by J. K. S. Reid. The Library of Christian Classics, vol. 22. Philadelphia: Westminster, 1954.

Catechesis Religionis Christianae, quae traditur in ecclesiis et scholis Palatinatus. Heidelberg: Schirat et Mayer, 1563.

"Consensus Tigurinus." In *Ioannis Calvini opera quae supersunt omnia*. Edited by Guilielmus Baum, Eduardus Cunitz, and Eduardus Reuss. Vol. 7. Brunswick: Schwetschke, 1868. English translation: Ian Bunting, "The *Consensus Tigurinus*." *Journal of Presbyterian History* 44 (1966): 45–61.

Erastus, Thomas. *Gründtlicher bericht, wie die wort Christi Das ist mein leib etc. zuuerstehen seien*. Heidelberg: Lück, 1562.

A Formula of Agreement. Presbyterian Church (U.S.A.). http://oga.pcusa.org/ecumenicalrelations/resources/formula.pdf.

"Formula of Concord [The Solid Declaration]." In *The Book of Concord: The Confessions of the Evangelical Lutheran Church*, edited by Robert Kolb and Timothy J. Wengert. Translated by Charles Arand et al. Minneapolis: Fortress Press, 2000.

Jud, Leo. "Catechismus. Christliche klare und einfalte ynleitung in den Willenn unnd in die Gnad Gottes [Larger Catechism]." 1534. In Maurits Gooszen, *De Heidelbergsche Catechismus: textus receptus met toelichtenden teksten* ("Catechismus"). Leiden: Brill, 1890.

———. "Der kürtzer Catechismus." 1541. In August Lang, *Der Heidelberger Katechismus und vier verwandte Katechismen*. Leipzig: Deichert, 1907.

"Kirchenordnung . . . [vom 15. November 1563]." In *Die evangelischen Kirchenordnungen des XVI. Jahrhunderts*, edited by Emil Sehling. Vol. 14, *Kurpfalz*. Tübingen: Mohr (Paul Siebeck), 1969.

"Ein Kurtze Ordenliche summa der rechten Waren Lehre unsers heyligen Christlichen Glaubens [1554 ed.]." In *Quellen zur Geschichte des kirchlichen Unterrichts in der evangelischen Kirche Deutschlands zwischen 1530 und 1600*, edited by Johann M. Reu. Pt. 1, *Quellen zur Geschichte des Katechismus-Unterrichts*. Vol. 1, *Süddeutsche Katechismen*. 1904. Reprint, Hildesheim: Olms, 1976.

Lang, August, ed. *Der Heidelberger Katechismus und vier verwandte Katechismen*. Leipzig: Deichert, 1907.

Lasco, Johannes à. *De catechismus, oft kinder leere, diemen te Londen, in de Duytsche ghemeynte, is ghebruyckende*. Translated into Dutch by Jan Utenhove. London: Steven Myerdman, 1551. http://eebo.chadwyck.com.

———. "Der Kleine Emder Katechismus (1554) in der Fassung von 1579." Edited by Alfred Rauhaus. In *Reformierte Bekenntnisschriften*, edited by Heiner Faulenbach et al. Vol. 1/3, *1550–1558*, edited by Judith Becker et al., Neukirchen-Vluyn: Neukirchener Verlag, 2007.

Luther, Martin. "Betbüchlein. 1522." In *D. Martin Luthers Werke: Kritische Gesamtausgabe*. Vol. 10, bk. 2. 1907. Reprint, Graz: Akademische Druck- und Verlagsanstalt, 1966.

———. "Dr. Martin Luther's Enchiridion: Der Kleine Katechismus." In *The Creeds of Christendom: With a History and Critical Notes,* edited by Philip Schaff. 6th ed. Vol. 3, *The Evangelical Protestant Creeds with Translations.* 1931. Reprint, Grand Rapids: Baker, 1990.

———. "Eine kurze Form der zehn Gebote, eine kurze Form des Glaubens, eine kurze Form des Vaterunsers. 1520." In *D. Martin Luthers Werke: Kritische Gesammtausgabe.* Vol. 7. 1897. Reprint, Graz: Akademische Druck- und Verlagsanstalt, 1966.

———. "The Large Catechism." In *The Book of Concord: The Confessions of the Evangelical Lutheran Church,* edited by Robert Kolb and Timothy J. Wengert, translated by Charles Arand et al. Minneapolis: Fortress Press, 2000.

———. "Personal Prayer Book, 1522." Translated by Martin H. Bertram. In *Luther's Works.* Edited by Helmut T. Lehmann. Vol. 43, *Devotional Writings II,* edited by Gustav K. Wiencke. Philadelphia: Fortress Press, 1968.

———. "The Small Catechism." In *The Book of Concord: The Confessions of the Evangelical Lutheran Church,* edited by Robert Kolb and Timothy J. Wengert, translated by Charles Arand et al. Minneapolis: Fortress Press, 2000.

Melanchthon, Philip. "Apology of the Augsburg Confession." In *The Book of Concord: The Confessions of the Evangelical Lutheran Church,* edited by Robert Kolb and Timothy J. Wengert, translated by Charles Arand et al. Minneapolis: Fortress Press, 2000.

———. "The Augsburg Confession." In *The Book of Concord: The Confessions of the Evangelical Lutheran Church,* edited by Robert Kolb and Timothy J. Wengert, translated by Charles Arand et al. Minneapolis: Fortress Press, 2000.

———. "Die Augsburgische Konfession [German and Latin texts]." In *Die Bekenntnisschriften der evangelisch-lutherischen Kirche,* 4th ed. Göttingen: Vandenhoeck & Ruprecht, 1959.

———. "Examen ordinandorum 1552." In *Melanchthons Werke in Auswahl,* edited by Robert Stupperich. Vol. 6, *Bekenntnisse und kleine Lehrschriften,* edited by Robert Stupperich. Gütersloh: Bertelsmann, 1955.

———. "Examen ordinandorum [1554]." In *CR.* Vol. 23, *Philippi Melanthonis opera quae supersunt omnia,* edited by C. G. Bretschneider and H. E. Bindseil. 1855. Reprint, New York: Johnson Reprint Corporation, 1963.

———. "Iudicium de Zwinglii doctrina" (1530). In *CR.* Vols. 1–28, *Philippi Melanthonis opera quae supersunt omnia.* Vol. 2. Edited by C. G. Bretschneider. 1835. Reprint, New York: Johnson Reprint Corporation, 1963.

———. "Loci Communes Theologici [1521]." Translated by Lowell J. Satre. In *Melanchthon and Bucer,* edited by Wilhelm Pauck. Library of Christian Classics, vol. 19. Philadelphia: Westminster, 1969.

———. "Loci theologici [1521]." In *CR.* Vols. 1–28, *Philippi Melanthonis opera quae supersunt omnia.* Vol. 21. Edited by C. G. Bretschneider and H. E. Bindseil. 1854. Reprint, New York: Johnson Reprint Corporation, 1963.

———. "Loci theologici [1543]." In *CR.* Vols. 1–28, *Philippi Melanthonis opera quae supersunt omnia.* Vol. 21. Edited by C. G. Bretschneider and H. E. Bindseil. 1854. Reprint, New York: Johnson Reprint Corporation, 1963.

———. "Responsio Philip. Melanth. ad quaestionem de controversia Heidelbergensi" In *CR.* Vols. 1–28, *Philippi Melanthonis opera quae supersunt omnia.* Vol. 9. Edited by C. G. Bretschneider. 1842. Reprint, New York: Johnson Reprint Corporation, 1963.

Micronius, Marten. *Den kleynen cathechismus, oft kinder leere der Duytscher Ghemeynte van Londen* (1552). London: Duvves, 1566. http://eebo.chadwyck.com.

———. "Een corte undersouckinghe des gheloofs (1553) in der Fassung von 1555," edited by J. Marius J. Lange van Ravenswaay. In *Reformierte Bekenntnisschriften*, edited by Heiner Faulenbach et al. Vol. 1/3, *1550–1558*, edited by Judith Becker et al. Neukirchen-Vluyn: Neukirchener Verlag, 2007.

Mörlin, Joachim. "Der Katechismus des Joachim W[M]örlin von 1547 resp. 1566." In *Quellen zur Geschichte des kirchlichen Unterrichts in der evangelischen Kirche Deutschlands zwischen 1530 und 1600*, edited by Johann M. Reu. Pt. 1, *Quellen zur Geschichte des Katechismusunterrichts*. Vol. 3, *Ost-, Nord-, und Westdeutsche Katechismen*. Sec. 2, bk. 2, *Texte*. 1920. Reprint, Hildesheim: Olms, 1976.

Müller, E. F. Karl. *Die Bekenntnisschriften der reformierten Kirche*. Leipzig: Deichert, 1903.

Olevianus, Caspar. *An Exposition of the Apostles' Creed*. Translated by Lyle D. Bierma. Classic Reformed Theology, edited by R. Scott Clark, vol. 2. Grand Rapids: Reformation Heritage Books, 2009.

———. *A Firm Foundation: An Aid to Interpreting the Heidelberg Catechism*. Translated and edited by Lyle D. Bierma. Texts and Studies in Reformation and Post-Reformation Thought, edited by Richard A. Muller. Grand Rapids: Baker, 1995.

Schaff, Philip, ed. *The Creeds of Christendom: With a History and Critical Notes*. 6th ed. 3 vols. 1931. Reprint, Grand Rapids: Baker, 1990.

Sehling, Emil, ed. *Die evangelischen Kirchenordnungen des XVI. Jahrhunderts*. Vol. 14, *Kurpfalz*. Tübingen: Mohr, 1957.

Ursinus, Zacharias. "Catechesis minor, perspicua brevitate christianam fidem complectens." In *Der Heidelberger Katechismus und vier verwandte Katechismen*, edited by August Lang. Leipzig: Deichert, 1907.

———. *The Commentary of Dr. Zacharias Ursinus on the Heidelberg Catechism*. Translated by G. W. Williard. Grand Rapids: Wm. B. Eerdmans, 1954.

———. *Corpus doctrinae Christianae*. Hannover: Aubrius, 1634.

———. *Grüntlicher Bericht vom heiligen Abendmal unsers Herren Jesu Christi*. Heidelberg: Mayer, 1564.

———. "The Larger Catechism." Translated by Lyle D. Bierma. In Lyle D. Bierma et al., *An Introduction to the Heidelberg Catechism: Sources, History, and Theology*. Texts and Studies in Reformation and Post-Reformation Thought, edited by Richard A. Muller. Grand Rapids: Baker Academic, 2005.

———. "The Smaller Catechism." Translated by Lyle D. Bierma. In Lyle D. Bierma et al., *An Introduction to the Heidelberg Catechism: Sources, History, and Theology*. Texts and Studies in Reformation and Post-Reformation Thought, edited by Richard A. Muller. Grand Rapids: Baker Academic, 2005.

———. "Theses complectentes breviter et perspicue summam verae Doctrinae de Sacramentis." In *Zachariae Ursini . . . volumen tractationem theologicarum*. Vol. 1. Neustadt: Harnisch, 1584.

———. "Theses de persona et officio unici mediatoris inter Deum et homines, domini nostri Iesu Christi." In *D. Zachariae Ursini . . . opera theological*, edited by Quirinus Reuter. Vol. 1. Heidelberg: Lancellot, 1612.

Zwingli, Ulrich. "Fidei Ratio" (1530). In E. F. Karl Müller, *Die Bekenntnisschriften der reformierten Kirche*. Leipzig: Deichert, 1903.

2. SECONDARY SOURCES

Althaus, Paul. *The Theology of Martin Luther*. Translated by Robert C. Schultz. Philadelphia: Fortress Press, 1966.

Alting, Heinrich. *Historia Ecclesiae Palatinae* (1644). In *Monumenta pietatis & literaria virorum in republica & literaria illustrium, selecta*, edited by Ludwig Christian Mieg and Daniel Nebel. Frankfurt: Maximillian, 1701, 130. Quoted in Gustav A. Benrath. "Die Eigenart der pfälzischen Reformation und die Vorgeschichte des Heidelberger Katechismus." *Heidelberger Jahrbuch* 7 (1963): 14.

Asendorf, Ulrich. "Luther's Small Catechism and the Heidelberg Catechism." In *Luther's Catechisms—450 Years: Essays Commemorating the Small and Large Catechisms of Dr. Martin Luther*, edited by David P. Scaer and Robert D. Preus, 1–7. Fort Wayne: Concordia Theological Seminary, 1979.

Bandstra, Andrew J. "Law and Gospel in Calvin and Paul." In *Exploring the Heritage of John Calvin*, edited by David E. Holwerda, 11–39. Grand Rapids: Baker, 1976.

Barth, Karl. *Learning Jesus Christ through the Heidelberg Catechism*. Translated by Shirley C. Guthrie Jr. Grand Rapids: Wm. B. Eerdmans, 1964.

Bavinck, Jan. *De Heidelbergsche Catechismus*. Vol. 2. 2nd ed. Kampen: Kok, 1913–14.

Benrath, Gustav A. "Die Eigenart der pfälzischen Reformation und die Vorgeschichte des Heidelberger Katechismus." *Heidelberger Jahrbuch* 7 (1963): 13–32.

Berkhof, Hendrikus. "The Catechism as an Expression of Our Faith." In Bard Thompson et al., *Essays on the Heidelberg Catechism*, 93–122. Philadelphia: United Church Press, 1963.

———. "The Catechism in Its Historical Context." In Bard Thompson et al., *Essays on the Heidelberg Catechism*, 76–92. Philadelphia: United Church Press, 1963.

Bierma, Lyle D. "Confessions and Ecumenicity: The Christian Reformed Church and Heidelberg Catechism 80." In *That the World May Believe: Essays on Mission & Unity in Honour of George Vandervelde*, edited by Michael W. Goheen and Margaret O'Gara, 145–54. Lanham, MD: University Press of America, 2006.

———. *The Covenant Theology of Caspar Olevianus*. Rev. ed. Grand Rapids: Reformation Heritage Books, 2005.

———. "How Should Heidelberg Catechism Q/A 60 Be Translated?" *Calvin Theological Journal* 26 (April 1991): 125–33.

———. "The Purpose and Authorship of the Heidelberg Catechism." In Lyle D. Bierma et al., *An Introduction to the Heidelberg Catechism: Sources, History, and Theology*, 49–74. Texts and Studies in Reformation and Post-Reformation Thought, edited by Richard A. Muller. Grand Rapids: Baker Academic, 2005.

———. "The Sources and Theological Orientation of the Heidelberg Catechism." In Lyle D. Bierma et al., *An Introduction to the Heidelberg Catechism: Sources, History, and Theology*, 75–102. Texts and Studies in Reformation and Post-Reformation Thought, edited by Richard A. Muller. Grand Rapids: Baker Academic, 2005.

———. "WARC, the Heidelberg Catechism, and the Concept of Life." Paper presented at the Theology Committee of the Caribbean and North American Area Council. Louisville, KY, February 2004.

———. "What Hath Wittenberg to Do with Heidelberg? Philip Melanchthon and the Heidelberg Catechism." In *Melanchthon in Europe: His Work and Influence beyond Wittenberg*, edited by Karin Maag, 103–21. Studies and Texts in Reformation and Post-Reformation Thought, edited by Richard A. Muller. Grand Rapids: Baker, 1999.

Bierma, Lyle D. et al. *An Introduction to the Heidelberg Catechism: Sources, History, and Theology*. Texts and Studies in Reformation and Post-Reformation Thought, edited by Richard A. Muller. Grand Rapids: Baker Academic, 2005.

Blake, Eugene Carson. "A Proposal toward the Reunion of Christ's Church." Sermon preached at Grace Cathedral, San Francisco, CA, December 4, 1960. http://keithwatkinshistorian.files.wordpress.com/2010/07/a-proposal-toward-the-reunion-of-christs-church.pdf.

Blocher, Henri. "The Atonement in John Calvin's Theology." In *The Glory of the Atonement-Biblical, Historical & Practical Perspectives: Essays in Honor of Roger Nicole*, edited by Charles E. Hill and Frank A. James III, 279–303. Downers Grove, Illinois: InterVarsity Press, 2004.

Boerke, Christa. "The People behind the Heidelberg Catechism." In *The Church's Book of Comfort*, edited by Willem van 't Spijker and translated by Gerrit Bilkes, 62–88. Grand Rapids: Reformation Heritage Books, 2009.

Bouwmeester, G. *Zacharias Ursinus en de Heidelbergse Catechismus*. The Hague: Willem de Zwijgerstichting, 1954.

Burchill, Christopher J. "On the Consolation of a Christian Scholar: Zacharias Ursinus (1534–83) and the Reformation in Heidelberg." *Journal of Ecclesiastical History* 37, no. 4 (1986): 565–83.

Busch, Eberhard. *Drawn to Freedom: Christian Faith Today in Conversation with the Heidelberg Catechism*. Translated by William H. Rader. Grand Rapids: Wm. B. Eerdmans, 2010.

Christian Reformed Church in North America. The Lord's Supper and the Roman Catholic Mass: A Discussion on Question and Answer 80 of the Heidelberg Catechism. http://www.crcna.org/site_uploads/uploads/Lord%27sSupper&RC Mass.pdf (accessed July 18, 2011).

Clark, R. Scott. *Caspar Olevian and the Substance of the Covenant: The Double Benefit of Christ*. Rutherford Series in Historical Theology. Edinburgh: Rutherford House, 2005.

Coenen, Lothar. "Gottes Bund und Erwählung." In *Handbuch zum Heidelberger Katechismus*, edited by Lothar Coenen, 128–34. Neukirchen-Vluyn: Neukirchener Verlag, 1963.

———. "Wort Gottes und Heiliger Geist." In *Handbuch zum Heidelberger Katechismus*, edited by Lothar Coenen, 81–90. Neukirchen-Vluyn: Neukirchener Verlag, 1963.

Couard, Ludwig. *Der Heidelberger Katechismus und sein Verhältnis zum kleinen lutherischen*. Gütersloh: Bertelsmann, 1904.

Culpepper, Robert H. *Interpreting the Atonement*. Grand Rapids: Wm. B. Eerdmans, 1966.

Dahlmann, A. E. "The Theology of the Heidelberg Catechism." *The Reformed Church Review*, 4th ser., 17 (April 1913): 167–81.

de Campos Júnior, Heber Carlos. "Johannes Piscator (1546–1625) and the Consequent Development of the Doctrine of the Imputation of Christ's Active Obedience." Ph.D. diss., Calvin Theological Seminary, 2009.

de Reuver, Arie. "De Augsburgse Confessie en de Heidelbergse Catechismus—een kritische vergelijking." *Theologia Reformata* 49, no. 4 (2006): 342–61.

den Hartogh, Gerrit. *Voorzienigheid in donker licht: Herkomst en gebruik van het begrip 'Providentia Dei' in de reformatorische theologie, in het bijzonder bij Zacharias Ursinus*. Heerenveen: Groen, 1999.

Ebrard, Johannes H. A. *Das Dogma vom heiligen Abendmahl und seine Geschichte*. 2 vols. Frankfurt: Zimmer, 1846.

Evangelical Dictionary of Theology, 2nd ed. Grand Rapids: Baker, 1984.

Gassmann, Benno. *Ecclesia Reformata: Die Kirche in den reformierten Bekenntnisschriften*. Freiburg: Herder, 1968.

George, Timothy. "The Atonement in Luther's Theology." In *The Glory of the Atonement-Biblical, Historical & Practical Perspectives: Essays in Honor of Roger Nicole*, edited by Charles E. Hill and Frank A. James III, 263–78. Downers Grove, Illinois: InterVarsity Press, 2004.

———. *Theology of the Reformers*. Nashville: Broadman, 1988.

Gerrish, Brian A. "Calvin Retrospect." *The Bulletin of the Institute for Reformed Theology* 8, no. 3 (2009): 3–9.

———. *Grace and Gratitude: the Eucharistic Theology of John Calvin*. Minneapolis: Fortress Press, 1993.

———. "Sign and Reality: The Lord's Supper in the Reformed Confessions." In *The Old Protestantism and the New: Essays on the Reformation Heritage*, 118–30. Chicago: University of Chicago Press, 1982.

Goeters, J. F. Gerhard. "Caspar Olevianus als Theologe." *Monatshefte für Evangelische Kirchengeschichte des Rheinlandes* 37–38 (1988—1989): 287–344.

——— "Christologie und Rechtfertigung nach dem Heidelberger Katechismus." In *Das Kreuz Jesu Christi als Grund des Heils*, edited by Ernst Bizer. Gütersloh: Mohn, 1967.

Good, James I. *The Heidelberg Catechism in Its Newest Light*. Philadelphia: Publication and Sunday School Board of the Reformed Church in the United States, 1914.

———. *The Origin of the Reformed Church in Germany*. Reading, PA: Daniel Miller, 1887.

Gooszen, Maurits. *De Heidelbergsche Catechismus: Textus Receptus met Toelichtende Teksten*. Leiden: Brill, 1890.

———. *De Heidelbergsche Catechismus en het boekje van de breking des broods, in het jaar 1563–1564 bestreden en verdedigd*. Leiden: Brill, 1892.

Gootjes, Nicolaas H. *The Belgic Confession: Its History and Sources*. Texts and Studies in Reformation and Post-Reformation Thought, edited by Richard A. Muller. Grand Rapids: Baker Academic, 2007.

Graafland, Cornelis. *Van Calvijn tot Comrie: Oorsprong en ontwikkeling van de leer van het verbond in het Gereformeerd Protestantisme*. Vol. 2. Zoetermeer: Boekcentrum, 1994.

Graffmann, Heinrich. *Unterricht im Heidelberger Katechismus*. Vol. 3. Neukirchen: Buchhandlung des Erziehungsvereins, 1951.

Gunnoe Jr., Charles D. "The Reformation of the Palatinate and the Origins of the Heidelberg Catechism, 1500–1562." In Lyle D. Bierma et al., *An Introduction to the Heidelberg Catechism: Sources, History, and Theology*, 15–47. Texts and Studies in Reformation and Post-Reformation Thought, edited by Richard A. Muller. Grand Rapids: Baker Academic, 2005.

———. "Thomas Erastus in Heidelberg: A Renaissance Physician during the Second Reformation, 1558–1580." Ph.D. diss., University of Virginia, 1998.

Guthrie Jr., Shirley G. Translator's preface to *Learning Jesus Christ through the Heidelberg Catechism*, by Karl Barth. Grand Rapids: Wm. B. Eerdmans, 1964.

Gyenge, Emerich. "Der Glaube, seine Gewissheit und Bewahrung." In *Handbuch zum Heidelberger Katechismus*, edited by Lothar Coenen, 113–27. Neukirchen-Vluyn: Neukirchener Verlag, 1963.

Hageman, Howard, "The Lasting Significance of Ursinus." In *Controversy and Conciliation: The Reformation and the Palatinate 1559–1583*, edited by Derk Visser, 227–39. Allison Park, PA: Pickwick, 1986.

Hartvelt, G. P. *Alles in Hem*. Vol. 1 of *Nieuwe Commentaar Heidelbergse Catechismus*. Aalten: Graafschap, 1966.

———. "De Avondmaalsleer van de Heidelbergse Catechismus en Haar Toepassing in de Prediking." *Homiletica en Biblica* 23 (1964): 121–40.

———. "Petrus Boquinus."*Gereformeerd Theologisch Tijdschrift* 62 (1962): 49–77.

———. *Tastbaar Evangelie*. Vol. 3 of Nieuwe Commentaar Heidelbergse Catechismus. Aalten: Graafschap, 1966.

———. *Verum Corpus: Een Studie over een Centraal Hoofdstuk uit de Avondmaalsleer van Calvijn*. Delft: Meinema, 1960.

Henss, Walter. *Der Heidelberger Katechismus im konfessionspolitischen Kräftespiel seiner Frühzeit*. Zurich: Theologischer Verlag, 1983.

Heppe, Heinrich. *Dogmatik des deutschen Protestantismus im sechzehnten Jahrhundert*. Vol. 1. Gotha: Perthes, 1857.

Hesse, Hermann. "Zur Sakramentslehre des Heidelberger Katechismus nach den Fragen 65–68." In *Theologische Aufsätze: Karl Barth zum 50. Geburtstag*, edited by E. Wolf, 467–89. Munich: Kaiser, 1936.

Hesselink, I. John. *Calvin's Concept of the Law*. Allison Park, PA: Pickwick, 1992.

———. *Calvin's First Catechism: A Commentary*. Columbia Series in Reformed Theology. Louisville, KY: Westminster John Knox Press, 1997.

Hodge, Charles. *The Biblical Repertory and Princeton Review* 20 (1848): 227–78.

Hollweg, Walter. "Die beiden Konfessionen Theodore von Bezas: Zwei bisher unbeachtete Quellen zum Heidelberger Katechismus." In *Neue Untersuchungen zur Geschichte und Lehre des Heidelberger Katechismus*, 124–52. Beiträge zur Geschichte und Lehre der Reformierten Kirche, edited by Paul Jacobs et al., vol. 13. Neukirchen: Neukirchener Verlag, 1961.

———. *Heinrich Bullingers Hausbuch: Eine Untersuchung über die Anfänge der reformierten Predigtliteratur*. Beiträge zur Geschichte und Lehre der Reformierten Kirche, vol. 8. Neukirchen: Verlag der Buchhandlung des Erziehungsvereins, 1956.

———. "Zur Quellenfrage des Heidelberger Katechismus." In *Neue Untersuchungen zur Geschichte und Lehre des Heidelberger Katechismus: Zweite Folge*, 38–47. Beiträge zur Geschichte und Lehre der Reformierten Kirche, edited by Hannelore Erhart et al., vol. 28. Neukirchen-Vluyn: Neukirchener Verlag, 1968.

Hutter, Ulrich. "Zacharias Ursinus und der Heidelberger Katechismus." In *Martin Luther und die Reformation in Ostdeutschland und Sudosteuropa: Wirkungen und Wechselwirkungen*, edited by Ulrich Hutter and Hans-Günther Parplies, 79–105. Beihefte zum Jahrbuch für Schlesische Kirchengeschichte 8. Sigmaringen: Jan Thorbecke, 1991.

Hyde, Daniel R. "The Holy Spirit in the Heidelberg Catechism." *Mid-America Journal of Theology* 17 (2006): 211–37.

Jacobs, Paul. *Theologie reformierter Bekenntnisschriften in Grundzügen*. Neukirchen Kreis Moers: Neukirchener Verlag, 1959.

Johnson, Marcus. "Luther and Calvin on Union with Christ." *Fides et Historia* 39, no. 2 (2007): 59–77.

Klooster, Fred H. "The Heidelberg Catechism—An Ecumenical Creed?" *Bulletin of the Evangelical Theological Society* 8, no. 1 (Winter 1965): 23–33.

———. "The Heidelberg Catechism: Origin and History." Photocopied manuscript, Calvin Theological Seminary, 1982.

———. *A Mighty Comfort: The Christian Faith according to the Heidelberg Catechism*. Grand Rapids: CRC Publications, 1990.

———. *Our Only Comfort: A Comprehensive Commentary on the Heidelberg Catechism*. 2 vols. Grand Rapids: Faith Alive, 2001.

Koch, Ernst. *Die Theologie der Confessio Helvetica Posterior*. Beiträge zur Geschichte und Lehre der Reformierten Kirche, edited by H. Erhart et al., vol. 27. Neukirchen-Vluyn: Neukirchener Verlag, 1968.

Korn, William E. "Die Lehre von Christi Person und Werk." In *Handbuch zum Heidelberger Ka- techismus*, edited by Lothar Coenen, 91–104. Neukirchen-Vluyn: Neukirchener Verlag, 1963.

Kreck, Walter. "Die Abendmahlslehre in den reformierten Bekenntnisschriften." In *Die Abendmahlslehre in den reformatorischen Bekenntnisschriften*. Munich: Kaiser, 1955.

Lang, August. *Der Heidelberger Katechismus: Zum 350 jährigen Gedächtnis seiner Entstehung*. Schriften des Vereins für Refomationsgeschichte, no. 113. Leipzig: Verein für Refomationsgeschichte, 1913.

———. "The Religious and Theological Character of the Heidelberg Catechism." *The Reformed Church Review*, 4th ser., 18 (October 1914): 456–71.

Latzel, Thorsten. *Theologische Grundzüge des Heidelberger Katechismus: Eine fundamentaltheologische Untersuchung seines Ansatzes zur Glaubenskommunikation*. Marburger Theologische Studien, edited by Wilfired Härle and Dieter Lührmann, vol. 83. Marburg: Elwert, 2004.

Lekkerkerker, Arie F. N. *Gespreken over de Heidelberger*. Wageningen: Zomer & Keunings, 1964.

Maag, Karin Y. "Early Editions and Translations of the Heidelberg Catechism." In Lyle D. Bierma et al., *An Introduction to the Heidelberg Catechism: Sources, History, and Theology*, 103–17. Texts and Studies in Reformation and Post-Reformation Thought, edited by Richard A. Muller. Grand Rapids: Baker Academic, 2005.

Manschreck, Clyde L. *Melanchthon: The Quiet Reformer*. New York: Abingdon Press, 1958.

Marcel, P. Ch. "Die Lehre von der Kirche und den Sakramenten." In *Handbuch zum Heidelberger Katechismus*, edited by Lothar Coenen, 135–58. Neukirchen-Vluyn: Neukirchener Verlag, 1963.

Marthaler, Berard. *The Catechism Today and Yesterday: The Evolution of a Genre*. Collegeville, MN: Liturgical Press, 1995.

McCord, James I. "The Heidelberg Catechism: An Ecumenical Confession." *The Princeton Seminary Bulletin* 56, no. 2 (February 1963): 12–18.

"More Than a Memorial." *The Christian Century* 80, no. 7 (February 13, 1963): 198.

Muller, Richard A. "Calvin on Sacramental Presence, in the Shadow of Marburg and Zurich." *Lutheran Quarterly* 23 (2009): 147–67.

———. *Christ and the Decree: Christology and Predestination in Reformed Theology from Calvin to Perkins*. Durham, NC: Labyrinth, 1986.

Neuser, Wilhelm. "Die Erwählungslehre im Heidelberger Katechismus." *Zeitschrift für Kirchengeschichte* 75 (1964): 309–26.

———. "Die Väter des Heidelberger Katechismus." *Theologische Zeitschrift* 35 (1979): 177–99.

Nevin, John W. *History and Genius of the Heidelberg Catechism*. Chambersburg, PA: Publication Office of the German Reformed Church, 1847.

———. Introduction to *The Commentary of Dr. Zacharias Ursinus on the Heidelberg Catechism*. Translated by G. W. Williard. Grand Rapids: Wm. B. Eerdmans, 1954.

Nischan, Bodo. "The 'Fractio Panis:' A Reformed Communion Practice in Late Reformation Germany." *Church History* 53 (1984): 17–29.

Peters, Albrecht. *Kommentar zu Luthers Katechismen*. Vol. 1, *Die Zehn Gebote; Luthers Vorreden*, edited by Gottfried Seebaβ. Göttingen: Vandenhoeck & Ruprecht, 1990.

Quere, Ralph W. "Christ's Efficacious Presence in the Lord's Supper: Directions in the Development of Melanchthon's Theology after Augsburg." *The Lutheran Quarterly* 29 (1977): 21–41.

Rauhaus, Alfred. "Untersuchungen zu Entstehung, Gestaltung und Lehre des Kleinen Emder Katechismus von 1554." Th.D. diss., University of Göttingen, 1977.

Richards, George W. *The Heidelberg Catechism: Historical and Doctrinal Studies*. Philadelphia: Publication and Sunday School Board of the Reformed Church in the United States, 1913.

Rohls, Jan. *Reformed Confessions: Theology from Zurich to Barmen*. Translated by John Hoffmeyer. Columbia Series in Reformed Theology. Louisville, KY: Westminster John Knox Press, 1997.

Rorem, Paul. "The *Consensus Tigurinus* (1549): Did Calvin Compromise?" In *Calvinus Sacrae Scripturae Professor: Calvin as Confessor of Holy Scripture*, edited by Wilhelm H. Neuser, 72–90. Grand Rapids: Wm. B. Eerdmans, 1994.

Saito, Isomi. "The Relation of the Law to Prayer in the Heidelberg Catechism." Th.M. thesis, Calvin Theological Seminary, 2003.

Schaff, Philip. "Geschichte, Geist und Bedeutung des Heidelberger Katechismus: Ein Beitrag zur dreihundertjährigen Jubilfeier." *Zeitschrift für die historische Theologie* 3 (1864): 328. Quoted in Bard Thompson et al., *Essays on the Heidelberg Catechism*, 91–92. Philadelphia: United Church Press, 1963.

Schilling, Heinz. "Confessionalization in the Empire: Religious and Societal Change in Germany between 1555 and 1620." In Heinz Schilling, *Religion, Political Culture and the Emergence of the Early Modern State: Essays in German and Dutch History*, 205–45. Studies in Medieval and Reformation Thought, vol. 50. Leiden: Brill, 1992.

Staedtke, Joachim. "Entstehung und Bedeutung des Heidelberger Katechismus." In *Warum Wirst Du Ein Christ Genannt?*, edited by Walter Herrenbrück and Udo Smidt, 11–23. Neukirchen Vluyn: Neukirchener Verlag des Erziehungsvereins, 1965.

Stupperich, Robert. *Melanchthon*. Translated by Robert H. Fischer. London: Lutterworth, 1965.

Sturm, Erdmann. *Der junge Zacharias Ursinus: Sein Weg vom Philippismus zum Calvinismus*. Neukirchen-Vluyn: Neukirchener Verlag, 1972.

Sudhoff, Karl. *C. Olevianus und Z. Ursinus: Leben und ausgewählte Schriften*. Leben und ausgewählte Schriften der Väter und Begründer der reformierten Kirche, vol. 8. Elberfeld: Friderichs, 1857.

Thompson, Bard. "Historical Background of the Catechism." In Bard Thompson et al., *Essays on the Heidelberg Catechism*, 8–30. Philadelphia: United Church Press, 1963.

———. "The Palatinate Church Order of 1563." *Church History* 23, no. 4 (1954): 339–54.

———. "Reformed Liturgies: An Historical and Doctrinal Interpretation of the Palatinate Liturgy of 1563, Mercersburg Provisional Liturgy of 1858, Evangelical and Reformed Order of 1944, and Their Sources." B.D. thesis, Union Theological Seminary (New York), 1949.

Venema, Cornelis P. *Heinrich Bullinger and the Doctrine of Predestination: Author of "the Other Reformed Tradition"?* Texts & Studies in Reformation and Post-Reformation Thought, edited by Richard A. Muller. Grand Rapids: Baker, 2002.

Verboom, Willem. *De Theologie van de Heidelbergse Catechismus*. Zoetermeer: Boekencentrum, 1996.

———. "Waardering voor de Augsburgse Confessie." *Reformatorisch Dagblad*. June 11, 2003. http://www.refdag.nl/opinie/opinie/waardering_voor_de_augsburgse_confessie_1_415196 (accessed July 26, 2010).

Verhey, Allen. *Living the Heidelberg: The Heidelberg Catechism and the Moral Life*. Grand Rapids: CRC Publications, 1986.

Visser, Derk. "The Covenant in Zacharias Ursinus." *The Sixteenth Century Journal* 18, no. 4 (1987): 531–44.

———. *Zacharias Ursinus, the Reluctant Reformer: His Life and Times*. New York: United Church Press, 1983.

Visser, L. L. J. "Die Lehre von Gottes Vorsehung und Weltregiment." In *Handbuch zum Heidelberger Katechismus*, edited by Lothar Coenen, 105–12. Neukirchen-Vluyn: Neukirchener Verlag, 1963.

Wallace, Ronald S. *Calvin's Doctrine of the Word and Sacraments*. Edinburgh: Oliver and Boyd, 1953; Tyler, TX: Geneva Divinity School Press, 1982.

Watson, Philip S. *Let God be God! An Interpretation of the Theology of Martin Luther*. Philadelphia: Muhlenberg, 1950.

Weismann, Christoph. *Eine Kleine Biblia: Die Katechismen von Luther und Brenz*. Stuttgart: Calwer, 1985.

———. *Die Katechismen des Johannes Brenz*. Vol. 1, *Die Entstehungs-, Text-, und Wirkungsgeschichte*, Spätmittelalter und Reformation Texte und Untersuchungen, edited by Heiko A. Oberman, vol. 21. Berlin: Walter de Gruyter, 1990.

Wengert, Timothy J. *Law and Gospel: Philip Melanchthon's Debate with John Agricola of Eisleben over Poenitentia*. Texts and Studies in Reformation and Post-Reformation Thought, edited by Richard A. Muller. Grand Rapids: Baker, 1997.

———. "Philip Melanchthon's 1522 Annotations on Romans and the Lutheran Origins of Rhetorical Criticism." In *Biblical Interpretation in the Era of the Reformation: Essays Presented to David C. Steinmetz in Honor of His Sixtieth Birthday*, edited by Richard A. Muller and John L. Thompson, 118–40. Grand Rapids: Wm. B. Eerdmans, 1996.

———. "'We Will Feast Together in Heaven Forever': The Epistolary Friendship of

John Calvin and Philip Melanchthon." In *Melanchthon in Europe: His Work and Influence beyond Wittenberg*, edited by Karin Maag, 19–44. Studies and Texts in Reformation and Post-Reformation Thought, edited by Richard A. Muller. Grand Rapids: Baker, 1999.

Wesel-Roth, Ruth. *Thomas Erastus*. Lahr: Schauenberg, 1954.

Winter, Friedrich. *Confessio Augustana und Heidelberger Katechismus in vergleichender Betrachtung*. Berlin: Evangelische Verlagsanstalt, 1954.

INDEX